£3·00

RECORDS OF CHRISTIANITY

RECORDS

OF

CHRISTIANITY

VOLUME I

In the Roman Empire

David Ayerst

A. S. T. Fisher

BASIL BLACKWELL

OXFORD

Printed in England by The Western Printing
Services Bristol and Bound at the Kemp Hall
Bindery.

CONTENTS

CHAPTER FOUR
CHRISTIAN WORSHIP IN THE SECOND CENTURY

CHAPTER FIVE
UNDER THE PHILOSOPHER KING

CHAPTER SIX
THE LONG PEACE

CHAPTER SEVEN
THE FIRST SYSTEMATIC PERSECUTIONS

CHAPTER EIGHT
THE FINAL STRUGGLE

CHAPTER NINE
THE EMPIRE BECOMES CHRISTIAN

CHAPTER TEN
MEN OF FAITH; AND POWER POLITICS

CHAPTER ELEVEN
JEROME AND THE BIBLE

CHAPTER TWELVE

THE PARTING OF THE WAYS

CHAPTER THIRTEEN

THE LIFE OF THE CHRISTIANS IN THE WEST

CHAPTER FOURTEEN

BEYOND THE BOUNDS

CHAPTER FIFTEEN
DARKNESS AND DAWN

ILLUSTRATIONS

INTRODUCTION

The purpose of this anthology is to illustrate from their own writings the life of Christians in the years between Nero's persecution and the death of Augustine. The extracts have been selected to enable us to overhear, so to speak, the kind of things they talked about among themselves, what they said to God and what they believed God said to them. We have also included something of what others said about them. The centuries with which we are concerned are a time when Christianity was one among many inter-acting faiths and philosophies—an open society like our own. We have tried to give the feel of this. Great men get more attention in these pages than ordinary men because great men write books and have books written about them, and because the doings of great men occupy much space in the thoughts of ordinary men. Many of the events described in these pages are great, too, by any reckoning. They changed men's lives, and they have changed the course of history.

This is not a source book for the development of Christian doctrine or the growth of the institutional church. There are excellent collections for this purpose which it would be folly to imitate. Our purpose is to introduce readers to some of the men through whom these great things were done and to portray them faithfully as Cromwell wanted to be painted, 'warts and all'. But it is not out of disrespect that we have omitted from the introductions the title Saint with which the Church later honoured many of them. It is to help readers feel their way back into the time when these were living men.

We hope that these extracts will serve both as an appetizer and a dessert for those who make a serious study of theology and church history. We believe that they will also provide a palatable main course for other Christian and non-Christian humanists, who share a general, less specialized interest in religion. They will, of course, find some passages which illustrate the main lines of theological and philosophical discussion and the climate in which it took place. This was, after all, a ruling passion among educated Christians and pagans alike. There is, therefore, a slight overlap between this anthology and standard source books for theological students. But most of this book is concerned with men and women in their less abstruse moments.

We have made this book as self-contained as possible, and have tried to take little for granted by way of general background information. Inquiry shows that Hadrian is still remembered because he built a wall (though many have never heard of Balbus who was the wall-builder *par excellence* in the editors' schooldays[1]). Titus is not even a name to many who will use this book. We had to choose between sending readers constantly to search a history of the Roman Empire and an atlas of the ancient world, and providing them with substantial introductions, notes, time charts and maps. We chose the latter course because many people will not have either a general Roman history or a classical atlas readily at hand. The introductions are printed in smaller type than the extracts to which they refer. The maps contain all the places which get more than a passing reference in the book, but only these places. Comparison with a general classical atlas, or for that matter with an ordinary atlas, will show that most of the principal cities of the Mediterranean world figure in the text as well, of course, as many minor places.

How should this book be used? Readers to whom this is largely new ground, and who find they need the introductions, will probably do well to treat it as an unfolding story, start at the beginning and move steadily forward. The world changed greatly in the four centuries which this book covers. The story starts in a world where the government found difficulty in making out what Christianity was; before it ends emperors have to accept the Church's discipline. It begins at a time when the Roman Empire seemed even more imperishable than did the British Empire between Queen Victoria's Jubilees; before it ends there had been as brisk a wind of change, though from another quarter, as that which has sprung up in our own days. It is well to tackle events of this magnitude in the order in which they occurred, at least when first one meets them.

Other readers will wish to use this anthology as a miscellany from which to draw illustrations for particular purposes. The table of contents and chapter headings give a general indication of the arrangement of the subject matter, and the index is full enough to enable scattered references to individual subjects, such as baptism, mystery

[1] 'Balbus murum aedificat'—Balbus builds a wall—was about the first Latin sentence most people learnt.

religions and heresy, to be easily assembled. Cross-references have been
provided in the text where they seem likely to be helpful. The source
of all biblical quotations has been provided. It should be mentioned
that, though at the beginning this book overlaps the period in which
the New Testament was being written, no passages from the Bible are
included among the extracts. The passages we might have chosen are
indicated in the introductions at the appropriate place.

The illustrations are grouped together for reasons of economy. They
are of two kinds. Some are there because they directly illustrate some
portion of the text, e.g. the head of Diocletian or Constantine's Chi-
Rho symbol. Illustrations of this kind are noted in the text at the
appropriate places. Other illustrations are there because they are by
themselves an essential part of the anthology. The pictures from the
catacombs, for instance, are a direct non-verbal expression of the
Christian imagination. Without their help we should have had no idea
—or, more probably, the wrong idea—of how the early Christians
visualized their Lord and felt about him.

ACKNOWLEDGEMENTS

The compilers and publishers would like to thank the following for permission to reproduce copyright material (the numbers refer to the extracts):

Burns and Oates for passages from J. M. Flood, *St Augustine*, 81C, 88B, and E. A. Foran, *The Augustinians*, 88C: The Regents of the California Press and Faber and Faber for excerpts from Peter Brown, *Augustine of Hippo*, 82F, G, 85: The Clarendon Press, Oxford, for extracts from M. R. James, *The Apocryphal N.T.*, 22, 82A; G. R. Driver and Leonard Hodgson, *Nestorius, The Bazaar of Heracleides*, 78A, C; F. Homes Dudden, *The Life and Times of St Ambrose*, 64: Constable for passages from Helen Waddell, *The Desert Fathers*, 47C, D, E, and *Mediaeval Latin Lyrics*, 74B, C: Harvard University Press and Loeb Classical Library for extracts from R. J. Deferrari, *St Basil, Letters*, 47A, 48C, D, 52, 53A, B, C; Wilmer C. Wright, *Works of the Emperor Julian*, 50D V: Longmans Green and the Paulist Newman Press for passages from R. T. Meyer, *Palladius, the Lausiac History*, 51, and L. Bieler, *The Works of St Patrick*, 80: The Lutterworth Press for extracts from R. P. C. Hanson, *Dialogue with Trypho*, 10A, 11, and S. Neill, *Crysostom and his Message*, 62: The Oxford University Press for passages from H. Bettenson, *Documents of the Christian Church*, 14, 23C, 84: Penguin Books for passages from Robert Graves, *Suetonius, the Twelve Caesars*, 3, and G. A. Williamson, *Eusebius, History of the Church*, 23A, B, 32C, 36B, D, 38, 41, 42 B, C: The Princeton University Press for an extract from C. C. Mierow, *Gothic History of Jordanes*, 90A, B: The S.C.M. for an extract from J. Foster, *After the Apostles*, 29A, and the S.C.M. and Westminster Press for passages from J. E. Oulton and H. Chadwick, *Alexandrian Christianity*, 10B, and S. L. Greenslade, *Early Latin Theology*, 61, 63: The S.P.C.K. for passages from B. J. Kidd, *Documents Illustrative of the History of the Church*, 82B, 83, 90C; C. K. Barrett, *The N.T. Background*, 9B; Dom G. Dix, *The Apostolic Tradition*, 15; F. R. M. Hitchcock, *St Irenaeus against the Heresies*, 21; M. C. McClure, *Pilgrimage of Etheria*, 46; W. K. L.

Clarke, *The Lausiac History of Palladius*, 47B; J. R. Stevenson, *A New Eusebius*, 59; S. G. A. Luff, *Early Christian Writing*, 43A, 48A, B, 72.

We are no less grateful to those earlier scholars whose work we have used in such major collections as *The Ante Nicene Christian Library*, 17, 20, 26, 39; *Nicene and Post-Nicene Fathers*, 44A, 45, 55, 57, 60B, 67B; *Library of the Fathers*, 29B, C, 31, 34, 37A, C, 54B; the Loeb *Select Letters of Jerome* (trans. by F. A. Wright), 56, 66B, 73, 86B. We hope that they would pardon the modifications, especially in punctuation, which we have made in the cause of easier reading; and we believe that they would have made similar changes themselves had they been alive today. Readers who have access to major or specialist libraries in which their works are found will discover much more to their pleasure than we have had room to include.

We are also indebted to the following for permission to reproduce photographs: Anderson, Rome, Plate 19: The Ashmolean Museum, Oxford, Plates 2a, 2b, 14b: The British Museum, Plates 14a, 26: J. Combier, Plate 22: J. Cutforth, Plate 16: Gabinetto Fotographico Nazionale, Plates 6, 7, 9, 17: Giraudon, Plate 29: Dr J. Grolenburg, Plates 23, 24: Hermer Verlag, Plate 15: Hulton Radio Times Picture Library, Plates 20, 23, 32: Kunsthistorisch Instuut Nijmegen, Plate 30: The Mansell Collection, Plates 4, 8, 18: Paul Popper, Plate 1: Pont. Comm. di Arch. Sacra, Rome, Plates 10, 11, 12, 13, 27, 28: John Rylands Library, Plate 4.

The compilers and publishers have made every effort to trace and acknowledge copyright material and, should anything have been inadvertently omitted, would be glad of any further information which could be included in another edition.

In particular we should like to thank Mr. R. S. Stanier for making three translations (extracts 28, 47F, 65); and the Dean of Christ Church, Dr Henry Chadwick, for his kindness in reading the book in proof and thus reducing the number of errors. For those which remain the editors are, of course, alone responsible. Mr J. A. Cutforth has given more time and thought, especially in regard to illustrations, than any author has a right to expect of his publisher.

CHAPTER ONE

FROM THE EMPEROR'S STANDPOINT
Claudius to Trajan

None of the four writers represented in Extracts 1 to 4 was a Christian. Three—Tacitus, Suetonius and Pliny—held high civil service appointments, were friendly with each other and with the emperors they served. Tacitus and Suetonius were outspoken in their criticisms of the earlier emperors, but they merely chronicle without disapproval their treatment of Christians. Neither they nor Pliny dissented from the official view. The fourth writer, Josephus, was a Jew, but one who stood high with the emperors Vespasian, Titus and Domitian and received from them a pension which enabled him to concentrate on writing his books.

The most important point which arises from these extracts is negative—how little Christianity had forced itself on the attention of these writers. As far as they are concerned, and the great world of which they were part, Christianity was not so much an underground movement as one which had not yet made its way into daylight.

I. NERO'S PERSECUTION
A.D. 64

In the year 64 there was a great fire at Rome which is still remembered in the English saying—'Nero fiddled while Rome burned.' Rumour said that the Emperor had himself started the fire. Attention had to be diverted. The Christians were blamed. They were easy game—a little known group, mixed up with the unpopular Jews—as Tertullian said a good deal later, 'If the Tiber has left its bed, if the Nile has not poured its waters over the fields, if there is an earthquake, if famine or pestilence threatens, the cry immediately arises, "The Christians to the lions!"' Nero's persecution, here described by Tacitus, diverted suspicion from Nero, but not for long.

C. Cornelius Tacitus was a boy at the time of the fire. He wrote this passage at least fifty years later. He held very distinguished appointments at court, and was the son-in-law of Agricola, Britain's most successful Roman governor. He was a writer with an unusually terse and salty style: e.g. in describing the 'pacification' of frontier districts, 'They make a desert and call it peace.'

Peter and Paul are believed to have been executed during this persecution. By this time the more important Epistles had been written, but none of the Gospels—Mark's followed soon after. The traditions about Peter—that he went into hiding but turned back when he met Jesus going into Rome to be crucified again (*Quo vadis?*); and that he was crucified upside down at his own request as unworthy to die in the same way as his Lord—are later, and are not given here.

Note that the Christians were not tried for the crime of being Christians, but for specific criminal acts, of which setting fire to the city was only one. It was only after the Neronian persecution, and as a result of the emperor's specific accusations against Christians, that the further stage was reached when being a Christian was by itself a sufficient cause for condemnation and death. It was certainly the assumption by the time of the emperor Trajan (Extract 4); it probably became so either during the reign of Titus or of his brother Domitian who has the reputation in Christian tradition of being the second great persecuting emperor in the year 95.

Early tradition put John's exile to Patmos and the visions he had there, recorded in the Book of Revelation, in Domitian's reign. Irenaeus, writing of the vision of Anti-Christ, said: 'Had there been any need for his name (Anti-Christ's) to be openly announced at the present time, it would have been stated by the one who saw the actual revelation. For it was seen not a long time back, but almost in my own lifetime, at the end of Domitian's reign.' Irenaeus might have added that he himself had been the pupil of Polycarp (pp. 22–9), who had been the pupil of John.

Source: Tacitus, *Annales* 15, 44.

But all human efforts, all the lavish gifts of the emperor, and the propitiations of the gods, did not banish the sinister belief that the conflagration was the result of an order. Consequently, to get rid of the report, Nero fastened the guilt and inflicted the most exquisite tortures on a class hated for their abominations, called Christians by the populace. Christus, from whom the name had its origin, suffered the extreme penalty during the reign of Tiberius at the hands of one of our procurators, Pontius Pilatus, and a most mischievous superstition thus checked for the moment, again broke out not only in Judaea, the first source of the evil, but even in Rome, where all things hideous and shameful from every part of the world find their centre and become popular. Accordingly, an arrest was first made of all who pleaded guilty; then, upon their information, an immense multitude was convicted, not so much of the crime of firing the city, as of hatred against mankind. Mockery of every sort was added to their deaths. Covered with the skins of beasts, they were torn by dogs and perished, or were nailed to crosses, or were doomed to the flames and burnt, to serve as a nightly illumination when daylight had expired. Nero offered his gardens for the spectacle, and was exhibiting a show in the circus, while he mingled with the people in the dress of a charioteer or stood aloft on a car. Hence, even for criminals who deserve extreme and exemplary punishment, there arose a feeling of compassion; for it was not, as it seemed, for the public good, but to glut one man's cruelty, that they were being destroyed.

2. THE FALL OF JERUSALEM

Two years after the fire of Rome there was a great rebellion against Rome in the Holy Land. It took four years to put down. Jerusalem was finally captured in 70 after the emperor Vespasian had returned home, leaving his son Titus in command.

The destruction of the Temple is described by Josephus in his *Jewish War*. Josephus was a Jew, born in 36 (about the time of the Crucifixion). At the beginning of the war he was a Jewish general, but he was captured at the siege of Jotapata in Galilee. He saw the later stages of the war, including the siege of Jerusalem, as an interpreter with the Romans. Titus sent him to promise mercy to the Jews if they surrendered so he 'went round about the wall, and tried to find a place that was out of reach of their darts and yet within their hearing, and besought them in many words to surrender themselves to the Romans'. Josephus gained the friendship of Titus, took his family name, Flavius, as if he had been his freed slave, went back with him to Rome where he settled down with a state pension and wrote his books. He remained a Jew, wrote a defence of Judaism, but gave up Jewish nationalism.

The Temple was the one started by Herod the Great in 20 B.C. It was the one in which Jesus worshipped, and whose destruction, according to the Gospels (e.g. Mark 14.28), he was charged with planning.

Only the 'Wailing Wall' survives, ever since a place of pilgrimage to Jews.

The destruction of the Temple brought great changes in both Christianity and Judaism. Many Jewish Christians, who up to this time were regarded by their fellow-Jews as of a heretical sect rather than of a different religion, left Jerusalem before the siege and settled at Pella (Mark 13:14–16 refers). They were regarded as having cut themselves off from Israel. This process was completed when, during the second Jewish war (133–5), the Nationalist leader, Bar-Cochba, was recognized by the great rabbi Akiba as Messiah. The umbilical cord which joined Christianity to Jerusalem and to Judaism was cut. Antioch, Alexandria and Rome replaced Jerusalem as the cities of first importance in the Christian world.

To the Jews the destruction of the Temple meant the end of animal sacrifice, and the acceleration of the development of Judaism as the religion of the Law as expounded and expanded by the rabbis in the Mishna and the Talmud. The failure of the two revolts against Rome, and the persecution which followed, put an end to the political expression of Jewish identity for 1800 years. But there had long been side by side with Jewish nationalism a non-political Jewish tradition which, while intensely Jewish in religion, was one of identification with the countries in which they lived. Philo of Alexandria, who died about the year 50, wrote of these Jews of the Dispersion:

'So populous are the Jews that no one country can hold them, and therefore they settle in very many of the most prosperous countries in Europe and Asia both in the islands and on the mainland, and while they hold the Holy City where stands the sacred Temple of the most high God to be their mother city, yet those (cities) which are theirs by inheritance from their fathers, grandfathers and even ancestors farther back, are in each case accounted by them to be their fatherland in which they were born and reared, while to some of these cities they came at the time of their foundation as immigrants, to the satisfaction of the founders.'

Source: Josephus, *Jewish War* (A) 6, 4 and (B) 7, 3.

A.   HOW THE TEMPLE WAS DESTROYED

                                              10 August, 70

So Titus resolved to storm the Temple the next day early in the morning, with his whole army, and to encamp round about the holy house. But as for that house, God had for certain long ago doomed it to the fire. And now that fatal day was come, according to the revolution of ages; it was the tenth day of the month *Lous* (*Ab*), upon which it was formerly burnt by the King of Babylon, although these flames took their rise from the Jews themselves and were occasioned by them. For upon Titus's retiring, the seditious lay still for a little while, and then attacked the Romans again, when those that guarded the holy house fought with those that quenched the fire that was burning the inner (court of) the temple. But these Romans put the Jews to flight, and proceeded as far as the holy house itself. At which time one of the soldiers, without staying for any orders and without any concern or dread upon him at so great an undertaking, and being hurried on by a certain divine fury, snatched somewhat out of the materials that were on fire, and being lifted up by another soldier, he set fire to a golden window, through which there was a passage to the rooms that were round about the holy house, on the north side of it. As the flames went upward, the Jews made a great clamour, such as so mighty an affliction required; and ran together to prevent it. And now they spared not their lives any longer, nor suffered anything to restrain their force, since that holy house was perishing, for whose sake it was that they kept such guard about it.

And now a certain person came running to Titus, and told him of this fire, as he was resting himself in his tent after the last battle. Whereupon he rose up in great haste and, as he was, ran to the holy house, in order to have a stop put to the fire. After him followed all his commanders, and after them followed the several legions in great astonishment. So there was a great clamour and tumult raised, as was natural upon the disorderly motion of so great an army. Then did Caesar, both by calling with a loud voice to the soldiers that were fighting, and by giving a signal to them with his right hand, order them to quench the fire. But they did not hear what he said, though he spake so loud, having their ears already dinned by a greater noise another way. Nor did they attend to the signal he made with his hand, as still some of them were distracted with fighting and others with passion. But as for the legions that came running thither, neither any persuasions nor any threatenings could restrain their violence, but each one's own passion was his commander at this time. And as they were crowding into the Temple together, many of them were trampled on by one another; while a great number fell among the ruins of the cloisters, which were still hot and smoking, and were destroyed in the same miserable way with those whom they had conquered. And when they were come near the holy house, they made as if they did not so much as hear Caesar's orders to the contrary, but they encouraged those that were before them to set it on fire. As for the seditious, they were in too great distress already to afford their assistance (towards quenching the fire). They were everywhere slain, and everywhere beaten. And as for a great part of the people, they were weak, and without arms, and had their throats cut wherever they were caught. Now round about the altar lay dead bodies heaped one upon another, as at the steps going up to it ran a great quantity of their blood, whither also the dead bodies that were slain above (on the altar) fell down.

And now, since Caesar was no way able to restrain the enthusiastic fury of the soldiers, and the fire proceeded on more and more, he went into the holy place of the Temple with his commanders, and saw it, with what was in it, which he found to be far superior to what the relations of foreigners contained, and not inferior to what we ourselves boasted of and believed about it. But as the flame had not as yet reached to its inward parts, but was still consuming the rooms that were about the holy house only, and Titus, supposing what the fact was, that the house itself might yet be saved, he came in haste and endeavoured to persuade the soldiers to quench the fire, and gave orders to Liberalius the centurion and one of those spearmen that were about him to beat the soldiers that were refractory with their staves and to restrain them. Yet were their passions too hard for the regards they had for Caesar and the dread they had of him who forbade them, as was their hatred of the Jews and a certain vehement inclination to fight them too hard for them also. Moreover, the hope of plunder induced many to go on, having this opinion, that all the places within were full of money, seeing that all round about it was made of gold. And besides, one of those that went into the place prevented Caesar, when he ran so hastily out to restrain the soldiers, and threw the fire upon the hinges of the gate, in the dark. Thereby the flame burst out from within the holy house itself immediately. Then the commanders retired, and Caesar with them, and then nobody any longer forbade those that were without to set fire to it. And thus was the holy house burnt down, without Caesar's approbation.

B.   THE TRIUMPH IN ROME   71

The date on which the victory festival was to take place was announced well in advance, and there was not a single person in the whole countless mass of citizens who stayed at home that day. Everyone went out and seized whatever spot they could find where it was possible merely to stand, leaving just enough room for the passing of the procession which they were to see.

During the hours of darkness the whole military force had been led out in companies and battalions by its officers and had been drawn up—not, as usual, near the gates of the palaces on the Palatine, but near the temple of Isis. For Titus and Vespasian had spent the night there, and now, as dawn began to break, they emerged, crowned in laurel wreaths and wearing the time-honoured purple clothes, and walked to the Octavian colonnade. There the Senate, the magistrates and those of Equestrian status were waiting for their arrival. A tribunal had been erected in front of the colonnade, with ivory chairs placed on it for them. As they walked forward to take their seats, all the soldiers raised an immediate cheer, paying abundant testimony to their valour, while Titus and Vespasian sat unarmed, dressed in silk garments and wearing their laurel wreaths. Vespasian acknowledged their acclaim, and, although they were keen to continue cheering, made a sign for silence. As all fell completely quiet, he rose, and, covering most of his head with a veil, made the traditional prayers. Titus followed him in doing likewise. After the prayers, Vespasian said a few words to the whole throng, and then dismissed the soldiers to have the customary breakfast provided at the generals' expense. He then walked to the gate, which got its name from the fact that all triumphal processions passed through it, where he and the others had a light meal. Afterwards, donning the triumphal robes and sacrificing to the gods stationed at the gate, they sent the procession on its way through the theatres to give the crowds a better view.

It is impossible to do justice in the description of the number of things to be seen and to the magnificence of everything that met the eye, whether in skilled craftsmanship, staggering richness or natural rarity. For almost all the remarkable and valuable objects which have ever been collected, piece by piece, by prosperous people, were on that day massed together, affording a clear demonstration of the might of the Roman Empire. The quantities of silver, gold and ivory, worked into every conceivable form, were not like those usually carried in a triumph, but resembled, as it were, a running river of wealth. Purple cloth of extreme rarity was carried along, some of it fashioned by Babylonian skill into accurate pictorial representations. Translucent gems, embedded in diadems or other objects, were borne in such profusion as to dispel any idea that they were rare. Images of the Roman gods passed by, wonderfully big and very skilfully worked, all of them made of expensive materials. Many kinds of beast were led along, all with their individual trappings. In charge of each part of the procession was a number of men in purple and gold costumes, while those selected for the triumph itself wore choice clothes of astonishing richness. Even the prisoners were worth seeing—no disordered mob, but the variety and beauty of their clothes diverted the eye from the disfigurement of their injuries.

The greatest amazement was caused by the floats. Their size gave grounds for alarm about their stability, for many were three or four stories high, and in the richness of their manufacture they provided an astonishing and pleasurable sight. Many were covered in cloth of gold, and worked gold or ivory was fixed on all of them. The war was divided into various aspects and represented in many tableaux which gave a good indication of its character. Here was a fertile land being ravaged, here whole detachments of enemy being slaughtered, others in flight and others being led off into captivity. Here were walls of colossal size being pounded down by siege-engines, here strongpoints being captured, and here well-defended fortifications overwhelmed. On one float the army could be seen pouring inside the walls, on another was a place running with blood. Others showed defenceless men raising their hands in entreaty, firebrands being hurled at temples or buildings falling on their owners. On yet others were depicted rivers, which, after the destruction and desolation, flowed no longer through tilled fields providing water for men and cattle, but through a land on fire from end to end. It was to such miseries that the Jews doomed themselves by the war. The craftsmanship and magnificence of the tableaux gave to those who had not witnessed the events as clear an idea of them as if they had been present. Standing on his individual float was the commander of each of the captured cities showing the way he had been taken prisoner. Many ships followed the floats.

Spoil in abundance was carried past. None of it compared with that taken from the Temple in Jerusalem, a golden table many stones in weight and a golden lampstand, similarly made, which was quite unlike any object in daily use. A centre shaft rose from a base, and from the shaft thin branches or arms extended, in a pattern very like that of tridents, each wrought at its end into a lamp. There were seven of these lamps, thus emphasizing the honour paid by the Jews to the number seven.[1] A tablet of the Jewish Law was carried last of all the spoil. After it came a large group carrying statues of victory, all of them made of ivory and gold. The procession was completed by Vespasian, and, behind him, Titus. Domitian rode on horseback wearing a beautiful uniform and on a mount that was wonderfully well worth seeing.

The procession ended up at the Temple of Jupiter on the Capitol, where the generals got down. They still had to wait for the traditional moment when the news was brought of the death of the enemy leader. In this case he was Simon, son of Giovas, who had passed in procession with the captives, and had been dragged under the lash, with his head in a noose, to a spot near the Forum. That is the traditional place at Rome for the execution of those condemned to death for war-crimes. When his end was

[1] See Plate 1.

announced and a general cheer had arisen, they started the sacrifices, and after completing them with the customary prayers, they retired to the palace. There they entertained some of the citizens to dinner, while for all the others preparations for banquets at their own homes had already been made.

For on that day the city of Rome made holiday for their victory in the war against the Jews, for the end of civil disorder, and for the rising expectation of peace and prosperity.

3. SUETONIUS ON CHRISTIANS, JEWS AND OTHERS   *c.* 52–96

We know from the New Testament that there were Christians in Rome before Paul got there in the year 61. The Jewish religion was officially permitted by the Roman emperors both before and after the great Jewish rebellions of 64–70 (Extract 2) and of 133–135. There was, however, frequent friction. Some of these troubles at least were caused by rows between Christian and non-Christian Jews. There had been trouble in Rome itself, for instance, during the reign of Claudius (41–54) which had led to the temporary expulsion of the Jews from the city. This trouble was probably of this nature if the Chrestus of this first extract is intended for Christ. Two of these expelled Jews, Aquila and his wife Priscilla, are mentioned in Acts 18, 2.

Suetonius, from whom these short extracts come, was a much duller writer than Tacitus but, like him, he was right at the centre of government affairs. He was, for instance, private secretary to the emperor Hadrian. His lives of Claudius and Nero deal with events that happened before he was born; but he was in his middle twenties by the time that Domitian took the action described in the two later extracts.

Politics and taxes play as big a part as religion in the events of the year 95. Money was scarce. The emperor needed more and more to pay for the army. The Jews used to pay a special Temple tax for the upkeep of the Temple at Jerusalem. It went on after the end of the Jewish war although there was no longer a temple to support. It went to the emperor instead. Domitian thought that it was not bringing all that it could be made to yield. He decided that two classes of people were escaping—first, those who lived as Jews without acknowledging the fact; and, secondly, Jews who concealed their origin. There is likelihood that the first were 'god-fearers'—Gentiles who were attracted to the Jewish religion and followed most of its practices, but stopped short of circumcision which would have made them proselytes. The second group are most likely to have been Jews who had become Christians, and by this period would no longer have regarded themselves, or been regarded, as part of the Jewish community.

Politics—the fear of a conspiracy—certainly entered into the case of Domitilla and her husband, Flavius Clemens. Domitian had expelled the philosophers from Rome in 93, disliking the free spirit of enquiry. He dreaded secret societies. In 95 he banished his niece, Flavia Domitilla and executed her husband, Flavius Clemens, who was his cousin. Suetonius suggests that Flavius was condemned on some trumped up charge, but does not specify its nature. He goes on to recount the story of the plot which resulted in Domitian's murder by, among others, Domitilla's steward. Dion Cassius, a hundred years later, says that the charge against Clemens and Domitilla was sacrilege. They and others had gone astray 'after the manner of the Jews'. The Christian, Eusebius, writing much later, but using earlier authorities—unfortunately in this instance he does not give a verbatim quotation as he often did—wrote: 'even historians who accepted none of our beliefs unhesitatingly recorded in their pages both the persecution and the martyrdoms to which it led. They also indicated the precise date, noting that in the fifteenth year of Domitian, Flavia Domitilla, ... was, with many others, because of their testimony to Christ, taken to the island of Pontia as a punishment.' (Eusebius 3. 18.) Clemens may have been a Christian; Domitilla certainly was. One of the earliest catacombs was on her land and was called by her name. (See Plates 9, 13, 28.)

Source: Suetonius: *The Twelve Caesars:* Claudius 25, Nero 16, Domitian 12 and 15, 17.

Because the Jews caused continual disturbances at the instigation of Chrestus, Claudius expelled them from Rome.... He completely abolished the cruel and savage rites of the Druids among the Gauls, which Augustus had only prohibited to Roman citizens. On the other hand he attempted to transfer the Eleusinian Mysteries[1] from Athens to Rome.

During his (Nero's) reign a great many public abuses were suppressed by the imposition of heavy penalties, and among the novel enactments were sumptuary laws limiting private expenditure; the substitution of a simple grain distribution for public

[1] See page 31.

banquets; and a decree restricting the food sold in wine-shops to green vegetables, dried beans and the like—whereas, before, all kinds of tasty snacks had been displayed. Punishments were also inflicted on the Christians, a sect professing a new and mischievous religious belief; and Nero ended the licence that the charioteers had so long enjoyed that they claimed it as a right: to wander merrily down the streets, swindling and robbing the populace. He likewise expelled from the City all pantomime actors and their hangers-on.

Being in financial difficulties through his costly buildings and entertainments, and the increases he had made to the soldiers' pay . . . Domitian resorted to every kind of extortion. . . . Besides other taxes, that on Jews was collected with extreme severity, and those were prosecuted who lived as Jews without publicly acknowledging Judaism, as well as those who kept their Jewish origin secret and did not pay the tax levied on their race. I remember as a boy being present when a man ninety years old was stripped and examined before the procurator and a crowded court to see whether he was circumcized or not.

The occasion of Domitian's murder was that he had executed, on some trivial pretext, his own extremely stupid cousin, Flavius Clemens, just before the completion of a consulship; though he had previously named Flavius's two small sons as his heirs. . . . All that has come to light about either the plot or the assassination is that his niece Domitilla's steward, Stephanus, had been accused of embezzlement; and that, when he approached the conspirators, they were already debating whether it would be better to murder Domitian in his bath or at dinner. Stephanus offered them his services which were accepted. . . .

4. HOW GOVERNORS SHOULD TREAT CHRISTIANS   112

Pliny's report asking how Christians should be treated and the emperor's reply to it mark the beginning of a period of greater tolerance. The setting of these letters is as follows. Pliny had been sent out as governor to a distant province to pull things together after a period of slack administration. Law and order must be enforced. This inevitably meant trouble for the Christians since technically they were always in the wrong, if challenged, because they would not sacrifice to the gods and burn incense before the emperor's statue. They had plenty of enemies to denounce them. There were by this time so many Christians along the Asiatic coast of the Sea of Marmora and the Black Sea (Pliny's province of Bithynia-Pontus) that people complained that the trade in sacrificial animals was doing badly. Compare the complaints against Paul at Ephesus (Acts 19. 23–41). It was the role of a governor to see that trade was not affected. Pliny could not have afforded to take no notice of the Christians even if he had wanted to.

At first Pliny enforced the law strictly, executing those provincials who admitted they were Christians. Christians who were Roman citizens he sent to Rome for judgment. Compare Paul's protest at Philippi and his appeal to Caesar (Acts 16. 35–39, and 25. 11–12). Up to this point Pliny merely administered the law and saw no reason to bother the emperor.

But his action against the Christians led to anonymous accusations, and the risk of a really great number of executions. Moreover Pliny's investigations to decide on the appropriate punishment in cases where the accused recanted or had already stopped being a Christian showed that Christians were not, as was usually thought, plain criminals but decent law-abiding citizens in their private lives. They tried to conform whenever they could in conscience—e.g. they had given up their club meals together (originally associated with the Eucharist) when Pliny had issued orders to enforce the emperor's general ban on private societies.

Pliny was a humane man. He asked the emperor what he should do. He got the answer he wanted from Trajan. Normally the answer would have been filed in the governor's archives and known only in the province, but the whole considerable correspondence between Pliny and Trajan was published, so that incidentally this ruling on how Christians were to be treated became widely known. Tertullian, for instance (see pp. 94–6, 98, 103–5), who lived in North Africa, was able to quote it verbatim.

Pliny (61–113) was a nephew and adopted son of the great naturalist of the same name. The elder Pliny was killed in the volcanic eruption of Vesuvius which destroyed Pompeii in 79; the younger Pliny wrote an account of the tragedy. Among the friends to whom he wrote letters was the historian Tacitus (see Extract 1). The emperor Trajan was a friend of Pliny as well as his master. Trajan was born about the

c

year 56. He was emperor from 98 to 117. Gibbon regretted how scanty was the first-hand evidence about him. 'There remains, however', he wrote, 'one panegyric far removed beyond the suspicion of flattery. Above two hundred and fifty years after the death of Trajan, the senate, in pouring out the customary acclamations on the accession of a new emperor, wished that he might surpass the felicity of Augustus, and the virtue of Trajan (felicior Augusto, *melior Trajano*).'

Notice that Christianity is established in villages as well as towns; note also that none of the three friends Tacitus, Suetonius and Pliny, who were all in high positions and in regular correspondence with one another, had any real knowledge of Christians or their religion until Pliny stumbled on it in the course of his duty as a provincial governor.

Source: Pliny, *Letters* 10, 96 and 97.

FROM PLINY TO THE EMPEROR TRAJAN

It is my rule, Your Majesty, to report to you anything that worries me, for I know well that you are best able to speed my hesitation or instruct me in my ignorance. I have never in the past been present at the investigations into Christians, and so I am at a loss to know the nature and extent of the normal questions and punishments. I have also been seriously perplexed whether age should make some difference, or whether the very young should be treated in exactly the same way as the more mature. Should the penitent be pardoned, or should no mercy be shown a man who has recanted if he has really been a Christian? Should the mere name be reason enough for punishment however free from crime a man may be, or should only the sins and crimes that attend the name be punished?

Till I hear from you, I have adopted the following course towards those who have been brought before me as Christians. First I have asked them if they were Christians. If they confessed that they were, I repeated my question a second and a third time, accompanying it with threats of punishment. If they still persisted in their statements, I ordered them to be taken out. For I was in no doubt that, whatever it was to which they were confessing, they had merited some punishment by their stubbornness and unbending obstinacy. There were others possessed by similar madness, but these I detailed to be sent to Rome, for they were Roman citizens.

Soon, as I investigated the matter, types began to multiply as so often happens, and charges started to spread. An anonymous notebook was presented with many names in it. Those who denied that they were or ever had been Christians I thought should be released, provided that they called on the gods in my presence, and offered incense and wine to your statue (which I had expressly brought in with the images of the gods for that very purpose), and, above all, if they renounced Christ, which no true Christian, I am told, can be made to do. Others informed against admitted that they were Christians but later denied it; they had been, but had given up, some three years past, some further back, and one person as long as 25 years ago. All of them reverenced your statue and the images of the gods, and renounced Christ.

They stated that the sum total of their fault or error was as follows. On a fixed day they used to assemble before dawn to sing an antiphonal hymn to Christ as to a god, and to bind themselves by oath not for any criminal purpose, but to commit no fraud, no robbery or adultery, to bear no false witness, and not to deny any debt when asked to pay up. After this it was their custom to separate and to reassemble to eat a common meal, all together and quite harmless. They claimed that they had stopped even that after my edict in which I followed your commands in banning society meetings. So I felt it all the more necessary to find out the truth under torture from two slave girls whom they called Deaconesses. But I found nothing but a depraved and groundless superstition.

So I postponed my enquiry to consult you. The matter seemed worth your attention, especially since the number of those slipping is great. Many people of all ages and classes and of both sexes are now being enticed into mortal peril and will be in the future. The superstition has spread like the plague, not only in the cities but in the villages and the countryside as well. I feel it must be stopped and checked. It is true that everyone is agreed that temples once deserted are now being attended once again, and that sacred ceremonies once neglected are again being performed. Victims for sacrifice are everywhere on sale, for which only an odd buyer could be found a short while ago. All this goes to show how many men could be saved if there is room for repentance.

THE EMPEROR'S REPLY

You have acted quite properly, Pliny, in examining the cases of those Christians brought before you. Nothing definite can be laid down as a general rule. They should not be hunted out. If accusations are made and they are found guilty, they must be punished. But remember that a man may expect pardon from repentance if he denies that he is a Christian, and proves this to your satisfaction, that is by worshipping our gods, however much you may have suspected him in the past. Anonymous lists should have no part in any charge made. That is a thoroughly bad practice, and not in accordance with the spirit of the age.

CHAPTER TWO

FOUR CHRISTIANS OF THE
SECOND GENERATION
Clement, Ignatius, Papias, Polycarp

Clement was bishop of Rome. He may have been the 'fellow worker' of Paul referred to in Philippians 4. 3, if that letter was written from Rome, but this can only be a guess. Ignatius was either the second or third bishop of Antioch, Peter was claimed by Antioch as its first bishop. He certainly visited it—Paul took a poor view of his behaviour there and said so in Galatians 2. 11–21. Papias and Polycarp were friends and pupils of John at Ephesus. Papias became bishop of Hierapolis, about a hundred miles up country from Ephesus; Polycarp, bishop of Smyrna.

There was clearly a great deal of letter writing between the churches in various towns in the first century. If there was as yet no empire-wide Christian organization, there was much communication both by letter and by personal visiting. Three of the four extracts in this chapter come from inter-church letters.

The remaining extract, that from Papias, deals with the process of gospel-making. Most of the Epistles in the New Testament belong to the first generation of Christians; most of the Gospels in the form in which we have them belong to the second generation.

5. THE SACKED BISHOPS OF CORINTH   c. 96

We know very little about the organization of the very early church. A good deal of what we do know comes, perhaps naturally, from places where things were going wrong. Corinth was one of the main Christian centres in the first century as well as a great trading city—Christianity took root first in towns. It had a reputation for troublesome disputes starting in New Testament times.

One of them occurred about the year 96 when the church of Corinth dismissed its bishops or presbyters. Pretty certainly the ejected men appealed to their friends in other churches for help. Rome, which had close ties with Corinth, sent a deputation of three men named in this extract, with a letter of introduction and advice from the head of the Roman church.

This was Clement who is reckoned third in succession to Peter as bishop of Rome. His name suggests that he may have been a freedman, i.e. an ex-slave, of Flavius Clemens and Domitilla (pages 11–12). This letter to Corinth hovered on the verge of admission to the New Testament for a considerable time. It was read at church services in Corinth at least as late as 170.

Notice that:

a. Clement supports the ejected bishops because they trace their authority back to the apostles;

b. the terms 'bishop' and 'presbyter' are interchangeable; and that there is more than one bishop—at least at Corinth church organization is still fluid;

c. it is the role of the bishops to 'offer the gifts', i.e. to celebrate the Eucharist;

d. the Roman church feels justified in offering strongly worded advice to the Corinthian church;

e. the language of the letter is Greek: Corinth was, of course, Greek-speaking; so, too, predominantly was the church at Rome in this period.

Source: Clement, *1st Letter to the Corinthians* 44; 65.

The Church of God which sojourns in Rome to the Church of God which sojourns in Corinth, to those who are called and sanctified by the will of God through our lord Jesus Christ. May grace and peace be multiplied to you from the supreme God through Jesus Christ . . .

Our apostles knew through our lord Jesus Christ that there would be strife for the title of bishop. For this reason, since they had received perfect foreknowledge, they appointed those already ordained and afterwards directed that, when these fell asleep, other attested men should succeed to their ministry. Therefore we consider that it is not just to discard from the ministry those appointed by the apostles, or by other notable men later, with the approval of the whole church, since they have ministered to the flock of Christ blamelessly, humbly, quietly, and unselfishly, as all have certified for many years. For our sin is not small if we reject as bishops those who have blamelessly and holily offered the gifts. Blessed are those presbyters who have already finished their course and have gained a fruitful and perfect release, for they have no fear that any one shall remove them from their appointed place. For we see that you have displaced some of those good governors from the ministry they have irreproachably fulfilled . . .

Quickly send back to us, in peace with gladness, our messengers Claudius Ephebus, Valerius Vito, and Fotunatus, that they may the sooner report the peace and concord we pray for and desire, and we may the sooner rejoice in your good health. The grace of our lord Jesus Christ be with you . . .

6. THE LAST LETTERS OF IGNATIUS   *c.* 114

Ignatius was bishop of Antioch, the capital of the great Roman province of Syria. He was arrested as a Christian and sent to Rome for sentence. On his way his escort allowed him to write letters to various Christian churches. The first extract, describing his journey, comes from Eusebius who, though he lived two hundred years later, based his work on contemporary documents many of which he copied into his book. For Eusebius see the Introduction and notes on pages 135 and 142. The second extract, in which Ignatius looks forward to his death, comes from his advance letter to the church at Rome.

Note that martyrdom is courted as a positive good, not looked on as something to be avoided if this was honourably possible. This is strange to us, but a fundamental part of early Christian feeling.

Trajan was still emperor. Note what even a humane pagan emperor could accept as a matter of course. The form of execution which Ignatius expected was to be thrown to the wild beasts at one of the Games, provided by the State for the amusement of the people of Rome and other great cities, where spectator sport was part of the way of life. This was not a form of torture specially laid on for Christians, but a regular method of capital punishment for ordinary criminals. 'As the condemned man had to be tortured to death, there seemed no reason for cheating the public, who could never have enough bloodshed, of such a spectacle.' (Paoli: *Rome, Its People, Life and Customs*, p. 252).

Note also the reference to heresies. A heresy is a belief which separates some Christians from the orthodox (those who hold 'the right teaching'). Of course to the heretics the roles were reversed—they were orthodox, their opponents, heretics. One heresy, common at this time in Ephesus, involved the belief that the god of Moses, who gave him the Law, was only an angel of the supreme God, and that Jesus was an ordinary man on whom the Holy Spirit came at his baptism and departed before his crucifixion.

Sources: A: An account of Ignatius' last journey, compiled by Eusebius from the letters of Ignatius; B: Ignatius, *Epistle to Romans*, quoted by Eusebius in *History of the Church* 3, 36.

A.   HIS LAST JOURNEY

Ignatius was sent from Syria to Rome and became food for wild beasts because of his witness for Christ. As he journeyed through Asia under the closest military guard, he encouraged the churches in the various cities where he stopped with sermons and exhortations, warning them especially to be on their guard against the heresies which were beginning to prevail and urging them to hold fast to the Apostolic tradition. And for safety's sake he thought it was essential to put that tradition in writing and fix its form. So when he reached Smyrna, where Polycarp was, he wrote one epistle to the church at Ephesus (in which he mentions its pastor Onesimus), another to the church at Magnesia on the river Maeander (in which he refers to a bishop Damas), and lastly one to the church at Tralles, whose bishop, he says, was then Polybius.

In addition to these he also wrote to the church at Rome, imploring them not to obtain his release from martyrdom and so rob him of his fervent hope.

These letters he wrote from Smyrna to the churches named. And after leaving Smyrna he wrote again from Troas to the Philadelphians and church at Smyrna, and particularly to Polycarp, the head of that church. He well knew that he was an apostolic man, and so he commended to him, as a true and good shepherd, the flock at Antioch and begged him to take great care of it.

B.   HIS DESIRE FOR MARTYRDOM

From Syria all the way to Rome I am fighting with wild beasts, on land and sea, by night and day, bound in the middle of ten leopards—a squad of soldiers—who only become worse the better they are treated. Their ill-treatment certainly teaches me discipleship, but 'I am not thereby justified' (1 Cor. 4, 4).

May I have joy of the beasts prepared for me! I pray that I may find them ready. I shall even coax them to devour me quickly, for they have been afraid to touch some people, and I don't want to be treated like that. If they are unwilling, I will force them. Forgive me, I know what is best for me. I do now begin to be a disciple. May nothing seen or unseen envy me, that I should attain to Jesus Christ. Let fire and cross, attacks of wild beasts, wrenching apart of bones, hacking of limbs, crushing of the whole body, tortures of the devil—let them all come upon me if only I may attain to Jesus Christ.

7. PAPIAS ON THE MAKING OF THE GOSPELS *c.* 120

Papias (*c.* 60–130), a close friend of Polycarp, was bishop of Hierapolis in Asia Minor near the junction of the roads inland from Smyrna and Ephesus. His great work, in five books, *Expositions of the Sayings of the Lord*, is lost apart from a few quotations in later authors. He had some written sources—he lived in the time of gospel-making—and collected much oral material. The loss is great.

Papias was what is called a Millenarian—that is to say he believed that Christ would reign on earth with his saints for a thousand years before taking them up with him to heaven. 'I suppose he got these notions,' Eusebius tartly remarked, 'by misinterpreting the apostolic accounts and failing to grasp what they had said in mystic and symbolic language. For he seems to have been a man of very small intelligence to judge from his books.' However that may have been, this belief had a great vogue among many leading second-century Christians. It was revived at the Reformation among the more extreme Protestants and has continued to be held among the more radical sects into the present age.

Mark's gospel is traditionally associated with Rome. Matthew's is clearly concerned with Jewish Christians and provided them with help in their arguments with non-Christian Jews. Behind its present Greek form there is probably an Aramaic document. Papias probably meant Aramaic, the common language of the country in Palestine at this time, when he said that Matthew's sayings were written in Hebrew. What relation there may have been between the Johns mentioned by Papias (it is not clear whether he refers to one or two people) and the Fourth Gospel, the Epistles of John and/or the Book of Revelation is something that nobody is sure about.

By the year 150 our four gospels were recognized as authentic and had begun to drive out their competitors, of which a good many were in existence. This was the time when Tatian reduced the four gospels to one continuous narrative in his *Diatessaron* (Through the Four) which for two hundred years was the standard text in use in the lands where Syriac was the language. Thirty years later the position of the four evangelists was so assured that Irenaeus could remark that of course there were four gospels just as there were four points of the compass.

Source: Eusebius, 3. 39.

I shall not hesitate to tell you, along with my interpretations, everything that I carefully learnt in time past from the Elders, and carefully remembered; for I can guarantee its truth . . .

Whenever anyone came who had been a follower of the Elders, I would enquire about their discourses, what was said by Andrew, or by Peter, or by Philip or Thomas or James, or by John or Matthew, or any other of the Lord's disciples, and what Aristion and the Elder John, the disciples of the Lord, were still saying. For I did not think that I could get as much profit from books as from the utterances of a living and abiding voice.

The Elder said this also: Mark, having become the interpreter of Peter, wrote down accurately, but in no order, everything that he remembered of what was said or done by the Lord. For he neither heard the Lord nor was he a follower of his, but he was later a follower of Peter, who had no intention of giving a connected account of the Lord's sayings but adapted his teaching to the occasion. So Mark was justified in writing down things as he remembered them, for he made it his one care not to omit anything that he had heard, or to set down any false statement about it.

Matthew compiled the Sayings in the Hebrew language, and each one interpreted them as he could.

8. THE MARTYRDOM OF POLYCARP
c. 155

Polycarp was bishop of Smyrna, now called Izmir, and the leading Christian figure in Roman Asia in the reign of the emperor Antoninus Pius. The conduct of Polycarp's trial and the nature of his death are an illuminating comment on the passage in Gibbon's *Decline and Fall*

of the Roman Empire in which he remarks: 'If a man were called to fix
the period in the history of the world during which the condition of
the human race was most happy and prosperous, he would, without
hesitation, name that which elapsed from the death of Domitian to the
accession of Commodus' (96–180).

Irenaeus, who knew Polycarp when he was a boy, wrote this about
him in a letter to a friend: 'What boys learn grows with their mind and
becomes a part of it, so that I can describe the very place where the
blessed Polycarp sat as he discoursed, his goings out and his comings in,
the manner of his life and his physical appearance, his discourses to the
people, and the accounts which he gave of his intercourse with John
and with the others who had seen the Lord' (quoted by Eusebius in his
history, 5. 20).

In the *Revelation of St John the Divine* (2, 10) there is a message to the
Church in Smyrna: 'Be thou faithful unto death and I will give thee
a crown of life'. This will serve as a good epitaph for Polycarp.

One of Polycarp's own letters, to the Philippians, survives and also
a letter to him from Ignatius. This account of his death was written by
the Church at Smyrna for the Church at Philomelium, and 'to all the
Holy Catholic Churches'.

The Church of God sojourning at Smyrna to the Church of
God sojourning at Philomelium, and to all the dioceses of the Holy
Catholic Church in every place, mercy and peace and love of God
the Father and of our Lord Jesus Christ be multiplied.

We write, brethren, to tell you of the events which befell them
that suffered martyrdom, and the blessed Polycarp, who, as it were,
by his martyrdom set his seal upon the persecution, and put an end
to it. For nearly all the preceding events came to pass in order that
to us the Lord might once again give an example of the martyrdom which resembles the Gospel story.

For he waited that he might be betrayed, just as was the Lord,
to the end that we too may become imitators of him, regarding
not only what concerns ourselves but also what concerns our
neighbours.

For it is the part of true and constant love that a man should
wish not only himself, but also all the brethren, to be saved.

Now blessed and noble were all the martyrdoms which took
place in accordance with the will of God; for we are bound to be

very reverent and to ascribe the power over all things to God. And who could fail to marvel at their nobility, their endurance, their love for their Master? Some were so torn by the scourges that the structure of their flesh to the inner veins and arteries was exposed to view; but they endured it, so that even the bystanders were moved to pity and lamentation. Some reached such a pitch of noble endurance that not one of them let cry or groan escape him, while they showed us all that, tortured as they were at that time, Christ's martyrs were absent from the flesh; or rather that standing by their side their Lord was in close converse with them. So, giving heed to the grace of Christ, they were despising the torments of the world, redeeming themselves at the cost of one short season from everlasting punishment. Cold to them was the fire of the inhuman tormentors; for they kept before their eyes their escape from the fire that is everlasting and is never quenched, while with the eyes of the heart they looked up at the good things reserved for them that have endured, which 'neither ear hath heard nor eye seen, neither have entered into the hearts of man' (1 Cor. 2. 9), but were being shown by the Lord to those who were now already no longer men but angels. In like manner they that were condemned to the beasts underwent awful punishments, being made to lie on prickly shells and buffeted, with various other forms of torture, to the end that, if it were possible, by means of their protracted punishment they might be turned to denial by him who was devising so many wiles against them—the devil.

But thanks be to God, for he verily prevailed against all. For the right noble Germanicus, by means of his endurance, turned their cowardice into courage. With signal distinction did he fight against the beasts. While the Proconsul, wishful to persuade him, was urging him to have compassion on his youth, in his eagerness to be released the sooner from their unrighteous and careless mode of life he used force to the wild beast and pulled it on himself. Now it was on this that all the multitude, amazed at the noble conduct of the Godbeloved and Godfearing race of the Christians, shouted out,

'Away with the Atheists. Let search be made for Polycarp.'

But one of them, Quintus by name, a Phrygian, lately arrived from his native province, when he saw the beasts, was afraid. It was he who had forced both himself and certain others to come forward of their own accord. After very earnest entreaty he had been persuaded by the Proconsul to take the oath and offer incense. Now, brethren, we do not commend those who surrender themselves, for not such is the teaching of the Gospel.

Now the most admirable Polycarp so soon as he heard (that he was being sought for) at first showed no dismay, but wished to remain in town. The majority, however, prevailed on him to withdraw. And withdraw he did, to a little estate not far from the city. There he spent his time with a few companions, occupied night and day in nothing but prayer for all men, and for the churches throughout the world, as indeed was his constant habit. And while praying he fell into a trance three days before his apprehension, and he saw his pillows being burned by fire. And he turned and said to them that were with him,

'I must needs be burned alive.'

Now his pursuers were persistent, so he shifted his quarters to another farm. Then straightway the pursuers arrived on the spot and, on failing to find him, they seized two slave-boys. One of these confessed under torture; for indeed it was impossible for him to evade pursuit, since they that betrayed him were of his own household. And the eirenarch, head of the police, who, as it befell, bore the same name (as our Lord's judge), being called Herod, made haste to bring him into the stadium, in order that he might be made a partner of Christ, and so fulfil his own appointed lot, and that his betrayers might undergo the punishment of Judas himself.

Accordingly, having the lad with them, on Friday at about supper time forth sallied constables and mounted men, with their usual equipment, hurrying as though 'against a thief' (Matt. 26. 55). Late in the day they came up together and found him in a cottage lying in an upper room. It was within his power to go away thence to another place, but he refused to do so, saying,

'God's will be done.'

So, on hearing of their arrival, he came down and conversed

with them, they all the while wondering at his age and his constancy, and at there being so much ado about the arrest of such an old man. Upon this he gave orders for something to be served for them to eat and drink, at that hour, as much as they would. He besought them withal to give him an hour that he might pray freely; and on their granting him this boon he stood up and prayed, being so full of the grace of God, that for the space of two hours he could not hold his peace, while the hearers were smitten with amazement, and many were sorry that they had come after so venerable an old man.

After remembering all, both small and great, high and low, who had ever been brought into communication with him and all the Catholic Church throughout the world, at last he brought his prayer to an end. The time had come for him to depart. They set him on an ass and brought him into the city, it being a high Sabbath. He was met by the eirenarch Herod, and by his father, Nicetes, who shifted him into their carriage, and tried to persuade him as they sat by his side, urging,

'Why, what harm is there in saying Caesar is Lord, and sacrificing, and the rest of it, and so saving thyself?'

At first he made no reply, but, as they were persistent, he said, 'I do not intend to do what you advise me.'

On their failing to persuade him they began to use terrible language and to drag him hurriedly down, so that as he was getting down from the carriage he grazed his shin. Without turning back, as though he had suffered no hurt, he fared on with speed, and was conducted to the stadium, where there was so great a tumult that it was impossible for anyone to be heard.

Now as Polycarp was entering into the stadium, there came a voice to him from heaven,

'Be strong, Polycarp, and play the man.'

The speaker indeed no one saw, but the voice was heard by those of our friends who were present. Then he was dragged forward, and great was the din of them that heard that Polycarp was arrested. So he was brought before the Proconsul, who asked him if he were the man himself? He assented, and the Proconsul tried to persuade him, urging,

'Have respect to thine old age,' and the rest of it, according to the customary form, 'Swear by the genius of Caesar; repent; say, "Away with the Atheists".'

Then Polycarp looked with a serious countenance on the multitude of lawless heathen gathered in the stadium, and he beckoned with his hand, and looked up to heaven with a groan, and said, 'Away with the Atheists.'

The Proconsul continued insisting and saying, 'Swear, and I release thee; revile the Christ.'

And Polycarp said, 'Eighty and six years have I served him, and he hath done me no wrong; how then can I blaspheme my King who saved me?'

The Proconsul continuing to persist, and to urge, 'Swear by the genius of Caesar,' he answered,

'If thou vainly fanciest that I would "swear by the genius of Caesar," as thou sayest, pretending that thou art ignorant who I am, hear plainly that I am a Christian. And if thou art willing to learn the doctrine of Christianity, appoint a day, and grant me a hearing.'

The Proconsul said, 'Persuade the people.'

Polycarp then said, 'Thee, indeed, I should have deemed worthy of argument, for we have been taught to render to authorities and powers ordained by God, honour as is meet, so long as it does us no harm, but I deem not this multitude worthy of my making my defence to them.'

The Proconsul said, 'I have wild beasts; if thou wilt not change thy mind I will throw thee to them.' Then he said, 'Bid them be brought: change of mind from better to worse is not a change that we are allowed; but to change from wrong to right is good.' Then again said the Proconsul to him, 'As thou despisest the beasts, unless thou change thy mind, I make thee to be destroyed by fire.'

Then Polycarp: 'Thou threatenest the fire that burns for a season, and after a little while is quenched; for thou art ignorant of the fire of the judgement to come, and of everlasting punishment reserved for the ungodly. But for what art thou waiting? Bring what thou wilt.'

While speaking these words and many more he was filled with

courage and gladness: his face grew full of grace, so that not only did it not fall, agitated at all that was being said to him, but on the contrary the Proconsul was amazed, and sent his own crier to make proclamation in the middle of the stadium thrice,

'Polycarp has confessed himself to be a Christian.'

No sooner was this proclaimed by the crier than the whole multitude, both of Gentiles and of Jews dwelling at Smyrna, with ungovernable rage and a loud voice began to shout—

'This is the teacher of Asia, the father of the Christians, the destroyer of our Gods, the man who teaches many not to sacrifice nor even to worship.' With these words they kept up their shout and continued asking Philip the Asiarch to let loose a lion at Polycarp.

'But,' said he, 'that is no longer in my power: the sports are over.' Thereupon it was their pleasure to yell with one accord that he should burn Polycarp alive. For the (prediction) of the vision about his pillow must needs be fulfilled, on the occasion of his seeing it burning while he was at prayer, and turning round and saying prophetically to his faithful friends,

'I must needs be burnt alive.'

This then was no sooner said than done, the mob in a moment getting together logs and faggots from the workshops and baths, the Jews as usual showing themselves specially zealous in the work. When the pyre had been made ready, Polycarp took off all his upper garments, and untied his girdle. He endeavoured also to take off his shoes, though he had never been in the habit of doing this, because every one of the faithful was eager to be the first to touch his bare body. For his good life's sake he had been treated with every honour even before his head was white. Forthwith then all the gear adapted for the pyre was put about him. They were on the point of fastening him with nails, but he said,

'Let me be as I am: he that gave me power to abide the fire will grant me too, without your making me fast with nails, to abide untroubled at the pyre.'

So they did not nail him, but they bound him to the stake. He put his hands behind him and was bound, like a goodly ram out of a great flock for an offering, a whole burnt offering made ready and acceptable to God. Then he looked up to heaven and said,

'O Lord God Almighty, Father of thy beloved and blessed Son Jesus Christ, by whose means we have received our knowledge of thee, God of Angels and Powers and of all creation and of the whole race of the just who live before thy face, I bless thee in that thou hast deemed me worthy of this day and hour; that I might take a portion in the number of the martyrs in the cup of Christ, to the resurrection of eternal life both of soul and body in the incorruption of the Holy Ghost. Among these may I today be welcome before thy face as a fat and acceptable sacrifice, as thou didst prepare and manifest beforehand and didst bring about its fulfilment, thou the faithful and true God. For this cause, yea and for all things I praise thee, I bless thee, I glorify thee through the everlasting and heavenly High Priest Jesus Christ thy beloved Son, through whom to thee with him and with the Holy Ghost be glory now and for the ages to come. Amen.'

When he had offered up his Amen and completed his prayer, the firemen kindled the fire. A great flame flashed out, and we to whom it was granted to see saw a marvel; and we moreover were preserved to the end that we might tell to the rest the tidings of what came to pass. The fire made the appearance of a vaulted roof, like a ship's sail filling out with the wind, and it walled about the body of the martyr in a ring. There was he in the midst, not like flesh burning, but like a loaf baking, or like gold and silver being fired in a furnace. Moreover we were aware of a fragrance as great as of frankincense or some other of the precious spices.

In the end, when the wicked ones had seen that his body could not be consumed by the fire they commanded an executioner to come up to him and to drive in a dagger. When he had so done there came out (a dove and) abundance of blood so that it put out the fire, and all the multitude marvelled at the mighty difference between the unbelievers and the elect, of whom one was this man, the most admirable Polycarp, who in our times was an apostolic and prophetic teacher, bishop of the holy Church in Smyrna; for every word which he uttered from his mouth was accomplished and will be accomplished.

D

CHAPTER THREE

CHRISTIANITY AND ITS RIVALS IN THE SECOND CENTURY
The Mysteries, the Philosophers, the Jews

In the second century as many men had as much need of a personal faith to live by as at any other time. They could not, for the most part, find it in the classical religion of the gods of Olympus. The old religion was, so to speak, the Established Church and, as such, it was a civic duty to support it—little more, at least for the educated. Allied to it was the homage or worship due to the emperor. Before long emperors were claiming divine honours: Domitian, for instance, liked to be greeted as 'Our Master and our God'. But, as Sir William Ramsay put it, the State interfered in religious matters only in so far as they had a political aspect and a bearing on patriotism and loyalty. In other respects the gods were left to defend themselves (deorum iniuriae dis curae).

Men turned, as they had long been doing, to beliefs that promised personal salvation, and that made sense of the universe and man's place in it. They found satisfaction in the mystery cults and in the various schools of philosophy. They turned to Christianity or to Judaism. They moved from one belief to another. They held several at the same time. Only Christianity and Judaism made exclusive claims. Many men came to Christianity through one of the other Ways. This chapter is designed to give a little insight into how men sought and came to find satisfaction in this period of spiritual rootlessness.

The last extract shows how a Christian philosopher thought people ought to behave.

9. THE MYSTERIES

The mystery religions, much older than Christianity, offered men release and initiation into life on a new plane. Little is known about these cults: to the uninitiated they were—mysteries.

There were many different Mysteries. From Greece came the Orphic and Eleusinian Mysteries. Orphism is associated with the myth of Orpheus who went to the underworld to bring back his dead wife. In it are found elements of atonement, the suffering of a god-man and immortality. The Eleusinian Mysteries were associated with the worship of Demeter, the earth goddess who left Olympus to retrieve her daughter Persephone, who had been carried off to earth. There are references both to seed-time and harvest and, later by the philosophers and perhaps also in the Mystery, to death, burial and immortality. Claudius wanted to transfer the Eleusinian Mysteries from Athens to Rome; Julian the Apostate, the emperor, who wanted to restore paganism, was initiated at Eleusis.

The most serious Mystery as a rival to Christianity was that of Mithras, one confined to men and very popular in the army. It was apparently brought from Persia by the soldiers of Alexander the Great. Mithra was a Persian sun-god, the slayer of the bull from whose blood all earthly life had sprung. He was always represented as fighting for right against wrong—hence, perhaps, its appeal to soldiers. Immortality was promised to initiates. Three small temples of Mithras have been found along Hadrian's Wall, and a larger one was recently uncovered in London.

From Egypt came the Isis–Osiris mystery, developed, like all the others, from a myth. Osiris, god of light, was killed by Set, god of darkness; Isis gathered the pieces of her brother together and reanimated him. Their son Horus slew Set. Initiates of the mystery were united in spirit with Osiris and shared his immortality. Apuleius' curious autobiographical novel, *The Golden Ass* (c. 150), describes the transformation of a lecherous dabbler in witchcraft into a devotee of the goddess Isis. The climax of the story, given in the first extract, has all the marks of a genuine spiritual experience.

The mystery of Cybele and Attis, the subject of the second extract, came originally from Asia Minor. In the literary form of the story the goddess Cybele loved Attis a shepherd who was unfaithful to her and was changed into a fir tree. As a mystery, Attis is identified with Adonis, Tammuz, the god of vegetation. Initiation involved baptism in bull's blood. The description of the consecration of a priest of Cybele, given here, is from the Christian poet, Prudentius, writing about the year 400 (*Peristephanon* 10, lines 1011–50). Priest-novices in a frenzy castrated themselves to give new life to the dead Attis. This Mystery lost its early orgiastic character, possibly under Christian influences, and became an emotional cult for women parallel to that of Mithras for men.

A.   APULEIUS IS INITIATED

In a dark night the goddess appeared to me in a vision, declaring in
words not dark that the day was come which I had wished for so
long; she told me what provision and charges I should be at for the
supplications, and that she had appointed her principal priest, one
Mithras, that was joined unto my destiny (as she said) by the
ordering of the planets, to be a minister with me in my sacrifices.

When I had heard these and the other divine commandments
of the high goddess, I greatly rejoiced, and arose before day to
speak with the great priest, whom I fortuned to espy coming out
of his chamber. The old man took me by the hand, and led me
courteously to the gate of the great temple, where, after that it
was religiously opened, he made a solemn celebration, and after
the morning sacrifice was ended, he brought out of the secret
place of the temple certain books written with unknown char-
acters . . . thence he interpreted to me such things as were necessary to the use and preparation of mine order.

This done, I diligently gave in charge to certain of my companions to buy liberally whatsoever was needful and convenient;
but part thereof I bought myself. Then he brought me, when he
found that the time was at hand, to the next baths, accompanied
with all the religious sort, and demanding pardon of the gods,
washed me and purified my body according to the custom: after
this, when two parts of the day were gone, he brought me back
again to the temple and presented me before the feet of the goddess, giving me a charge of certain secret things unlawful to be
uttered, and commanding me generally before all the rest to fast
by the space of ten continual days, without eating of any beast or
drinking of any wine: which things I observed with a marvellous
continency.

Then behold the day approached when the sacrifice of dedication should be done; and when the sun declined and evening
came, there arrived on every coast a great multitude of priests,
who according to their ancient order offered me many presents
and gifts. Then were all the laity and profane people commanded
to depart, and when they had put on my back a new linen robe,

the priest took my hand and brought me to the most secret and sacred place of the temple. Thou wouldest peradventure demand, thou studious reader, what was said and done there: verily I would tell thee if it were lawful for me to tell, thou wouldest know if it were convenient for thee to hear; but both thy ears and my tongue should incur the like pain of rash curiosity. Howbeit I will not long torment thy mind, which peradventure is somewhat religious and given to some devotion; listen therefore, and believe it to be true.

Thou shalt understand that I approached near unto hell, even to the gates of Proserpine, and after I was ravished through all the elements, I returned to my proper place: about midnight I saw the sun brightly shine, I saw likewise the gods celestial and the gods infernal, before whom I presented myself and worshipped them. Behold now have I told thee, which although thou hast heard, yet it is necessary that thou conceal it; wherefore this only will I tell, which may be declared without offence for the understanding of the profane.

When morning came and the solemnities were finished, I came forth sanctified with twelve stoles and in a religious habit, whereof I am not forbidden to speak, considering that many persons saw me at that time . . . In my right hand I carried a lighted torch, and a garland of flowers was upon my head, with white palm-leaves sprouting out on every side like rays; thus I was adorned like unto the sun, and made in fashion of an image, when the curtains were drawn aside and all the people compassed about to behold me. Then they began to solemnize the feast, the nativity of my holy order.

I began to say in this sort: 'O holy and blessed dame, the perpetual comfort of human kind, who by thy bounty and grace nourishes all the world, and bearest a great affection to the adversities of the miserable as a loving mother, thou takest no rest night or day, neither art thou idle at any time in giving benefits and succouring all men as well on land as sea; thou art she that puttest away all storms and dangers from men's life by stretching forth thy right hand, whereby likewise thou dost unweave even the inextricable and tangled web of fate, and appeasest the great tempests of fortune, and keepest back the harmful course of the stars. The gods supernal do honour thee; the gods infernal have thee in reverence; thou dost make all the earth to turn, thou givest light to the sun, thou governest the world, thou treadest down the power of hell. By thy means the stars give answer, the seasons return, the gods rejoice, the elements serve: at thy commandment the winds do blow, the clouds nourish the earth, the seeds prosper, and the fruits do grow. The birds of the air, the beasts of the hill, the serpents of the den, and the fishes of the sea do tremble at thy majesty: but my spirit is not able to give thee sufficient praise, my patrimony is unable to satisfy thy sacrifices; my voice hath no power to utter that which I think of thy majesty, no, not if I had a thousand mouths and so many tongues and were able to continue for ever. Howbeit as a good religious person, and according to my poor estate, I will do what I say: I will always keep thy divine appearance in remembrance, and close the imagination of thy most holy godhead within my breast.'

When I ended my oration to the great goddess, I went to embrace the great priest Mithras, now my spiritual father, clinging upon his neck and kissing him oft, and demanding his pardon, considering I was unable to recompense the good which he had done me: and after much talk and great greetings and thanks I departed from him straight to visit my parents and friends, after I had been so long absent. And so within a short while after, by the exhortations of the goddess I made up my packet and took shipping towards the city of Rome, and I voyaged very safely and swiftly with a prosperous wind to the port of Augustus (Ostia), and thence travelling by chariot, I arrived at that holy city about the twelfth day of December in the evening. And the greatest desire which I had there was daily to make my prayers to the sovereign goddess Isis, who, by reason of the place where her temple was builded, was called Campensis, and continually is adored of the people of Rome: her minister and her worshipper was I, a stranger to her church but not unknown to her religion.

B.   THE CONSECRATION OF A PRIEST OF CYBELE

The high priest who is to be consecrated is brought down under ground in a pit dug deep, marvellously adorned with a fillet, binding his festive temples with chaplets, his hair combed back under a golden crown, and wearing a silken toga caught up with Gabine girding.[1]

Over this they make a wooden floor with wide spaces, woven of planks with an open mesh; they then divide or bore the area and repeatedly pierce the wood with a pointed tool that it may appear full of small holes.

Hither a huge bull, fierce and shaggy in appearance, is led, bound with flowery garlands about its flanks, and with its horns sheathed; yea, the forehead of the victim sparkles with gold, and the flash of metal plates colours its hair.

Here, as is ordained, the beast is to be slain, and they pierce its breast with a sacred spear; the gaping wound emits a wave of hot blood, and the smoking river flows into the woven structure beneath it and surges wide.

Then by the many paths of the thousand openings in the lattice the falling shower rains down a foul dew, which the priest buried within catches, putting his shameful head under all the drops, defiled both in his clothing and in all his body.

Yea, he throws back his face, he puts his cheeks in the way of the blood, he puts under it his ears and lips, he interposes his nostrils, he washes his very eyes with the fluid, nor does he even spare his throat but moistens his tongue, until he actually drinks the dark gore.

Afterwards, the flamens draw the corpse, stiffening now that the blood has gone forth, off the lattice, and the pontiff, horrible in appearance, comes forth, and shows his wet head, his beard heavy with blood, his dripping fillets and sodden garments.

This man, defiled with such contagions and foul with the gore of the recent sacrifice, all hail and worship at a distance, because profane blood and a dead ox have washed him while concealed in a filthy cave.

[1] A special way of wearing the toga for religious ceremonies.

10. THE PHILOSOPHERS

There was much intellectual life in the second century. Although higher education was not formally organized in universities as it is today, there may well have been proportionately as many serious students. Many of them were concerned not only with knowledge but with knowledge applied to solve their personal problems of living. This is the way by which many notable men became Christians. No doubt the same ferment of ideas took some who had been Christians on to other beliefs. An account of one such traveller in the reverse direction is given later in Extract 18. But here our concern is with what proved to be the main stream. Justin Martyr and Clement of Alexandria have both left accounts of their intellectual and spiritual pilgrimage. They must stand as examples of a steady traffic.

A.   HOW JUSTIN BECAME A CHRISTIAN   c. 160

Justin Martyr (c. 100–165) wrote his account when he was a man of sixty. He looked back to his own conversion about thirty years before. He tells the story in the form of a dialogue with a Jew, Trypho, a fictional character, but the story of his own student years is probably autobiography. The dialogue takes place in a colonnade or cloister where men of all philosophies and faiths would gather to argue, discuss, teach or gossip. The place is presumably Ephesus where Justin was teaching in 130. The intellectual curiosity of the time and place, and the free debate to which it gave rise, are clearly portrayed in this extract. It was thus that Christianity often made its way. The dialogue is fiction, but the debate it describes is fact.

The four rival schools of philosophy to which Justin attached himself in turn before he became a Christian all had their origins in Greece long before the birth of Jesus. The Stoics were the followers of Zeno who taught at Athens in the Stoa (the Greek word for 'porch') about 300 B.C. In Justin's time the leading Stoic was the emperor himself, Marcus Aurelius, of whom Gibbon wrote: 'At the age of twelve years he embraced the rigid system of the stoics, which taught him to submit his body to his mind, his passions to his reason; to consider virtue as the only good, vice as the only evil, all things external as things indifferent. . . . His life was the noblest commentary on the teachings of Zeno. He was severe to himself, indulgent to the imperfections of others, just and beneficent to all mankind.' His *Meditations*, written in camp during his military campaigns on the Danube, is a classic of the disciplined moral life.

The Peripatetics, literally the 'walking philosophers', got their name from the fact that their founder Aristotle (384–322 B.C.), Alexander the Great's tutor, walked about as he taught in the shady walks which surrounded the Lyceum, which was his headquarters in Athens. He made a systematic study of all fields of human knowledge. His *Ethics* was, and is, of fundamental importance in Christian ethical thought.

The Pythagoreans were the oldest established of the four schools. Their founder, Pythagoras, remembered today mainly as a mathematician, worked in southern Italy, then part of the Greek world, about 525 B.C. He paid great attention to music and aesthetics as the basis of a harmonious life. The reincarnation of souls was one of the beliefs of the Pythagoreans.

Plato (428–347 B.C.) was the disciple of Socrates, and wrote his own works in the form of dialogues between Socrates and his followers. His thought has influenced Christians as deeply as Aristotle's, especially at Alexandria in the time of the Roman empire and much later at and after the Renaissance.

It is worth noting that Aristotle was accused by the people of Athens of impiety and went into exile in the last year of his life before his trial came on; that Pythagoras and his disciples were attacked in the temple where they taught by the townspeople, who set the building on fire, burning to death most of those inside including, according to one report, Pythagoras himself; and that Socrates was executed for impiety by the Athenians.

Source: Justin, *Dialogue with Trypho.*

I attached myself to a Stoic teacher. And when I had studied a long time with him, since no further information about God came to me (for he was not a believer in God himself and he did not think this doctrine essential), I rid myself of this teacher and went to another, who called himself a Peripatetic and had a reputation as a shrewd man. And when he had put up with me for the first few days he decided then that the scale of his fees should be determined, so that our association should not be without profit. That was why I left him, thinking that he was no philosopher at all. But as my soul was still bursting to hear the peculiar and choice secret of philosophy, I moved on to a man who was very well spoken of, a Pythagorean, one who had devoted much thought to philosophy.

And when I was anxious to become a hearer and disciple of his and entered into conversation with him, he said,

'Well? Have you studied music and astronomy and geometry? Or do you think that you will perceive any of the things which assist towards happiness, unless you have first learnt the studies which will detach the soul from tangible things and will render it able for intellectual things, so that it can contemplate the Beautiful and the Truly Good?'

When he had greatly praised these disciplines and declared them essential he sent me away, because I had acknowledged that I did not know them. I was upset therefore, as well I might be, because I was disappointed, and all the more because I conjectured that he did have some knowledge; but again when I contemplated the time which I would be likely to spend on those disciplines, I could not bear to postpone everything for so long.

In this state of resourcelessness it occurred to me to try the Platonists, for their fame was considerable. And consequently I constantly associated with a very learned man who had very recently come to live in our town, and who was eminent among the Platonists, and I was making progress and improving more and more every day. Their conception of the bodiless things was attracting me greatly and the contemplation of the Ideas was exciting my mind, and I thought that I had become wise in a short time, and in my stupidity I hoped to have a vision of God straight away, for this is the objective of Plato's philosophy.

Now when I was in this state of mind. . . . I made a journey to a place which was not far from the sea. When I was near the spot where I intended to be quite alone, an old man . . . began almost shadowing me. I turned round to him, stopped, and inspected him keenly.

He said: 'Do you know me?'

'No,' I said.

'Then,' said he, 'why are you looking at me like that?'

'I am surprised,' I said, 'that you happen to be in the same place as I am, because I did not expect to see anybody else here.'

'I am looking for some of my slaves,' he said. 'They have run away from me, so I have made a personal visit to look for them, in case they turn up anywhere here. But what are you doing here?' he asked me.

'I am spending the time here for my own enjoyment,' I said. 'My discourse with myself meets no hindrance here, and places like these are conducive to the study of ideas.'

'So you study ideas, do you?' said he, 'and you never study deeds nor truth nor try to be a man of action rather than an academic?' [The old man then put Justin through a rigorous Socratic examination until finally Justin asked:]

'What teacher could anyone employ then, or how could anyone get any assistance, if the truth is not in these philosophers?'

'There were men a very long time ago more ancient than those reputed to be philosophers, blessed and righteous and dear to God. They spoke by a divine spirit and they oracularly predicted future events which are now taking place. They are called prophets . . . Their writings remain to this day and it is possible for anyone who studies them to gain much enlightenment about first principles, and the final consummation and everything which a philosopher ought to know, if a man will but believe them. They have not set out their accounts with formal argument, but as witnesses of the truth worthy of belief, as if they were above all formal argument. . . . You should pray above all that the gates of light may be opened to you, for these things are not intelligible and comprehensible to everybody unless God and his Christ give understanding to a man.'

. . . This man told me these facts, and many others, which there is not time now to relate, and then departed, enjoining me to investigate them, and I never saw him again. Immediately a fire was lit in my soul, and a desire for the prophets seized me and for those men who are friends of Christ; as I turned over his words in my mind I found this the only reliable and profitable philosophy. In fact this is the way and these the means whereby I am a philosopher. . . .

B.   CLEMENT OF ALEXANDRIA

Alexandria was the second city of the empire with a population of

half a million, and its most learned one. It was there that the Jewish
thinker, Philo, had lived and studied both the Bible and the Greek
philosophers, especially Plato, bringing the two into fruitful contact.
Similarly it was there that Christians tried hardest to reconcile their
religion and philosophy.

Clement was born, probably in Athens, about the middle of the
second century. In his writings he gives a summary account of his own
student years, which took him to Italy and Greece as well as to Egypt.
It was there that he found his last and most important teacher, the
Christian Pantaenus, about the year 180. The reference at the end of
the first extract is to the fact that Sicilian honey was reckoned to be
the best in the world. It means that Pantaenus had the best wisdom,
not necessarily that he was a Sicilian.

In the second and third extracts he makes clear what he permanently
owed to the Greeks and brought with him from their teaching into his
Christian faith.

Source: Clement of Alexandra, *Stromateis* 1: 11, 2, and 5.

This book is not written to show off my skill as a writer; it is
rather that I am treasuring up notes for my old age, a remedy for
forgetfulness. They are intended simply as a picture and rough
sketch of those clear and living teachings and of those blessed and
truly honourable men whom I was privileged to hear. Of them,
one was an Ionian who taught in Greece. Others were in Magna
Graecia [Southern Italy or Sicily]; of them one came from Coele-
Syria, the other from Egypt. Others lived in the East; of these one
was an Assyrian, one a Palestinian Hebrew. After I met the last
(who was first of them in importance) I abandoned further search,
having discovered him hiding in Egypt. A truly Sicilian bee, he
drew honey from the flowers in the meadow of the apostles and
prophets, and implanted in the souls of his pupils pure knowledge . . .

. . . Neither can the Greeks be fairly condemned by those who
have merely glanced over their writings since they cannot be
understood by any who have not carefully perused them, and unveiled, as it were, the science there taught. For amid their many
modes of teaching, their disciples were at least led towards true
principles; nor can that philosophy be pernicious, as some contend,

by which it is clear that the image of truth—that divine gift—was bestowed upon the Greeks.

Indeed, before the coming of the Lord, philosophy was needful to the Greeks for the purification of their lives, and even now it is useful towards piety, as supplying a rudimentary teaching for those who may afterwards receive the faith upon conviction. For God is indeed the cause of all good things: of some pre-eminently and directly, as of the old and new covenant. Of others indirectly, by means of reason and argument, as philosophy, which probably he gave to the Greeks before the Lord himself came in order to call them also to his service. For philosophy acted the part of a schoolmaster to the Greeks, as the Mosaic Law did to the Jews, for the purpose of bringing men to Christ, thus preparing the way for such as were to be further perfected by him. We know that the truth is one only; but into it, as into a great river, many streams flow from different quarters. . . .

C.   AN OPPONENT'S VIEW   *c.*1 75

Celsus was a pagan philosopher who made a strong attack on much in Christianity in his *True Logos*, written about 175. This book itself does not survive, but the greater part of it is to be found in the answer to it that Origen, an Alexandrian Christian philosopher, wrote about seventy years later—a sign of the influence that Celsus had had. Celsus praised the moral teaching of Christianity, but regarded the miraculous element in it, and the exclusive claims made for it, as thoroughly obscurantist. He disliked what he took to be the Christian praise of ignorance in such passages[1] as that in which Christ thanked his heavenly Father that 'thou didst hide these things from the wise and understanding, and didst reveal them unto babes'; and that in which Paul admitted to the Corinthians that 'not many wise after the flesh, not many mighty, not many noble' are called to be Christians. This Celsus said, had become a Christian boast. They said, 'Let no cultured person draw near, none wise, none sensible, for all that sort of thing we consider evil; but if any one is ignorant, wanting in sense or culture, if any is a fool, let him come boldly.' Origen's answer was that, while the church certainly included slaves, women and children, who needed—and got—simple instruction, it also had other well-educated members—and

1 Matt. 11, 25 and 1 Cor. 1, 26.

'when we have an abundance of intelligent hearers we then venture to include in our discourse those things among us which are especially noble and divine'.

Celsus could draw a highly graphic picture of how he thought Christianity spread.

Source: Origen, *Contra Celsum* 3, 55.

In private houses we see workers in wool and leather, fullers, and the most uneducated and rustic people, who do not dare to utter a word in the presence of their elders and wiser masters, yet when they get hold of the children privately, and any women as ignorant as themselves, they pour forth these wonderful statements: that they should pay no attention to their father or teachers, but only to themselves; that the former are foolish and stupid, and neither know nor are able to do anything really good because they are busied with futile trifles; that they alone know how men ought to live, and that, if the children do as they say, they will be happy themselves and make their home happy also. While they are speaking, they may see one of the school-teachers approaching, or one of the more educated class, or even the father himself. Then the more timid of them become afraid, but the bolder ones incite the children to throw off the yoke whispering that they cannot explain any good thing in the presence of father and teachers. . . . but, if they liked, they could go with the women or their play-mates to the women's quarters or to the leather shop or to the fuller's shop, and so achieve perfection. With words like these they win them over.

II. THE JEWS

Justin's *Dialogue with Trypho* is, as explained in the previous section, a fictional discussion between a Christian (Justin) and a Jew. Justin had been born in the Biblical Shechem, then called Neapolis—one of many Newtowns. It is now Nablus and is the home of the few remaining Samaritans. There were many more in Justin's time. He indeed thought of himself as a Samaritan although he was not circumcized. He was thoroughly acquainted with the Judaism of his day, and in this Dialogue he is clearly not unsympathetic to Jews. It was written in Rome towards the end of his life, about 160, but it is set some thirty years earlier just after the collapse of the last Jewish revolt against the

Romans, that of Bar-Cochba for whom Trypho and his friends had been fighting.

The discussion on both sides is tolerant and fair-minded; the arguments which Trypho uses are arguments which in fact Jews of his day employed; and the dialogue ends with Trypho unconvinced but willing to pursue the argument further another day—a reasonable enough conclusion.

The Dialogue makes it clear that proselytes were still a numerous enough class to be worth bringing into the discussion in 130 and, no doubt, in 160, or Justin would hardly have included them in a book meant to be read by Christians and Jews of that time.

Source: Justin Martyr, *Dialogue with Trypho.*

JUSTIN TALKS WITH A JEW

I was walking early one morning in the covered walk belonging to the Colonnade when a man, with some companions, met me, and said, 'Hullo, Philosopher!' And so saying he turned and walked along beside me, and his friends turned along with him. I in turn greeted him, and said, 'Well?'

He answered: 'I was taught in Argos by Corinthus the Socratic philosopher that people who wear the sort of dress which you are wearing . . . should be treated courteously and associated with in case some profit might result from the association, either to the other man or to me. . . .'

' "But who art thou, bravest of mortal men?" ' [a quotation from Homer] was how I playfully replied to him.

'I am called Trypho,' he said; 'I am a Hebrew, from the circumcision, a refugee from the present war, and have spent a long time in Greece and in Corinth.'

'Then,' said I, 'how could you possibly derive as much benefit from philosophy as you do from your own Lawgiver and from the prophets?'

'Why not? Do not the philosophers occupy all their discussion with the subject of God?' was his reply.

[There follows a long philosophical discussion at the end of which Justin describes how he became a Christian—see page 38. Justin ended his account of his conversion thus:]

'If therefore you are concerned about yourself and are anxious to gain salvation, and trust in God ... it is possible for you to know God's Christ, to become initiated and to be happy.'

... Trypho's companions laughed, but he smiled and said:

'I accept the rest of your opinions and am impressed with your enthusiasm for religion. But it would be better for you to follow the philosophical system of Plato ... than to be deceived by false words and follow worthless men. . . . If you wish to be persuaded by me (for I have already regarded you as a friend), first undergo circumcision . . . and do all the things that are written in the law, and then perhaps one day there will be mercy for you from God. ... You have received a futile rumour, and have invented some sort of Christ for yourselves, and for his sake you are now un-reflectingly going into perdition.'

'My dear man,' I said, 'may you receive pardon and be forgiven. . . . I will show you, if you pay attention, we have not put our trust in empty legends nor in arguments incapable of proof, but in a religion full of a divine spirit and bursting with power and blossoming with grace.'

At this his companions again burst into laughter and made an unseemly uproar. So I got to my feet and prepared to go off. But he took hold of my coat and said that he would not let me go until I had done what I had promised.

'Well,' said I, 'your companions must not ... behave in this rude way. But if they choose to they can listen quietly ... I suggest that we should retire somewhere and, having had a rest, finish our argument.' Trypho agreed ... and we ... went into the space in the middle of the Colonnade, but two of his companions, joking and laughing at our earnestness, went off. When we reached the place where there are stone seats on each side, Trypho's companions sat down on one of them and one of the men started a conversation about the war in Judaea, and they began talking among themselves.

When they had finished I began speaking to them again thus:

'My friends, is the only fault which you have to find with us that we do not live according to the law. . . . Or do imputations against our life and behaviour circulate among you? What I mean is, do you also believe about us that we are allegedly cannibals and that after a banquet we extinguish the lights and have orgies of unnatural intercourse; or do you only condemn in us . . . that we believe in a creed which is, as you think, a false one?'

'This last point is what amazes us,' said Trypho, 'but as for the popular assertions, they are not worth believing. . . . You try to convert us as if you knew God, though you keep none of the customs which the proselytes do. If therefore you have any defence to make to this and can show in any way that you have a ground of hope, even though you do not keep the law, this is what we would be particularly glad to hear . . .'

At that I answered him, 'Trypho, there will never be any other God, nor was there from eternity, except the creator and orderer of this universe. We do not imagine that you have one God and we another, but that same God who "brought out" your fathers from the land of Egypt "with a strong hand and a high arm." We have not hoped in any other, for none exists, but on this same one as you do, the God of Abraham and Isaac and Jacob. But we have not hoped in him through Moses nor through the law, otherwise we should be doing just what you do. . . .' [There follows a great exchange of proof texts. Justin argues in the way that moderns find most disconcerting in Paul's epistles; Trypho's arguments are to be found also in rabbinical literature of the period—Justin was well informed.]

I again took up the argument at the point where originally I had stopped in my demonstration that (Christ) was born from a Virgin. . . .

Trypho answered, 'The passage does not say, "Behold, the virgin shall conceive in the womb and bring forth a son", but "Behold, the young woman shall conceive . . ." and so on, as you said. The whole prophecy is to be applied to Hezekiah, and it is demonstrable that the events happened to Hezekiah according to the prophecy. And in the legends of those who are called the Greeks it is related that Perseus was born of Danae while she was a virgin after he who is called Zeus among them had flowed into her in the form of a stream of gold. You ought to be ashamed of retailing the same tales as the Greeks, and should say rather that

E

this Jesus was born as a human being from human beings, and, if you are demonstrating from the Scriptures that he is the Christ, you should say that he earned the appointment as Christ by his perfect behaviour in obedience to the law, but you should not dare to tell fairy stories, in case you are convicted of the same futility as the Greeks.'

I replied to this. . . . 'You can be sure, Trypho, that the very stories which he who is called the devil deceitfully caused to be told among the Greeks, just as he operated through the wise men of Egypt and the false prophets in the time of Elijah, have confirmed my understanding and faith in the Scriptures. For when they say that Dionysus was born as the son of Zeus as a result of his intercourse with Semele, and when they relate that this Dionysus was the inventor of the vine, and that he was torn in pieces and died and rose again and went up to heaven, and when they introduce an ass into his mysteries, can I not recognize that he has imitated the prophecy spoken beforehand by the patriarch Jacob and recorded by Moses (Gen. 49 : 11, 12)? . . .

'When those who hand on the mysteries of Mithras relate that he was born from a rock and call the place a cave where they initiate into their traditions those who believe in him, can I not perceive that in this case they are imitating the saying of Daniel that "A stone was cut without hands from a great mountain", and a similar passage in Isaiah, the whole of whose utterances they attempted to imitate? For they have arranged that words urging right conduct should be spoken in their rites.' (Daniel 2 : 34; Isaiah 33 : 16.)

. . . When I had finished Trypho remained silent for some time, and then said: 'You perceive that it was not deliberately that we met together in this discussion. I confess that I enjoyed the encounter greatly, and I know that my companions feel as I do. We found more than we expected or than we once thought it possible to expect. . . . But (said he) since you are about to make a journey by sea and are expecting daily to sail, do not hesitate if you go away to think of us as your friends.'

. . . After that we parted. They wished me for the future a safe journey and preservation from all evil. When I gave them my good wishes, I said, 'I cannot pray any better prayer for you, my friends, than that you may recognize that every man is granted the opportunity of happiness through this religion, and that you may resolutely become what we are, recognizing that Jesus is the Christ of God.'

12. 'HEALTHY MINDS AND HEALTHY BODIES':
A Schoolmaster's Lectures to Christians   *c.* 190

Clement of Alexandria was not only interested in the philosophy of Christianity. He concerned himself greatly with down-to-earth instruction on the elements of good manners and considerate behaviour, believing that these had a real part in Christian life. The following extracts come from his book, *The Paedagogus* or, as in this translation, Instructor. The word means the slave who used to accompany a Greek boy to his classes and gymnastic exercises, looking after him and keeping him from harm or, perhaps better, out of harm's way. This, then, is the comparatively humble but important role that Clement saw for the practical moral instruction contained in his book. Note that Clement quotes as freely from the Greek classics as from the Bible. The book is clearly written for a settled Christian society from which the thought of persecution and martyrdom is far removed. It was in fact, however, not far away, and in 202 Clement had to give up his headship of the Christian Academy in Alexandria and leave the city to escape from persecution.

The *agapë* or Love-feast was a feature of the early Church. It seems to have been a Christian communal meal, at first preceding the Eucharist (see I Cor. 11, 17–34). Later, the Eucharist was celebrated in the morning, the *agapë* in the evening. It was presumably this meal that the Christians of Bithynia gave up on Pliny's orders (page 13).

The game Phaininda (p. 52) was a type of net-ball, judging from a passage in Athenaeus' *Doctors at Dinner* I, 14. A player takes the ball, gives it to one and escapes another. There are shouts of 'I have it! A long one! Over his head! Down! Up! A Short Pass.'

FOOD

Some men, in truth, live that they may eat, as the irrational creatures, 'whose life is their belly, and nothing else'. But the Instructor enjoins us to eat that we may live. For neither is food our business, nor is pleasure our aim; but both are on account of our life here, which the Word is training up to immortality. Wherefore also there is discrimination to be employed in reference to food. And it is to be simple, truly plain, suiting precisely simple and artless children—as ministering to life, not to luxury. And the life to which it conduces consists of two things—health and strength; to which plainness of fare is most suitable, being conducive both to digestion and lightness of body, from which come growth, and health, and right strength, not strength that is wrong or dangerous and wretched, as is that of athletes produced by compulsory feeding.

We must therefore reject different varieties, which engender various mischiefs, such as a depraved habit of body and disorders of the stomach, the taste being vitiated by an unhappy art—that of cookery, and the useless art of making pastry. For people dare to call by the name of food their dabbling in luxuries, which glides into mischievous pleasures. Antiphanes, the Delian physician, said this variety of viands was the one cause of disease; but there are people who dislike the truth, and through various absurd notions abjure moderation of diet, and put themselves to a world of trouble to procure dainties from beyond seas.

For my part, I am sorry for this disease. But they are not ashamed to sing the praises of their delicacies, giving themselves great trouble to get lampreys in the Straits of Sicily, the eels of the Maeander, and the kids found in Melos, and the mullets in Sciathus, and the mussels of Pelorus, the oysters of Abydos, not omitting the sprats found in Pipara, and the Mantinican turnip; and furthermore, the beetroot that grows among the Ascraeans. They seek out the cockles of Methymna, the turbots of Attica, and the thrushes of Daphnis, and the reddish-brown dried figs, on account of which the ill-starred Persian marched into Greece with five hundred thousand men. Besides these, they purchase birds from Phasis, the Egyptian snipes, and the Median peafowl. Altering these by means of condiments, the gluttons gape for the sauces. 'Whatever earth and the depths of the sea, and the unmeasured space of the air produce,' they cater for their gluttony. In their greed and solicitude, the gluttons seem absolutely to sweep the world with a drag-net to gratify their luxurious tastes.

These gluttons, surrounded with the sound of hissing frying-pans, and wearing their whole life away at the pestle and mortar, cling to matter like fire. More than that, they emasculate plain food, namely bread, by straining off the nourishing part of the grain, so that the necessary part of food becomes matter of reproach to luxury. There is no limit to epicurism among men. For it has driven them to sweetmeats, and honey-cakes, and sugar-plums; inventing a multitude of desserts, hunting after all manner of dishes. A man like this seems to me to be all jaw, and nothing else.

Some, speaking with unbridled tongue, dare to apply the name *agapë* to pitiful suppers, redolent of savour and sauces. They dishonour the saving work of the Word, the consecrated *agapë*, with pots and pouring of sauce, and by drink and delicacies and smoke desecrate that name. They are deceived in their idea, having expected that the promise of God might be bought with suppers. Gatherings for the sake of mirth and such entertainments we name rightly suppers, dinners, and banquets, after the example of the Lord. But such entertainments the Lord has not called *agapœ*.

DRINK

Towards evening, about supper-time, wine may be used, when we are no longer engaged in more serious readings. Then also the air becomes colder than it is during the day; so that the failing natural warmth requires to be nourished by the introduction of heat. But even then it must only be a little wine that is to be used; for we must not go on to intemperate potations. Those who are already advanced in life may partake more hilariously of the bowl, to warm by the harmless medicine of the vine the chill of age, which the decay of time has produced. For old men's passions are not, for the most part, stirred to such agitation as to drive them to the shipwreck of drunkenness. For being moored by reason and time, as by anchors, they stand with greater ease the storm of passions which rushes down from intemperance. They also may be permitted to indulge in pleasantry at feasts. But to them also let the limit of their potations be the point up to which they keep their reason unwavering, their memory active, and their body unmoved and unshaken by wine.

One Artorius, in his book *On Long Life* (for so I remember), thinks that drink should be taken only till the food be moistened, that we may attain to a longer life. It is fitting, then, that some apply wine by way of physic, for the sake of health alone, and others for purposes of relaxation and enjoyment. For first wine makes the man who has drunk it more benignant than before, more agreeable to his boon companions, kinder to his domestics, and more pleasant to his friends. But when intoxicated, he becomes violent instead.

It has therefore been well said,

> 'Wine drunk in season and to satisfy
> Is joy of heart and gladness of soul.'[1]

And it is best to mix the wine with as much water as possible . . . For both are works of God; and so the mixture of both, of water and of wine, conduces together to health, because life consists of what is necessary and of what is useful. With water, then, which is the necessary of life, and to be used in abundance, there is also to be mixed the useful.

By an immoderate quantity of wine the tongue is impeded; the lips are relaxed; the eyes roll wildly, the sight, as it were, swimming through the quantity of moisture; and compelled to deceive, they think that everything is revolving round them, and cannot count distant objects as single. 'And, in truth, methinks I see two suns,'[2] said the Theban old man in his cups. For the sight, being disturbed by the heat of the wine, frequently fancies the substance of one object to be manifold. And there is no difference between moving the eye or the object seen. For both have the same effect on the sight, which, on account of the fluctuation, cannot accurately obtain a perception of the object. And the feet are carried from beneath the man as by a flood, and hiccuping and vomiting and maudlin nonsense follow: 'for every intoxicated man', according to the tragedy,[3]

---

[1] Ecclesiasticus 31. 28.   [2] Pentheus in Euripides, *Bacchae*.
[3] Attributed to Sophocles.

'Is conquered by anger, and empty of sense,
And likes to pour forth much silly speech;
And is wont to hear unwillingly,
What evil words he with his will hath said.'

... The miserable wretches who expel temperance from conviviality, think excess in drinking to be the happiest life; and their life is nothing but revel, debauchery, baths, excess, urinals, idleness, drink. You may see some of them, half-drunk, staggering, with crowns round their necks like wine jars, vomiting drink on one another in the name of good fellowship; and others, full of the effects of their debauch, dirty, pale in the face, livid, and still above yesterday's bout pouring another bout to last till next morning. It is well, my friends, it is well to make our acquaintance with this picture at the greatest possible distance from it, and to frame ourselves to what is better, dreading lest we also become a like spectacle and laughing-stock to others.

EXERCISE

The gymnasium is sufficient for boys, even if baths are within reach. And even for men to prefer gymnastic exercises by far to the baths, is perchance not bad, since they are in some respect conducive to the health of young men, and produce exertion—emulation to aim at not only a healthy habit of body, but courageousness of soul. When this is done without dragging a man away from better employments, it is pleasant, and not unprofitable. Nor are women to be deprived of bodily exercise. But they are not to be encouraged to engage in wrestling or running, but are to exercise themselves in spinning, and weaving, and superintending the cooking if necessary. And they are, with their own hand, to fetch from the store, what we require. And it is no disgrace for them to apply themselves to the mill. Nor is it a reproach to a wife —housekeeper and helpmeet—to occupy herself in cooking, so that it may be palatable to her husband. And if she shake up the couch, reach drink to her husband when thirsty, set food on the table as neatly as possible, and so give herself exercise tending to sound health, the Instructor will approve of a woman like this, who 'stretches forth her arms to useful tasks, rests her hands on the distaff, opens her hand to the poor, and extends her wrist to the beggar'.[1]

She who emulates Sarah is not ashamed of that highest of ministries, helping wayfarers. For Abraham said to her, 'Haste, and knead three measures of meal, and make cakes.'[2] 'And Rachel, the daughter of Laban, came,' it is said, 'with her father's sheep.'[3] Nor was this enough; but to teach humility it is added, 'for she fed her father's sheep'. And innumerable such examples of frugality and self-help, and also of exercises, are furnished by the Scriptures.

In the case of men, let some strip and engage in wrestling; let some play at the small ball, especially the game they call Phaininda, in the sun. To others who walk into the country, or go down into the town, the walk is sufficient exercise. And were they to handle the hoe, this stroke of economy in agricultural labour would not be ungentlemanly.

But let not such athletic contests, as we have allowed, be undertaken for the sake of vainglory, but for the exuding of manly sweat. Nor are we to struggle with cunning and showiness, but in a stand-up wrestling bout, by disentangling of neck, hands, and sides. For such a struggle with graceful strength is more becoming and manly, being undertaken for the sake of serviceable and profitable health. But let those others, who profess the practice of illiberal postures in gymnastics, be dismissed. We must always aim at moderation.

It is respectable for a man to draw water for himself, and to cut billets of wood which he is to use himself. Attending to one's own wants is an exercise free of pride—as, for example, putting on one's own shoes, washing one's own feet, and also rubbing one's self when anointed with oil. To render one who has rubbed you the same service in return, is an exercise of reciprocal justice; and to sleep beside a sick friend, help the infirm, and supply him who is in want, are proper exercises.

---

[1] Proverbs 31, 19–20 (Septuagint version).   [2] Genesis 18, 6.
[3] Genesis 29, 9.

VESSELS

And so the use of cups made of silver and gold, and of others inlaid with precious stones, is out of place, being only a deception of the vision. For if you pour any warm liquid into them, the vessels becoming hot, to touch them is painful. On the other hand, if you pour in what is cold, the material changes its quality, injuring the mixture, and the rich potion is hurtful. Away, then, with Thericleian cups and Antigonides, and Canthari, and goblets, and Lepastæ, and the endless shapes of drinking vessels, and wine-coolers, and wine-pourers also. For, on the whole, gold and silver, both publicly and privately, are an invidious possession when they exceed what is necessary, seldom to be acquired, difficult to keep, and not adapted for use.

The elaborate vanity, too, of engraved glass vessels, more apt to break on account of the art, teaching us to fear while we drink, is to be banished from our well-ordered constitution. And silver couches, and pans and vinegar-saucers, and trenchers and bowls; and besides these, vessels of silver and gold, some for serving food, and others for other uses which I am ashamed to name, of easily cleft cedar and thyine wood, and ebony, and tripods fashioned of ivory, and couches with silver feet and inlaid with ivory, and folding-doors of beds studded with gold and variegated with tortoiseshell, and bed-clothes of purple and other colours difficult to produce, proofs of tasteless luxury, cunning devices of envy and effeminacy,—are all to be relinquished, as having nothing whatever worth our pains . . . It is a farce, and a thing to make men laugh outright, for men to bring in silver urine vases and chamber pots of crystal as they usher in their counsellors, and for silly rich women to get gold receptacles for excrement made; so too, being rich, they cannot even ease themselves except in a superb way. I would that in their whole life they deemed gold fit for dung.

BEDS

How, in due course, we are to go to sleep in remembrance of the precepts of temperance, we must now say. For after the meal, having given thanks to God for our participation in these enjoyments and the (happy) passing of the day, our talk must be turned

to sleep. Magnificence of bed-clothes, gold-embroidered carpets
... and long fine robes of purple, and costly fleecy cloaks, and
manufactured rugs of purple, and mantles of thick pile, and
couches softer than sleep, are to be banished.

For besides the reproach of voluptuousness, sleeping on downy
feathers is injurious, when our bodies fall down as into a yawning
hollow, on account of the softness of the bedding.

For they are not convenient for sleepers turning in them, on
account of the bed rising into a hill on either side of the body. Nor
are they suitable for the digestion of the food, but rather for
burning it up, and so destroying the nutriment. But stretching
one's self on even couches, affording a kind of natural gymnasium
for sleep, contributes to the digestion of the food. And those that
can roll on other beds, having this, as it were, for a natural gymnasium for sleep, digest food more easily, and render themselves
fitter for emergencies. Moreover, silver-footed couches argue
great ostentation; and the ivory on beds, the soul having left the
body, is not permissible for holy men, being a lazy contrivance for
rest.

We must not occupy our thoughts about these things, for the
use of them is not forbidden to those who possess them; but solicitude about them is prohibited, for happiness is not to be found in
them. On the other hand, it savours of cynic vanity for a man to
act as Diomede,—

'And he stretched himself under a wild bull's hide,'[1]—

Ulysses rectified the unevenness of the nuptial couch with a
stone. Such frugality and self-help was practised not by private
individuals alone, but by the chiefs of the ancient Greeks. But why
speak of these? Jacob slept on the ground, and a stone served him
for a pillow; and then was he counted worthy to behold the vision
—that was above man. And in conformity with reason, the bed
which we use must be simple and frugal, and so constructed that,
by avoiding the extremes (of too much indulgence and too much
endurance), it may be comfortable: if it is warm, to protect us;
if cold, to warm us. But let not the couch be elaborate, and let it

[1] *Iliad*, 16, 155.

have smooth feet; for elaborate turnings form occasionally paths for creeping things which twine themselves about the incisions of the work, and do not slip off.

Especially is a moderate softness in the bed suitable for manhood; for sleep ought not to be for the total enervation of the body, but for its relaxation. Wherefore I say that it ought not to be allowed to come on us for the sake of indulgence, but in order to rest from action. We must therefore sleep so as to be easily awaked. For it is said, 'Let your loins be girt about, and your lamps burning; and ye yourselves like to men that watch for their lord, that when he returns from the marriage, and comes and knocks, they may straightway open to him. Blessed are those servants whom the Lord, when he cometh, shall find watching.' . . .[1] Wherefore we ought often to rise by night and bless God. For blessed are they who watch for him, and so make themselves like the angels, whom we call 'watchers'. But a man asleep is worth nothing, any more than if he were not alive.

[1] Luke 12, 35-7.

CHAPTER FOUR

CHRISTIAN WORSHIP IN THE SECOND CENTURY

Converts to the Jewish faith were baptized; the Christian Eucharist or Last Supper was instituted at a Jewish ritual meal (possibly the Kiddush of the Passover, a rite of sanctification). It is not surprising, therefore, that many Jewish traces can be found in these earliest detailed accounts of the two Christian sacraments.

Notice that a simple form of the so-called Apostle's Creed can be extracted from the three-fold questions put to those who are being baptized, in our third extract. The Jewish stress on the importance of 'living water'—running water—is interesting. The use of baptistries and fonts had yet to come.

13. FROM THE DIDACHE $\qquad$ c. 120

Date and authorship are unknown and its importance much disputed. It is, however, generally accepted as the earliest Church 'Order', though probably only of some isolated community in Syria, c. 100–130. This community has bishops and deacons, but no presbyters; instead, there are travelling prophets:

'Elect for yourselves bishops and deacons worthy of the Lord, men that are gentle and not covetous, true men and approved . . . for these are they that are honoured of you with the prophets and teachers.'

Prophets and teachers are noted at Antioch in Acts 13, 1, and Paul speaks of them as coming after Apostles in the diversities of gifted ones in the Church (1 Cor. 12, 28). These travelling prophets could celebrate the Eucharist, but many were frauds. The *Didache* directs that if any should stay more than two days and ask for money, he should not be accepted. 'By their ways shall be known the false prophet and the true.'

The *Didache* seems to show a stage of development where the travelling prophets are beginning to lose status and be replaced by resident priests. If such a one was prepared to stay in a community and work for a living, then he was to be welcomed and must receive his share of first-fruits, 'for the prophets are your high priests'.

A rudimentary form of the prayer for 'the whole state of Christ's Church' is given in the thanksgiving at the end of the Eucharist in section 10 of the *Didache*.

Source: The Didache or *The Teaching of the Lord through the Twelve Apostles to the Gentiles*, chapters 7, 14, 9.

Baptize in the name of the Father and of the Son and of the Holy Spirit, in living water; but if you have no running water, baptize in other water, and if you cannot in cold, in warm. If you have neither, pour water thrice upon the head in the name of the Father and of the Son and of the Holy Spirit. And before the baptism let the baptizer and the baptized fast, and any others who can. And order the baptized to fast for one or two days before.

On the Day of the Lord, gather together, break bread and *eucharistize*,[1] after confessing your sins, so that your offering may be pure. But let none who has a quarrel with his neighbour join your assembly until they are reconciled (Matt. 5, 23–4), so that your offering shall not be defiled.

Concerning the Eucharist, *eucharistize* thus: First for the cup, 'We give thee thanks, our Father, for the holy vine of thy child David, which you made known to us through thy child Jesus. To thee be glory for ever.' And for the broken bread: 'We thank thee, our Father, for the life and knowledge which thou hast revealed to us through thy child Jesus. To thee be glory for ever. As this broken bread was scattered on the hills but was gathered together and made one, so let thy Church be gathered together from the ends of the earth into thy kingdom, for thine is the glory and the power through Jesus Christ for ever.'

But let none eat or drink of your Eucharist except those who have been baptized into the name of the Lord. For the Lord has said about this, 'Give not that which is holy to the dogs.'[2]

14. FROM JUSTIN   c. 155

Much of our knowledge of the daily life of the early Christian Church comes from the work of the 'apologists', those who tried to make a reasoned account of their faith and religious practices, generally in a

---

[1] This Greek word meant both 'bless' and 'give thanks', and as both meanings are implied here, the word has been left untranslated.   [2] Matt. 7, 6.

direct appeal to the Roman emperor, but sometimes in answer to a written attack. The earliest apologist was Quadratus who addressed the emperor Hadrian in A.D. 124, but only a fragment survives in Eusebius' *Church History*. The most important apologies which survive are those of Justin Martyr, Tertullian, and Origen.

Justin taught for a time in Ephesus and then opened a school in Rome. In about A.D. 150 he addressed the first of his two apologies to the emperor Antoninus Pius, his sons, the Senate and the Roman people, demanding justice for Christians and a proper investigation into the charges commonly laid against them. One such charge was cannibalism, resulting from vague rumours about the Eucharist, so Justin gives a particularly detailed account of the Eucharist. Justin was concerned to show that Christianity had no rites that were secret, unlike the so-called mystery religions of Mithras, Cybele, and others (Extract 9) which were becoming popular in Rome. His *Second Apology*, addressed to the Senate, was written early in the reign of Marcus Aurelius.

Source: Justin Martyr, *First Apology* 1, 65–7.

After thus washing him who has been persuaded and has given his assent, we bring him to those that are called brethren, where they are assembled, to offer prayers in common, both for ourselves and for him who has been illuminated and for all men everywhere, with all our hearts, that as we have learned the truth so we may also be counted worthy to be found good citizens and guardians of the commandments, that we may be saved with an eternal salvation.

We salute one another with a kiss when we have ended the prayers. Then is brought to the president of the brethren bread and a cup of water and wine. And he takes them and offers up praise and glory to the Father of all things, through the name of his Son and of the Holy Ghost, and gives thanks at length that we are deemed worthy of these things at his hand. When he has completed the prayers and thanksgiving all the people present assent by saying 'Amen.' Amen in the Hebrew tongue signifies 'So be it.' When the president has given thanks and all the people have assented, those who are called deacons with us give to those present a portion of the Eucharistic bread and wine and water, and carry it away to those that are absent.

This food is called with us the Eucharist, and of it none is allowed to partake but he that believes that our teachings are true, and has been washed with the washing for the remission of sins and unto regeneration, and who so lives as Christ directed. For we do not receive them as ordinary food or ordinary drink; but as by the word of God, Jesus Christ our Saviour took flesh and blood for our salvation, so also, we are taught, the food blessed by the prayer of the word which we received from him, by which, through its transformation, our blood and flesh is nourished, this food is the flesh and blood of Jesus who was made flesh. For the Apostles in the memoirs made by them, which are called gospels, have thus narrated that the command was given; that Jesus took bread, gave thanks, and said,

'This do ye in remembrance of me; this is my body.' And he took the cup likewise and said, 'This is my blood,' and gave it to them alone.

This very thing the evil demons imitated in the mysteries of Mithras, and commanded to be done. For, as you know, or can discover, bread and a cup of water are set out in the rites of initiation with the repetition of certain words.

Now we always thereafter remind one another of these things; and those that have the means assist them that are in need; and we visit one another continually. And at all our meals we bless the maker of all things through his son Jesus Christ and through the Holy Ghost. And on the day which is called the day of the sun there is an assembly of all who live in the towns or in the country; and the memoirs of the apostles or the writings of the prophets are read, as long as time permits. Then the reader ceases, and the president speaks, admonishing us and exhorting us to imitate these excellent examples. Then we arise all together and offer prayers; and, as we said before, when we have concluded our prayers, bread is brought, and wine and water, and the president in like manner offers up prayers and thanksgivings with all his might; and the people assent with 'Amen.' And there is the distribution and partaking by all of the eucharistic elements; and to them that are not present they are sent by the hand of the deacons. And they that are prosperous and wish to do so give what they will, each after his choice. What is collected is deposited with the president, who gives aid to the orphans and widows and such as are in want by reason of sickness or other cause; and to those also that are in prison, and to strangers from abroad, in fact to all that are in need he is a protector.

We hold our common assembly on the day of the sun, because it is the first day, on which God put to flight darkness and chaos (lit. matter) and made the world, and on the same day Jesus Christ our saviour rose from the dead; for on the day before that of Saturn they crucified him; and on the day after Saturn's day, the day of the sun, he appeared to his apostles and disciples and taught them these things, which we have also handed on to you for your consideration.

15. FROM *The Apostolic Tradition*   *c.* 215

This is listed as one of the writings of Hippolytus on the statue of him in the Vatican Library (Plate 7). Though written about 215, it is a deliberately conservative work, written in Greek, and looking backward to traditional practices in Rome.

These extracts are from sections 16–23, but the central consecration prayer, from the liturgical section 4, has been inserted in its place in the Eucharist. Note the practice of child baptism.

INSTRUCTION TO CATECHUMENS

Those who come forward for the first time to hear the word shall first be brought to the teachers at the house before all the people come in. And let them be examined as to the reason why they have come forward to the faith. And those who bring them shall bear witness for them whether they are able to hear. Let their life and manner of living be enquired into, and whether slave or free.

If one be the slave of a believer and his master permit him, let him hear. If his master do not bear witness to him, let him be rejected. If his master be a heathen, let him be taught to please his master that there be no scandal. . . .

If a man be a pandar who supports harlots, either let him desist or be rejected. If a man be a sculptor or a painter he shall be taught not to make idols: if he will not desist, let him be rejected.

If a man teach children worldly knowledge, it is indeed well if he desist, but if he has no other trade by which to live, let him have forgiveness.

If a man be an actor or one who makes shows in the theatre . . . a charioteer likewise, or one who takes part in the games or who goes to the games . . . a gladiator or a trainer of gladiators, a huntsman or one concerned with wild beast shows . . . a priest of idols or a keeper of idols—either let him desist or be rejected.

If a catechumen or a baptized Christian wishes to become a soldier, let him be cast out, for he has despised God . . .

A magician shall not even be brought for consideration. A charmer or an astrologer or an interpreter of dreams or a clipper of fringes of clothes[1] or a maker of amulets, let them desist or be rejected.

If a man's concubine be a slave, let her hear on condition that she have reared her children, and if she consorts with him alone. But if not let her be rejected. If a man have a concubine, let him desist and marry legally; and if he will not, let him be rejected.

Let a catechumen be instructed for three years; but if a man be earnest and persevere well in the matter, let him be received, because it is not the time that is judged, but the conduct.

Each time the teacher finishes his instruction, let the catechumens pray by themselves apart from the faithful. And let the women stand in the assembly by themselves, both the baptized women and the women catechumens. But after the prayer is finished the catechumens shall not give the kiss of peace, for their kiss is not yet pure. But the baptized shall embrace one another, men with men and women with women; but let not men embrace women. Moreover let all the women have their heads veiled with a scarf but not with one of linen only, for that is not a sufficient covering . . .

And when they are chosen who are set apart to receive baptism, let their life be examined, whether they lived piously as catechumens, whether they 'honoured the widows', visited the sick, fulfilled every good work. If those who bring them bear witness to them that they have done thus, then let them hear the gospel . . .

---

[1] Apparently worn to protect the wearer from evil.

And let those who are to be baptized be instructed to wash and cleanse themselves on the fifth day of the week; and if any woman be menstruous she shall be put aside and be baptized another day.

Those who are to receive baptism shall fast on the Friday and the Saturday. And on the Saturday the bishop shall assemble those who are to be baptized in one place, and shall bid them all to pray and bow the knee. And laying his hand on them he shall exorcize every evil spirit to flee away from them and never to return to them henceforward. And when he has finished exorcizing let him breathe on their faces and seal their foreheads and ears and noses, and let him raise them up.

BAPTISM AND CONFIRMATION

At the hour when the cock crows they shall first pray over the water. When they come to the water, let the water be pure and flowing.

And they shall put off their clothes.

And they shall baptize the little children first. And if they can answer for themselves, let them answer; but if they cannot, let their parents answer or someone from their family.

And next they shall baptize the grown men; and last the women, who shall have loosed their hair and laid aside the gold ornaments. Let no one go down to the water having any alien object with them.

At the time determined for baptizing the bishop shall give thanks over the oil and put it into a vessel, and it is called the Oil of Thanksgiving. And he shall take other oil and exorcize over it, and it is called Oil of Exorcism. And let a deacon carry the Oil of Exorcism and stand on the left hand, and another deacon shall take the Oil of Thanksgiving and stand on the right hand. And when the presbyter takes hold of each one of those who are to be baptized, let him bid him renounce, saying:

'I renounce thee, Satan, and all thy service and all thy works.'

And when he has said this let the presbyter anoint him with the Oil of Exorcism, saying:

'Let all evil spirits depart far from thee.'

Then after these things let him give him over to the presbyter who stands at the water. And let them stand in the water naked. And let a deacon likewise go down with him into the water.

Let him who baptizes lay hand on him, saying:

'Dost thou believe in God the Father Almighty?'

'I believe.'

Let him forthwith baptize him once, having his hand upon his head. And after, let him say:

'Dost thou believe in Christ Jesus, the Son of God,

Who was born of Holy Spirit and the Virgin Mary,

Who was crucified in the days of Pontius Pilate,

And died,

And rose the third day living from the dead

And ascended into the heavens,

And sat down at the right hand of the Father,

And who will come to judge the living and the dead?'

And when he says, 'I believe', let him baptize him the second time. And again let him say,

'Dost thou believe in the Holy Spirit in the holy Church,

And the resurrection of the flesh?'

And he who is being baptized shall say, 'I believe.' And so let him baptize him the third time.

And afterwards when he comes up he shall be anointed by the presbyter with the Oil of Thanksgiving, saying:

'I anoint thee with the holy oil in the Name of Jesus Christ.'

And so, each one drying himself, they shall now put on their clothes, and after this let them be together in the assembly.

And the bishop shall lay his hand upon them, invoking and saying:

'O Lord God, who didst count these worthy of deserving the forgiveness of sins by the water of regeneration, make them worthy to be filled with thy Holy Spirit and send upon them thy grace, that they may serve thee according to thy will; to thee is the glory, to the Father and to the Son with the Holy Ghost in the holy Church, both now and ever and world without end. Amen.'

After this, pouring the consecrated oil and laying his hand on his head, he shall say:

'I anoint thee with holy oil in God the Father Almighty and Christ Jesus and the Holy Ghost.'

And sealing him on the forehead he shall give him the kiss and say:

'The Lord be with you.'

And he who has been sealed shall say:

'And with thy spirit.'

And so shall the bishop do to each one severally.

Thenceforward they shall pray together with all the people; but they shall not previously pray with the faithful before they have undergone these things. And after the prayers, let them give the kiss of peace.

THE EUCHARIST

Then let the oblation at once be brought by the deacons to the bishop, and he shall *eucharistize*[1] first the bread into the representation of the flesh of Christ; and the cup mixed with wine for the anti-type of the blood which was shed for all who have believed in him; and milk and honey mingled together in fulfilment of the promise which was made to the Fathers, wherein he said, 'I will give you a land flowing with milk and honey'; which Christ indeed gave—his flesh, whereby they who believe are nourished like little children, making the bitterness of the heart sweet by the sweetness of his word; water also, for an oblation for a sign of the laver, that the inner man also, which is spirit, may receive the same as the body. And the bishop shall give an explanation concerning all these things to them who receive.

[Then[2] the bishop, laying his hand on the oblation, shall say, giving thanks:

BISHOP: The Lord be with you.
PEOPLE: And with thy spirit.
BISHOP: Lift up your hearts.
PEOPLE: We have them with the Lord.
BISHOP: Let us give thanks unto the Lord.
PEOPLE: It is meet and right.
BISHOP: We render thanks to thee, O God, through thy

[1] See note on p. 57.   [2] Transferred from section 4; see p. 60.

beloved child Jesus Christ, whom in the last times thou didst send to us to be a Saviour and Redeemer and the Angel of thy counsel; who is thy Word inseparable from thee, through whom thou madest all things and in whom thou wast well-pleased; whom thou didst send from heaven into the Virgin's womb and who, conceived within her, was made flesh and demonstrated to be thy Son, being born of Holy Spirit and a Virgin; who, fulfilling thy will and preparing for thee a holy people, stretched forth his hands for suffering that he might release from sufferings them who have believed in thee; who when he was betrayed to voluntary suffering that he might abolish death, and rend the bonds of the devil, and tread down hell, and enlighten the righteous, and establish the limit,[1] and demonstrate the resurrection:

Taking bread and giving thanks to thee said: 'Take eat: this is my Body which is broken for you.' Likewise also the cup, saying: 'This is my Blood which is shed for you. When ye do this ye do my anamnesis.'[2]

Doing therefore the anamnesis of his death and resurrection, we offer to thee the bread and the cup, making eucharist to thee because thou hast made us worthy to stand before thee and minister as priests to thee. And we pray that thou wouldest send thy Holy Spirit upon the oblation of thy holy Church and grant to all who partake to be united, that they may be fulfilled with the Holy Spirit for the confirmation of faith in truth, that we may praise and glorify thee through thy child Jesus Christ, through whom glory and honour be unto thee with the Holy Spirit in thy holy Church now and for ever and world without end. Amen.]

And when (the bishop) breaks the Bread in distributing to each a fragment, he shall say:

'The Bread of heaven in Christ Jesus.'

And he who receives shall answer, 'Amen.' And the presbyters (but if there are not enough of them the deacons also) shall hold

---

[1] Probably a reference to the number of the elect; cf. Mark 13. 27 and Rev. 7. 4.

[2] Memorial or Remembrance are not adequate translations of this Greek work, the translator explains. It is a re-calling before God of a past event in such a way that its consequences take effect in the present.

the cups and stand by in good order and with reverence: first he
that holdeth the water, second he who holds the milk, third he
who holds the wine. And they who partake shall taste of each cup,
he who gives it saying thrice:

'In God the Father Almighty.'

And he who receives shall say, 'Amen.'

'And in the Lord Jesus Christ'.

'Amen.'

'And in the Holy Spirit in the holy Church'.

'Amen.'

So shall it be done to each one.

And when these things have been accomplished, let each one be
zealous to perform good works and to please God, living righteously, devoting himself to the Church, performing the things
which he has learnt, advancing in the service of God.

16. MORNING HYMN OF THE EASTERN CHURCH

Christians have always used the ancient hymns of the Jews, the
Psalms, and Paul mentions 'psalms, hymns, and spiritual songs' (Col.
3, 16 and Eph. 5, 19). The younger Pliny wrote in 112 that Christians
sang a hymn at daybreak (see p. 15), and such hymns at daybreak and
sunset, 'Office hymns' as they came to be called in monastic times, are
very ancient. The oldest surviving hymn is Greek, Φῶς ἱλαρὸν, and
it is still used in the Vespers of the Orthodox Church. Basil (d. 379)
mentions it as ancient in his book, *Of the Holy Spirit*: 'We cannot say
who was the author of those expressions in the Thanksgiving at the
Lighting of the Lamps; but it is an ancient form which the people
repeat, and no one has ever yet been accused of impiety for saying,
"We hymn the Father and the Son and the Holy Spirit of God"'

John Keble translated it and his reasonably close version appears in
Hymns Ancient and Modern: 'Hail, gladdening light'. Robert Bridges
made a poetical approximation for the *Yattendon Hymnal*: 'O gladsome
grace'.

> O laughing light of the pure glory
> Of the immortal Father of heaven,
> The holy one, the blessed one,
> Jesus Christ!

Coming to the time of the setting of the sun,
We see the light of evening
And hymn the Father, Son,
And Holy Spirit of God.

Worthy art thou at every time
To be hymned with holy voices,
O Son of God, the giver of life;
So all the world extols thee.

CHAPTER FIVE

UNDER THE PHILOSOPHER KING

Marcus Aurelius (161–180) was the best man among the Roman emperors; he was a firm and wise ruler; he was a thoughtful writer on the moral life, almost painfully honest with himself, whose *Meditations* have never ceased to be read. It might have been expected that, of all the Roman emperors, he would have been the one who would have responded with toleration to the plea put forward by Justin in his two Apologies—the first addressed jointly to Antoninus Pius and Marcus Aurelius, his adopted son; the second addressed to the Senate of Rome just after the accession of Marcus Aurelius. This did not happen. Without introducing any new laws against Christianity, or giving any orders for a general witch hunt, Marcus Aurelius showed that he considered the existing laws just and saw to it that they were enforced with greater strictness. This chapter contains abundant evidence that government by a man, who almost completely filled Plato's specification for the just ruler, could yet amount to persecution of men holding unpopular opinions.

17. JUSTIN BECOMES JUSTIN MARTYR   165

Justin was writing and teaching in Rome. Teaching involved controversy. One with whom Justin argued none too kindly was Crescens, a philosopher who belonged to the school known as Cynics (see page 72). Justin denounced him in his *Apology* as 'a lover not of wisdom but of showing off. He does not deserve the name of philosopher, seeing that he publicly criticises what he does not understand, alleging that Christians are godless and impious . . . For if he lashes out at us without studying Christ's teaching he is most unscrupulous and much worse than simple people, who as a rule refrain from arguing and making false statements on subjects they know nothing about . . .' Justin, as he stated in the same passage, expected to be denounced to the authorities by Crescens. He was.

Tatian (see page 22), who was at this time a pupil of Justin, has left us an even more unflattering picture of Crescens: a man who 'went beyond everyone in his offences against boys, and was passionately devoted to money-making. He urged others to despise death, but was so afraid of it himself that he did his best to compass the death of Justin —as though death was a calamity—simply because by preaching the truth Justin convicted the philosophers of gluttony and fraud.'[1]

The description given here of the trial of Justin and some of his pupils comes from a contemporary Christian account based on the official court report.

In the time of the lawless partisans of idolatry, wicked decrees were passed against the godly Christians in town and country, to force them to offer libations to vain idols; and accordingly the holy men having been apprehended, were brought before the prefect of Rome, Rusticus by name. And when they had been brought before his judgment-seat, Rusticus the prefect said to Justin,

'Obey the gods at once, and submit to the Emperors.'

Justin said, 'To obey the commandments of our Saviour Jesus Christ is worthy neither of blame nor of condemnation.'

Rusticus the prefect said, 'What kind of doctrines do you profess?'

Justin said, 'I have endeavoured to learn all doctrines, but I have acquiesced at last in the true doctrines, those namely of the Christians, even though they do not please those who hold false opinions.'

Rusticus the prefect said, 'Are those the doctrines that please you, you wretched fellow?'

Justin said, 'Yes, since I adhere to them with right dogma.'

Rusticus the prefect said, 'What is the dogma?'

Justin said, 'That belief by which we worship the God of the Christians, whom we reckon to be one from the beginning, the maker and fashioner of the whole creation, visible and invisible; and the Lord Jesus Christ the Son of God, who had also been preached beforehand by the prophets as about to be present with the race of men, the herald of salvation and teacher of good disciples. And I, being a man, think that what I can say is insignificant in comparison with the boundless divinity, acknowledging a certain prophetic power, since it was prophesied concerning him of

[1] Quoted by Eusebius.

whom I now say that he is the Son of God. For I know that of old the prophets foretold his appearance among men.'

Rusticus the prefect said, 'Where do you assemble?'

Justin said, 'Where each one chooses and can; for do you fancy that we all meet in the very same place? Not so, because the God of the Christians is not circumscribed by place; but, being invisible, fills heaven and earth, and everywhere is worshipped and glorified by the faithful.'

Rusticus the prefect said, 'Tell me where you assemble, or into what place do you collect your followers?'

Justin said, 'I live above one Martinus, at the Trinothinian Bath; and during the whole time (and I am now living in Rome for the second time) I am unaware of any other meeting than his. And if any one wished to come to me, I communicated to him the doctrines of truth.'

Rusticus said, 'Are you not then a Christian?'

Justin said, 'Yes; I am a Christian.'

Then said the prefect Rusticus to Chariton, 'Tell me further, Chariton, are you also a Christian?'

Chariton said, 'I am a Christian by the command of God.'

Rusticus the prefect asked the woman Charito, 'What say you, Charito?'

Charito said, 'I am a Christian by the grace of God.'

Rusticus said to Euelpistus, 'And what are you?'

Euelpistus, a servant of Caesar, answered, 'I too, am a Christian, having been freed by Christ, and by the grace of Christ, I partake of the same hope.'

Rusticus the prefect said to Hierax, 'And you, are you a Christian?'

Hierax said, 'Yes, I am a Christian, for I revere and worship the same God.'

Rusticus the prefect said, 'Did Justin make you Christians?'

Hierax said, 'I was a Christian, and will be a Christian.'

And Pæon stood up and said, 'I too am a Christian.'

Rusticus the prefect said, 'Who taught you?'

Pæon said, 'From our parents we received this good confession.'

Euelpistus said, 'I willingly heard the words from Justin. But from my parents also I learned to be a Christian.'

Rusticus the prefect said, 'Where are your parents?'

Euelpistus said, 'In Cappadocia.'

Rusticus says to Hierax, 'Where are your parents?'

And he answered and said, 'Christ is our true father, and faith in him is our mother; and my earthly parents died; and I, when I was driven from Iconium, came here.'

Rusticus the prefect said to Liberianus, 'And what say you? Are you a Christian, and unwilling to worship the gods?'

Liberanus said, 'I too am a Christian, for I worship and reverence the only true God.'

The prefect says to Justin, 'Hearken, you who are called learned, and think that you know true doctrines; if you are scourged and beheaded, do you believe that you will ascend into heaven?'

Justin said, 'I hope that if I endure these things, I shall have his gifts. For I know that to all who have thus lived, there abides the divine favour until the completion of the whole world.'

Rusticus the prefect said, 'Do you suppose, then, that you will ascend into heaven to receive some recompense?'

Justin said, 'I do not suppose it, but I know and am fully persuaded of it.'

Rusticus the prefect said, 'Let us then now come to the matter in hand, and which presses. Having come together, offer sacrifice with one accord to the gods.'

Justin said, 'No right-thinking person falls away from piety to impiety.'

Rusticus the prefect said, 'Unless you obey, you shall be mercilessly punished.'

Justin said, 'Through prayer we can be saved on account of our Lord Jesus Christ, even when we have been punished, because this shall become to us salvation and confidence at the more fearful and universal judgment-seat of our Lord and Saviour.'

Thus also said the others martyrs: 'Do what you will; for we are Christians and do not sacrifice to idols.'

Rusticus the prefect pronounced sentence, saying: 'Let those who have refused to sacrifice to the gods and to yield to the command of the emperor be scourged, and led away to suffer the punishment of decapitation, according to the laws.'

The holy martyrs having glorified God, and having gone forth to the accustomed place, were beheaded, and perfected their testimony in the confession of the Saviour. And some of the faithful having secretly removed their bodies, laid them in a suitable place, the grace of our Lord Jesus Christ having wrought along with them, to whom be glory for ever and ever. Amen.

18. PRISON-VISITING: The Strange Career of Peregrinus

In the same year that Justin was executed, Lucian wrote the book from which Extract 18 is taken. It illustrates the compassion and courage which moved Christians who had escaped arrest to visit their friends in prison. It also introduces a man whom Christianity could not hold. Justin and Clement had come to Christianity through the non-Christian philosophers (Extracts 10 and 32); Peregrinus moved in the reverse direction. The extract refers to the time when as a young man Peregrinus was imprisoned in Syria as a Christian, but was released by the governor lest he should pose as a martyr. Some time later Peregrinus was excommunicated for profaning the Christian rites. In Egypt he joined the Cynics, a school of philosophers whose name comes from the Greek word for dog. Diogenes (c. 412–323 B.C.) was one of their founders. They were strong in the first and second centuries of the Christian era. They were so like the Stoics in their teaching that the poet Juvenal said that a Cynic only differed from a Stoic by the cut of his cloak. (For Stoics see notes to Extract 10.) Peregrinus moved to Rome but was expelled for insulting the emperor. He then taught in Athens but after a period of success became unpopular by the violence of his attacks on others. He set fire to himself as a gesture at the Olympic Games. Lucian saw his death and then wrote about his career in his book, *On the Death of Peregrinus* (165).

Lucian was the greatest wit and satirist among Greek prose writers. His scorn was aimed principally at the follies of the gods of Olympus and the 'humbug' of philosophers. Peregrinus, who had been forced to leave his home town in Asia Minor because he was thought to have killed his father, was a natural target. One might have expected the Christians, too, to have come in for a full-scale attack from Lucian as well as such glancing blows as those given here. It suggests that Lucian had not had much, if any, contact with them. It is only fair to Peregrinus to say that he had devoted friends who thought highly of him.

Source: Lucian of Samosata, *On the Death of Peregrinus.*

When Peregrinus was imprisoned, the Christians, taking the matter to heart, left no stone unturned in the endeavour to rescue him. Then, when this was found to be impossible, they looked after his wants in every other respect with unremitting care and zeal. And from the first break of day old women—widows they are called—and orphan children might be seen waiting about the doors of the prison; while their officers, by bribing the keepers, succeeded in passing the night inside with him. Then various meals were brought in, and sacred formulas of theirs were repeated; and this fine fellow Peregrinus—for he still bore this name —was entitled a new Socrates by them.

Moreover there came from certain of the cities in Asia deputies sent by the Christian communities to assist and advise and console the man. Indeed the alacrity they display is incredible, when any matter of the kind is undertaken as a matter of public concern; for in short they spare for nothing. Accordingly, large sums of money came to Peregrinus at that time from them, on the plea of his bonds, and he made no inconsiderable revenue out of it. For the poor wretches have persuaded themselves that they will be altogether immortal and will live for ever, and with this end in view they actually despise death and the greater part of them give themselves up voluntarily.

19. THE MARTYRS OF VIENNE AND LYONS 177

Southern France had been a Roman province (hence its modern name Provence) for nearly 300 years. Its chief coastal towns had been Greek colonies from an even earlier date—Marseilles was founded by the Greeks in 600 B.C. There were close trade links between southern France and Asia Minor in the second century. There were also close religious links. Pretty certainly Christianity came to Provence from Asia Minor. This letter from the Christians of Vienne and Lyons, towns on the northern border of the Province, was written to the Christians of the Roman province of Asia, which included the hill country of Phrygia. Two of the martyrs came from there. So too did one of the

presbyters, Irenaeus, who escaped because he had been sent on a mission
to Rome with a letter pleading for an understanding view to be taken
of the Montanists, a sect of ecstatic enthusiasts which had just come
into existence in Phrygia (Extract 23).

The persecution seems to have begun as a mob attack. The procedure
followed by the authorities corresponds closely with that described in
the letters between Pliny and Trajan sixty-five years earlier. Those who
maintained their Christian faith were executed for that sufficient reason.
Those who recanted were put back for further investigation to see
what other crimes they might have committed. They were executed
for 'manslaughter and abominable impurity'—presumably on the
strength of the persistent rumours of cannibalism associated with the
Eucharist. Those who were Roman citizens were put back until the
emperor's decision was known. Notice that these Christians were still
observing the old Jewish rule against drinking blood (see Leviticus 3.
17 and Acts 15. 20).

On his return from his journey to Rome Irenaeus was elected bishop
of Lyons in place of the martyred Pothinus. He spent the rest of his life
there, learnt the Celtic language of the country people and feared that
it was corrupting his Greek style. He maintained his concern for the
Christians of his native Asia Minor and read bishop Victor of Rome a
firm lecture when he broke off relations with them because of differences about the day on which Easter was to be observed: 'The dispute
is not only about the day,' he wrote, 'but also about the actual character
of the fast . . . In spite of that, they all lived in peace with one another,
and so do we: the divergency in the fast emphasizes the unanimity of
our faith.'

The servants of Christ who sojourn in Vienne and Lyons in Gaul
to the brethren throughout Asia and Phrygia who hold the same
faith and hope with us of redemption: peace, grace, and glory from
God the Father and Christ Jesus our Lord.

The magnitude of the tribulation in these parts, and the intensity of the fury of the heathen against the saints, and the variety of
the sufferings which the blessed martyrs endured, we are neither
able to state with accuracy nor indeed is it possible for them to be
put into words. For the adversary darted upon us with all his
might, giving us a foretaste of what to expect at his coming, which
about to be. He practised every device to train and exercise his

own agents against the servants of God, so that not only were we excluded from houses and baths and markets, but actually the mere appearance of any one of us in any place whatever was forbidden.

But the grace of God was our general in the fight, rescuing the weak and ranging them in battle-array as strong pillars, enabling them through patient endurance to draw upon themselves all the violence of the Evil One; and indeed they advanced to close quarters with him, enduring every form of reproach and punishment; finally, making light of their sufferings, they hastened to Christ, truly showing that the sufferings of this present time are not worthy to be compared with the glory that shall be revealed to us-ward (Rom. 8. 18).

First, they nobly endured all that had to be borne at the hands of the mob and rabble; they were hooted, assaulted, pulled about, plundered, stoned, and forced to barricade themselves in; in fact they suffered every indignity which an infuriated mob is accustomed to inflict upon its supposed adversaries and foes. At length, being brought into the forum by the tribune and chief men of the city, they were examined in the presence of the whole multitude, and having confessed (their Christianity), were put into prison to await the arrival of the governor. Subsequently, when they were brought before him and he was treating us with great harshness, Vettius Epagathus, one of the brethren, a man filled with the fulness of love towards God and towards his neighbour, intervened. His life as a citizen was so upright that, although so young a man, he equalled the testimony borne to the aged Zacharias, for 'he walked in all the commandments and ordinances of the Lord blameless' (Luke 1. 6), being also tireless in every act of service to his neighbour, very zealous towards God, and fervent in spirit. Being of such a character, he could not endure that such unreasonable judgment should be given against us; and so, being highly indignant, he asked to be permitted to testify on behalf of the brethren, to the effect that there is nothing impious or sacrilegious amongst us.

But those around the judgment-seat shouted him down (for he was a man of influence), and the governor refused the just claim

which he thus put forward, merely asking if he were himself also
a Christian; and when he confessed it with a clear voice, he was
himself also taken into the order of the witnesses [i.e. martyrs],
being designated 'the Christians' advocate', having the Advocate
in himself, the Spirit in greater measure than Zacharias (cf. Luke
1. 67), as he showed by the fulness of his love, being well pleased
to lay down even his own life for the defence of the brethren.
For he was, and is, a genuine disciple of Christ, following the
Lamb whithersoever he goeth (Rev. 14. 4).

Then the rest were assorted into two groups; manifestly, some
were ready to be proto-martyrs [of Gaul] and with all eagerness
completed the confession of their witness, but manifestly others
were not ready and untrained, weak as yet and unable to bear the
strain of a great contest. Of these about ten miscarried, who caused
us great grief and sorrow unmeasured, and also hindered the eagerness of the others not yet arrested, who, although suffering all
terrors, were nevertheless constantly present with the confessors,[1]
and would not leave them. Then, indeed, were we all greatly
anxious, through uncertainty as to their confession, not because
we dreaded the punishments to be endured, but because we looked
to the end, and feared lest any might fall away. Each day, however, those who were worthy were arrested, and filled up the
others' places, so that there were gathered together from the two
Churches all the zealous ones who had done most to establish our
way of life. They arrested also certain heathen domestic slaves of
ours, for the governor ordered that we should all be examined in
public; and these falling into a plot of Satan, and fearing the tortures which they saw the saints suffering, on being instigated to
this course by the soldiers, falsely accused us of Thyestean banquets and Oedipodean intercourse,[2] and of other deeds of which
it is not lawful for us either to speak or think nor even to believe
that the like is ever done amongst mankind. These statements
being reported, all were infuriated against us, so that if there were
any who from ties of kinship had hitherto been lenient, even these

[1] In these early years the name was given to those who declared their faith
but were not necessarily martyred.

[2] Thyestes ate his sons; Oedipus had children by his mother.

were now greatly enraged and mad with anger against us. Then that was fulfilled which was spoken by our Lord: 'The time shall come wherein every one that killeth you will think that he doeth God service' (John 16. 2). Hereupon the holy witnesses endured punishments beyond all description, Satan being ambitious that some of the slanders might be admitted by them also. The whole wrath of the populace and of the governor and of the soldiers was directed in excessive measure against Sanctus, a deacon from Vienne, and against Maturus, a very recent convert but a noble warrior, and against Attalus, a native of Pergamum, who had ever been a pillar and a foundation (1 Tim. 3. 15) of our Church, and against Blandina, through whom Christ showed that what men regard as worthless and uncomely and despicable is deemed worthy of great glory by God, because of that love towards him which is manifested in power and not boasted of in mere show (1 Cor. 1. 25 f.). For while we were all afraid for her, and her earthly mistress (who was herself also one of the witnesses) dreaded lest she should be unable through bodily weakness boldly to make confession, Blandina was filled with such power that she was set free from and raised above those who tortured her. They, using every kind of torture in turn from morning to evening, had to confess that they were conquered, since they had nothing left which they could any longer do to her, and they marvelled at breath remaining in her when her whole body was lacerated and laid open, testifying that one of the tortures by itself was sufficient to end life, let alone so many and such great ones. But the blessed woman, like a noble athlete, grew in strength as she proclaimed her faith, finding refreshment and freedom from pain in saying, 'I am a Christian, and we do nothing vile.'

Sanctus also nobly endured with boundless and super-human courage all the outrages put upon him, the ungodly hoping that from the persistency and magnitude of his tortures something would be heard from his lips of the Christians' unlawful doings; but with such confidence did he array himself against them, that he did not even tell his own name or race or city, nor whether he were a slave or free, but to all their interrogations he returned answer in the Latin tongue, 'I am a Christian.' This he owned for

G

name, for city, for race, for everything besides, nor did the heathen
hear from him any other word. On this account there was kindled
a great rivalry against him on the part of the governor and the
torturers, so that when no other form of torture remained to be
inflicted on him, as a last resort they affixed hot brazen plates to
the tenderest parts of his body. These were burned, but he remained unmoved and unyielding, steadfast in his confession,
refreshed and strengthened by the heavenly fountain of the water
of life (John 7. 38) which springs from the heart of Christ. His
poor body was a witness to his sufferings, being one entire wound
and scar, drawn together and battered out of all human shape. In
him Christ suffered and achieved great glory, bringing the adversary to naught, and showing that nothing can frighten us where the
Father's love is, nor hurt us where is Christ's glory. And when
after some days the wicked men again tortured this witness, thinking that, if they repeated the same punishments upon his limbs,
which were so swollen and inflamed that he could not bear the
touch of a hand, they would overcome him, or that, dying under
his tortures, he would strike fear into the rest, not only did nothing
of this sort happen, but contrary to all human expectation he
lifted his head and straightened his body under the second tortures, recovering his own former appearance and the use of his
limbs, so that by the grace of Christ the second torture became
for him no punishment but a means of healing.

Biblias, too, one of those who had denied Christ, was brought
again to the torture; the devil thought that he had gulped her
down, and wished to damn her further as a slanderer by forcing
her to say wicked things about us, she being one already crushed
and cowardly. But under the torture she recovered her senses, and,
as it were, awoke from a deep sleep, being reminded by the temporal anguish of the eternal punishment in Gehenna; and she
determinedly contradicted the slanders, saying, 'How could those
persons eat children to whom it is not lawful to eat the blood even
of irrational animals?' Thereupon she confessed herself a Christian,
and was added to the order of martyrs.

The tyrannous punishments being thus brought to naught by
Christ through the patient endurance of the blessed, the devil

conceived other contrivances—close confinement in the prison in the dark, and in a most loathsome situation, clamping the feet in the stocks, stretching them apart to the fifth hole, and other cruelties such as enraged underlings who are full of the devil are wont to inflict upon their prisoners. So that very many were suffocated in the prison—those whom the Lord willed thus to depart, showing forth his glory. For some who had suffered such acute tortures that it seemed impossible for them to continue to live even with every nursing care, remained alive in the prison, destitute indeed of all human care, but strengthened and empowered in body and soul by the Lord, exhorting and encouraging the rest. Whereas the younger ones, and those only just arrested, whose bodies had not been accustomed to torture, could not bear the confinement, and died in the prison.

Now the blessed Pothinus, who had been entrusted with the bishopric of Lyons, and was more than ninety years of age and quite feeble in body, scarce indeed able to breathe from long bodily weakness, yet strengthened by spiritual zeal because of his blessed desire for martyrdom, was himself haled to the judgment-seat. Though his body was broken down with age and disease, his soul was preserved within him in order that Christ might triumph through it. And he, being brought to the judgment-seat, and escorted by the police-magistrates and rabble with all kinds of hooting as though he were the Christ, rendered a glorious witness (cf. 1 Tim. 6. 13). Being asked during his examination by the governor who the God of the Christians was, he replied, 'If thou art worthy, thou shalt know.' Thereupon he was mercilessly mauled and buffeted with all kinds of blows, the nearest ones assailing him with hands and feet, not even respecting his age, while those at a distance hurled at him whatever each could lay hold of, every one thinking it a gross carelessness and impiety if any act of cruelty were omitted; for so they thought to avenge their own gods. Thus, scarcely breathing, he was cast into prison, and after two days yielded up his spirit.

Hereupon a remarkable instance of God's providence occurred, and the measureless mercy of Jesus was shown—an occurrence seldom happening in the brotherhood, but not beyond the power of Christ. For those who on their first arrest had denied Christ were imprisoned along with the others and shared their miseries— for not even in the present time was their denial of any benefit to them—while those who confessed what they were, were imprisoned as 'Christians', no other charge being brought against them. The former were detained as guilty of manslaughter and abominable impurity, being punished two-fold in comparison with the latter. The confessors were comforted by the joy of martyrdom and the hope of the things promised and the Father's Spirit, while the recanters were greatly tormented by their conscience, so that their very faces distinguished them from all the rest when they were let out. The confessors came forth joyously, with glory and much grace blended in their faces, so that even their bonds encircled them like beautiful decorations, as a bride is decked with fringes of cunningly-worked gold, and they were scented with the sweet savour of Christ (2 Cor. 2. 15), so that some fancied they had actually been anointed with earthly ointment. But the others were dejected, ashamed and downcast, brimful of disgrace. Besides being reviled by the heathen as contemptible cowards and branded as murderers, they had lost the all-worthy and glorious and life-giving Name. The rest beholding this were strengthened, and when arrested, confessed unhesitatingly, giving no heed to the suggestions of the devil . . .

Subsequently their martyrdoms embraced every kind of death. For out of flowers of every shape and colour they wove a crown and offered it to the Father. It was indeed right that such noble athletes, who had patiently undergone manifold contests and had greatly conquered, should receive the splendid crown of incorruption.

Accordingly Maturus and Sanctus and Blandina and Attalus were led forth to the beasts in the amphitheatre, to give the heathen public an exhibition of cruelty, a day for beast-fighting being granted directly on our account. Maturus and Sanctus once more went through every form of punishment in the amphitheatre, just as though they had suffered nothing before, or rather as having already in many bouts defeated their opponent and were now contending for the crown itself. They again ran the gauntlet of whips, which is customary on such occasions, and the mauling by the beasts, and all else that the maddened populace yelled for and demanded. Finally they were placed in the iron chair and choked with the reek of their own roasted flesh. Nor did they even then desist, but became even more mad against them in their desire to break their patience. Yet even so they heard nothing from Sanctus but that word of confession which he had constantly uttered from the first. These two, then, their life having been preserved through all this great and varied agony, were at last sacrificed, having been made a spectacle to the world (1 Cor. 4. 9) throughout that day in place of all the usual gladiatorial combats.

Now Blandina, hanging upon a stake, was exposed as food for the wild beasts that were driven in. And because she seemed to be hanging on a cross, and because of her intense prayers, she inspired great courage in the combatants, for in this contest they saw, with their outward eyes in the form of their sister, him who was crucified for them, that he might persuade those who believe on him that all who suffer for the glory of Christ have an abiding fellowship with the living God. And when none of the beasts would touch her, she was taken down from the stake and sent back again to the prison, being reserved for another contest, in order that, being victorious in many trials, she might make the condemnation of the crooked serpent irrevocable (Isa. 27. 1), and encourage the brethren; for she, small and weak and despised as she was, put on Christ (Gal. 3. 27), the great and conquering Athlete, and having defeated the adversary in many contests, won through conflict the incorruptible crown.

Attalus also was loudly demanded by the people, for he was a man of note. He readily entered the contest because of his good conscience, since he had been genuinely trained in the Christian rule and had ever been a witness amongst us of the truth. He was led round the amphitheatre, having in front a tablet on which had been written in Latin, THIS IS ATTALUS THE CHRISTIAN. The people indeed were bursting with eagerness for him, but the governor, hearing that he was a Roman, bade him be put back again with the rest of those prisoners concerning whom he had written to Caesar, and was awaiting an answer.

The intervening period was not idle nor fruitless. For through their influence most of the lapsed were restored, being both conceived anew and endowed with fresh life; and they learned to confess, and living now and nerved, they went to the tribunal to be again interrogated by the governor, God who desires not the death of a sinner (Ezek. 33. 11), but is gracious to the penitent, shedding sweetness on them.

Now the rescript of Caesar was that they should be put to death by torture, but that those who recanted should be released.

Therefore, at the beginning of the public festival held here, which is thronged with men who attend it from all nations, the governor brought the blessed ones to his tribunal as a spectacle, and displayed them to the crowd. Whereupon he again examined them, and those who appeared to be Roman citizens he beheaded, the rest he sent to the beasts. And Christ was greatly glorified in the case of those who had previously denied him but now confessed him, contrary to the expectation of the heathen. Moreover these were examined separately, as certain to be released; but when they confessed, they were added to the order of the witnesses, those only remaining without who had no longer any trace of faith, nor of respect for their wedding garment (Matt. 22. 11), nor idea of the fear of God, slandering the Way by their manner of life, being truly the sons of perdition (cf. John 17. 12). But all the rest were added to the Church (Acts 2. 47).

Amongst those examined was Alexander a Phrygian, a physician by profession, who had spent many years in Gaul, and was known to almost every one for his love to God and boldness in the Word, for he was not without a share of apostolic grace. This man, standing by the judgment-seat, and with a nod encouraging the others to their confession, appeared to the bystanders as though in pains of travail. And the populace, exasperated at seeing those who had before recanted once more confessing, hooted at Alexander as the cause of this. Then the governor, turning his attention to him, asked him who he was, and on his replying 'A Christian,' he fell into a rage and condemned him to the beasts. On the next day he and Attalus entered the arena; for the governor, to please the people, had ordered even Attalus again to the beasts. These men suffered all the instruments of torture in the amphitheatre, and having endured a magnificent contest, at last were themselves sacrificed. Alexander neither murmured nor groaned at all, but conversed with God in his heart, while Attalus, when placed upon the iron chair and roasted, the fumes from his poor body being borne aloft, said to the crowd in Latin, 'Lo, this it is to eat men, and you are doing it; we neither eat men, nor practise any wickedness.' And when asked what name God has, he replied, 'God has not a name as a man has.'

Finally, on the last day of the gladiatorial games, Blandina was again brought forward with a lad of about fifteen, named Ponticus. These two had been brought in each day to witness the punishment of the others, and had been pressed to swear by the idols. And because they remained constant and set them at naught, the mob grew furious, so that they neither pitied the youth of the boy nor respected the sex of the woman. They made them pass through every form of terrible suffering, and through the whole round of punishments, urging them to swear after each one, but they were unable to effect this. For Ponticus, excited to zeal by his sister, so that even the heathen saw that it was she who encouraged and strengthened him, yielded up his spirit after nobly enduring every punishment. And the blessed Blandina, last of all, like a noble mother who had encouraged her children, and sent them forward as conquerors to the King, herself endured all the conflicts of her children and hastened after them, rejoicing and exulting in her death, like one invited to a bridal feast rather than thrown to the beasts. For after scourging, after the beasts, after the roasting, she was at last enclosed in a net and thrown to a bull. Time after time the animal tossed her, and being no longer sensible of her sufferings on account of her hope and firm hold on the things entrusted to her and her communion with Christ, she also was sacrificed; and even the heathen themselves confessed that never yet amongst them had a woman suffered so many and great tortures.

Yet not even thus was their madness and cruel hatred towards the saints satiated. For being savage and barbarous tribes, incited by the Wild Beast, they were not easily appeased, their malice finding another peculiar opportunity in the dead bodies ... For they cast to dogs those who had been suffocated in the prison, carefully guarding them by night and by day lest any one should be buried by us. Then they gathered together the remains left by the wild beasts and by the fire—how mangled and how charred!—and the heads of the others with their severed bodies, and guarded them from burial for many days with a watch of soldiers ... We were overwhelmed with sorrow because we could not bury the bodies in the earth. For night did not help us to do this, nor could bribes persuade nor entreaty move to pity; but in every way they guarded them, looking upon it as a great point gained if they prevented them being buried.

For six days the bodies of the martyrs were publicly exhibited and exposed to the open air, and then they were burnt and reduced to ashes by the godless, and swept away in the river Rhone which flows close by, to prevent any relic of them being seen any longer upon the earth. And this they did, imagining that they could conquer God, and deprive them of their new birth. In their own words:

'Now they can have no hope of a resurrection; through trusting in that they bring to us a foreign and strange religion, and despise terrible sufferings, and are willing with joy to die. Now let us see whether they will rise again, and if their God is able to succour them and rescue them out of our hands.'

20. AFRICAN MARTYRS   180

On July 17, 180 Carthage, the rich, dissolute capital of Roman North Africa, was the scene of the trial of seven men and five women from the neighbouring town of Scillium. Their offence was that they were Christians who refused to swear by the 'genius' of the emperor. The account of their trial is bald, official, moving in its simplicity. Their conviction and execution was inevitable. The report is the first documentary evidence of the existence of Christianity in any part of Africa except Egypt.

The language of government and of educated people in this part of the Roman empire was Latin, not Greek. During the next two hundred years Africa was to be the main centre of Christian thought in the Latin West. But Latin was an imposed culture. Carthage had been Rome's most dangerous enemy in the days before the empire. Its people were called by the Romans 'Poeni' and the wars are known as the Punic wars. These names point to the origin of Carthage as a Phoenician colony from Tyre. The language of these first Semitic settlers survived, 'the language,' as Hodgkin put it, 'in which Hiram spoke to Solomon and Jezebel to Ahab was still spoken from Tangier to Tripoli at the time of the Christian era.' And he quotes Augustine: 'Ask our country people what they are and they will answer in the Punic speech, "Canani". What is this but a slightly corrupt form of Canaanites?'

The Scillitan martyrs represent, so to speak, a hang-over from the reign of the good Marcus Aurelius to that of the undeniably bad Commodus. Marcus Aurelius had died in March, probably at Vienna. His son, who was engaged in the same frontier war, hurried back to Rome. Quite possibly had the good emperor died earlier the Scillitan martyrs might have lived, for by one of the ironies of history the reign of the quite impossible Commodus was one in which the church had peace.

When Praesens for the second time, and Claudianus were the consuls, on the seventeenth day of July, at Carthage, there were set in the judgment-hall Speratus, Nartzalus, Cittinus, Donata, Secunda, and Vestia.

Saturninus the proconsul said: 'You can win the indulgence of our lord the emperor, if you return to a sound mind.'

Speratus said: 'We have never done ill, but when ill-treated we have given thanks; because we pay heed to OUR EMPEROR.'

Saturninus the proconsul said: 'We too are religious, and our religion is simple, and we swear by the genius of our lord the emperor, and pray for his welfare, as you also ought to do . . .'

Speratus said: 'The empire of this world I know not; but rather, I serve that God, whom no man hath seen nor, with these eyes, can see. I have committed no theft; but if I have bought anything I pay the tax; because I know my Lord, the King of kings, and Emperor of all nations.'

Saturninus the proconsul said to the rest: 'Cease to be of this persuasion.'

Speratus said: 'It is an ill persuasion to do murder, to speak false witness.'

Saturninus the proconsul said: 'Be not partakers of this folly.'

Cittinus said: 'We have none other to fear, save only our Lord God, who is in heaven.'

Donata said: 'Honour to Caesar as Caesar; but fear to God.'

Vestia said: 'I am a Christian.'

Secunda said: 'What I am, that I wish to be.'

Saturninus the proconsul said to Speratus: 'Dost thou persist in being a Christian?'

Speratus said: 'I am a Christian.' And with him they all agreed.

Saturninus the proconsul said: 'Will you have a space to consider?'

Speratus said: 'In a matter so straightforward there is no considering.'

Saturninus the proconsul said: 'What are the things in your chest?'

Speratus said: 'Books and epistles of Paul, a just man.'

Saturninus the proconsul said: 'Have a delay of thirty days, and bethink yourselves.'

Speratus said a second time: 'I am a Christian.' And with him they all agreed.

Saturninus the proconsul read out the decree from the tablet: 'Speratus, Nartzalus, Cittinus, Donata, Vestia, Secunda, and the rest having confessed that they live according to the Christian rite, since after opportunity offered them of returning to the custom of the Romans they have obstinately persisted, it is determined that they be put to the sword.'

Speratus said: 'We give thanks to God.'

Nartzalus said: 'Today we are martyrs in heaven; thanks be to God.'

Saturninus the proconsul ordered it to be declared by the herald: 'Speratus, Nartzalus, Cittinus, Veturius, Felix, Aquilinus, Laetantius, Januaria, Generosa, Vestia, Donata, and Secunda, have I ordered to be executed.'

They all said: 'Thanks be to God.'

CHAPTER SIX

THE LONG PEACE
Two Generations of Growth

The Long Peace is the name given to the time from 211 to 250 when Christians were not persecuted, though they were not formally tolerated. Armistice might be a better term. The period might well be extended backward to the death of Marcus Aurelius in 180 with a partial break in the reign of Septimus Severus (193–211) and again in 235 under Maximin.

This was a period of degradation in the Roman State. It started with the sordid reign of Commodus. This was followed by the first half of the ninety years of the barrack-room emperors, who were made and unmade in bewildering rapidity by troops anxious for the large cash payments which a new emperor would make them. During these years the only reigns of any length or quality were those of Septimus and Alexander Severus.

But decay in the government was the opportunity for the Church. During these two generations (seventy years) Christians grew in numbers and diversified in belief and practice—if that is a permissible way of describing what is more usually regarded as an outcrop of heresies. But, in truth, heresy and orthodoxy were not clear-cut divisions. The two extremes are easily identifiable, but there is a great deal of shading off in between which was intellectually and spiritually fertile.

21. ONE FAITH EVERYWHERE   c. 180

Shortly after Irenaeus became bishop of Lyons he wrote his most important book, *Against Heresies*. He wrote in Greek, but for most of the book we have only a translation into bad Latin. In this passage he points out that there are now Christians 'scattered over the whole world even to its extremities'—an obvious exaggeration, but the list of places and peoples with which the extract ends makes it clear that it was already empire-wide.

He summarizes the main points of Christian belief in words that were to be echoed almost precisely in the Nicene creed. But the title itself of his book makes it clear that he exaggerates when he claims that the Church everywhere believes this faith 'as if it had but one mind'. This claim could only be sustained if all Christians who thought differently on one point or another were to be regarded as non-Christians—and this Irenaeus, the pacific (that is the meaning of his name) would have been reluctant to do.

The tradition of the Church in France makes Irenaeus a martyr under Septimus Severus, but there is no evidence for this earlier than Gregory, bishop of Tours, in the late sixth century.

Source: Irenaeus, *Against Heresies* 1, 2.

The Church, although scattered over the whole world even to its extremities, received from the Apostles and their disciples the faith in one God, the Father Almighty, Maker of heaven and earth, the seas and all that in them is, and in one Christ Jesus, the Son of God, who became incarnate for our salvation, and in the Holy Ghost, who by the prophets proclaimed the dispensations, the advents, the virgin birth, the passion and resurrection from the dead, the bodily ascension of the well-beloved Christ Jesus our Lord into heaven, and his Parousia [advent] from the heavens in the glory of the Father to gather up all things in himself and to raise the flesh of all mankind to life, in order that *everything in heaven and in earth and under the earth shall bow the knee* (Phil. 2. 10 f.) to Christ Jesus our Lord and God, our Saviour and our King, according to the will of the invisible Father, and that every tongue should *confess* to him, and that he should pronounce a just judgment upon all, and dismiss the spirits of wickedness and the angels who transgressed and became apostate, and the ungodly, unrighteous, lawless and profane into everlasting fire, but in his graciousness should confer life and the reward of incorruption and eternal glory upon those who have kept his commandments and have abided in his love either from the beginning of their life or since their repentance.

This *Kerygma*[1] and this faith the Church, although scattered over the whole world, diligently observes, as if it occupied but one

---

[1] Kerygma ('preaching', derived from the Greek word for herald) denotes what the Church proclaims, in contrast to Didache, instruction.

house, and believes as if it had but one mind, and preaches and teaches as if it had but one mouth. And although there are many dialects in the world, the meaning of the tradition is one and the same.

For the same faith is held and handed down by the Churches established in the Germanies, the Spains, among the Celtic tribes, in the East, in Libya, and in the central portions of the world. But as the sun, the creation of God, is one and the same in all the world, so is the light of the *Kerygma* of the truth which shines on all who desire to come to the knowledge of the truth.

22. A GNOSTIC HYMN

Gnosticism was a weird and complicated amalgam of Christian and pagan thought, a mystery religion (see Chapter 3). A 'gnostic' was 'in the know', an 'enlightened' one. There were many forms of Gnosticism. Valentinus, Basilides and Marcion were the founders of its chief schools, which had become separate sects by the middle of the second century.

All agreed that the Supreme God, remote and unknowable, had given rise to four succeeding pairs of 'aeons' or emanations—the Eight from whom issued a further Twelve, and Ten, making a 'pleroma', a Whole of thirty. All but the Ten are referred to in the following Gnostic ritual hymn. Sophia, Wisdom, the lowest or furthest of the aeons, produced Demiurgos, the creator of the material universe—to the Gnostics matter was evil. A divine spark had been trapped in certain persons and the further emanations of Christ and the Holy Spirit had been sent to redeem this spiritual element from the gross enveloping clay. In this way the humanity of Christ disappears.

This is full-grown Gnosticism: from the Christian standpoint manifestly a heresy. But there were also many truly Christian thinkers, among them some of the greatest minds in the history of theology, whose philosophy followed some of the same lines as Gnosticism. Among them the greatest was Origen.

Irenaeus, Tertullian and Hippolytus were all active in writing against the Gnostics. They prevailed. But the Gnostics can still be studied in their writings as well as those of their opponents. They wrote their own Gospels and Acts which can be found in M. R. James' *The Apocryphal New Testament*. This hymn, for instance, comes from the 'Acts of John' and was attributed to Leucius, a companion of the apostle—but there is no good evidence for such a person, or for so early a date for the hymn.

Glory be to thee, Father. (And we, going about in a ring, answered him:) Amen.
Glory be to thee, Word: Glory be to thee, Grace. Amen.
Glory be to thee, Spirit: Glory be to thee, Holy One: Glory be to thy glory. Amen.
We praise thee, O Father; we give thanks to thee, O Light, wherein darkness dwelleth not. Amen.
  Now whereas we give thanks, I say:
I would be saved, and I would save. Amen.
I would be loosed, and I would loose. Amen.
I would be wounded, and I would wound. Amen.
I would be born, and I would bear. Amen.
I would eat, and I would be eaten. Amen.
I would hear, and I would be heard. Amen.
I would be thought, being wholly thought. Amen.
I would be washed, and I would wash. Amen.
Grace danceth. I would pipe; dance ye all. Amen.
I would mourn; lament ye all. Amen.
The number Eight singeth praises with us. Amen.
The number Twelve danceth on high. Amen.
The Whole on high hath part in our dancing. Amen.
Whoso danceth not, knoweth not what cometh to pass. Amen.
I would flee, and I would stay. Amen.
I would adorn, and I would be adorned. Amen.
I would be united, and I would unite. Amen.
A house I have not, and I have houses. Amen.
A place I have not, and I have places. Amen.
A temple I have not, and I have temples. Amen.
A lamp am I to thee that beholdest me. Amen.
A mirror am I to thee that perceivest me. Amen.
A door am I to thee that knockest at me. Amen.
A way am I to thee a wayfarer. Amen.
Now answer thou unto my dancing.

23. 'THE NEW PROPHECY' IN ASIA

About the middle of the second century a new prophetic movement began in the heart of Asia Minor where Montanus began to 'speak in tongues' and proclaim that the New Jerusalem was soon to descend on two small Phrygian towns. Associated with him were two women, Maximilla and Prisca, who also had the gift of prophecy, or speaking with tongues—ecstatic speech that needed interpreting. Just as the Gnostics had the tradition of a secret succession of initiates going back to New Testament times, so the followers of the New Prophecy, or Montanists, claimed to be the heirs in true descent of such people as Agabus (Acts 11. 28 and 21. 10) and the four daughters of Philip the Deacon (Acts 21. 8–9). Whatever may be thought of this claim, there clearly was a 'fresh outpouring of the Spirit' of this kind in the second century. This seems to have been provoked by three other features of Christianity in the second half of the second century: the growing worldliness of the churches as their numbers increased; their tightening organization; and, in the last quarter-century, the belief arising from persecution that these were the last days before the coming again of Christ.

The Montanists stood for a new standard of moral obligation, especially with regard to marriage, fasting and martyrdom. They were at first a fervent evangelical group within the church; but they soon came into conflict with the local bishops. These tried to convince the Montanists of the error of their ways, but on at least two occasions they failed to get a hearing. They spread among other churches stories— some of them admittedly only hearsay—of the outrageous lives of the new prophets and prophetesses. In the end, but only after considerable difficulty (see page 74) they persuaded churches in other parts of the empire, including in 202 the Roman church, to break off all relations with the Montanists. Meanwhile in Asia Minor the Montanists had established their own organization and paid prophetic ministry.

The three extracts represent the official view. Reading between the lines, it is possible to detect what the Montanists were doing. The first two extracts come from Eusebius who quotes, first from the book of an unknown presbyter or bishop dedicated to Abercius, bishop of Hieropolis in Phrygia (see Extract 31); and, secondly, from an other-wise unknown writer called Apollonius. Both writers had first-hand experience of Montanism in its middle period when it had been driven out of the church and was becoming a separate sect. The third extract is from Hippolytus (see Extract 27).

Sources: A: Eusebius, *Church History*, Book 5, 16; B: Do. Book 5, 18; C: Hippolytus, *Refutation of All Heresies* 8, 19.

A. BY AN UNKNOWN WRITER 193

A little while ago I visited Ancyra [the modern Ankara] in Galatia and found the local church deafened with the noise of this new craze—not prophecy, as they call it, but pseudo-prophecy, as I shall shortly prove. So far as I was able, the Lord helping me, I spoke out for days on end in the church about these matters, and replied to every argument they put forward. The church was delighted and confirmed in the truth while the enemy were repulsed for the time being and the opposition demoralized. . . .

In a certain village in that part of Mysia over against Phrygia, Montanus, they say, first exposed himself to the assaults of the adversary through his unbounded lust for leadership. He was one of the recent converts, and he became possessed of a spirit, and suddenly began to rave in a kind of ecstatic trance, and to babble in a jargon, prophesying in a manner contrary to the custom of the Church which had been handed down by tradition from the earliest times.

Some of them that heard his bastard utterances rebuked him as one possessed of a devil . . . remembering the Lord's warning to guard vigilantly against the coming of false prophets. But others were carried away and not a little elated, thinking themselves possessed of the Holy Spirit and of the gift of prophecy. And he also stirred up two women and filled them with the bastard spirit so that they uttered demented, absurd and irresponsible sayings . . . And these people blasphemed the whole Catholic Church under heaven, under the influence of their presumptuous spirit, because the Church granted to the spirit of false prophecy neither honour nor admission. For the faithful in Asia met often and in many places throughout Asia upon this matter . . . and rejected the heresy, and thus these people were expelled from the Church and debarred from communion. . . .

It is thought that both Montanus and Maximilla were driven

out of their minds by a spirit, and hanged themselves, at different times; and on the occasion of the death of each, it was said on all sides that this was how they died, putting an end to themselves just like the traitor Judas. In the same way it is commonly asserted that Theodotus, that wonderful fellow, the first trustee, shall we say, of their 'prophecy', was once raised aloft and taken up to heaven, where he experienced an unnatural ecstasy and entrusted himself to the spirit of deception, only to be sent spinning and perish miserably. That at any rate is how they say it happened. But we must not imagine that without seeing them we know the truth about such things, my friend; it may have been in this way, it may have been in some other way that death came to Montanus, Theodotus and their female associate. . . .

When all their arguments have been disposed of and they have nothing to say, they try to take refuge in the martyrs, alleging that they have a great number and that this is a convincing proof of the power of what in their circles is called the prophetic spirit. But this seems to be as false as false can be, for some of the other heretical sects have immense numbers of martyrs, but this is surely no reason why we should approve of them or acknowledge that they have the truth. . . . Whenever members of the Church called to martyrdom for the true Faith meet any of the so-called martyrs of the Phrygian sect, they part company with them and have nothing to do with them till their own fulfilment, because they will not be associated with the spirit that spoke through Montanus and the women. That this is true, and that it occurred in our own time in Apamea on the Maeander, in the case of Gaius and Alexander and the other martyrs from Eumenea (in Phrygia), is perfectly clear.

B.   BY APOLLONIUS   196

What sort of person this upstart teacher is, his own actions and teaching show. This is the man who taught the dissolution of marriages, who laid down the law on fasting, who renamed Pepuza and Tymion, insignificant towns in Phrygia, as Jerusalem, in the hope of persuading people in every district to gather there, who appointed agents to collect money, who contrived to make

H

the gifts roll in under the name of 'offerings', and who has sub-
sidized those who preached his message, in order that gluttony
may provide an incentive for teaching it.

It is thus evident that these prophetesses, from the time they
were filled with the spirit, were the very first to leave their husbands. How then could they lie so blatantly as to call Priscilla a
virgin?

If they deny that their prophets have accepted gifts, they will
surely admit this, that if they are proved to have accepted them
they are no prophets: I can provide endless proof of this. All the
fruits of a prophet must be submitted to examination. Tell me,
does a prophet dye his hair? Does a prophet paint his eyelids? Does
a prophet do business as a moneylender? Let them say plainly
whether these things are permissible or not, and I will prove that
they have been going on in their circles.

c.   BY HIPPOLYTUS   c. 210–20

They have been deceived by two females, Priscilla and Maximilla
by name, whom they hold to be prophetesses, asserting that into
them the Paraclete spirit entered . . . They magnify these females
above the Apostles and every gift of grace, so that some of them
go so far as to say that there is in them something more than
Christ. These people agree with the Church in acknowledging the
Father of the universe to be God and Creator of all things, and
they also acknowledge all that the Gospel testifies of Christ. But
they introduce novelties in the form of fasts and feasts, abstinences
and diets of radishes, giving these females as their authority. . . .

24. TERTULLIAN:

The Scholar who Distrusted Intellectuals   c. 155–c. 222

Tertullian's father was a centurion in the Roman army; he himself
was a lawyer. Both professions left their mark indelibly on the way he
saw and presented the Christian faith, and marshalled his arguments in
controversy. He was by temperament an advocate, not a judge. He
delighted in paradox. His writings contain more sayings gripping and
memorable today than any of the other early Christians. He was,
moreover, the first great Christian writer in Latin. In the words of
Harnack, 'Tertullian in fact created Christian Latin literature. . . .

Cyprian polished the language ... Augustine, again, stood on the shoulders of Tertullian and Cyprian; and these three North Africans are the fathers of the Western churches.'

Tertullian worked as a lawyer in Rome. It was probably there when he was about forty that he was converted to Christianity. By 197 he was back in Carthage where he had been born and brought up. There he embarked at once on a major series of books intended both for external and internal use. In his *Apology*, or Defence of Christianity, he wrote for non-Christians explaining what Christians believed and what they did—things about which the outside world was either grossly ignorant or deliberately misinformed. In his book *On the Objections of the Heretics* Tertullian was concerned with issues that would hardly have interested the great non-Christian world. Both were written before the outbreak of persecution in Carthage under Septimus Severus. So, too, was *On the Evidence of the Soul*.

The extracts come from these books. Tertullian had had a first-rate literary education. He knew the historians from Herodotus to Tacitus; he had a thorough knowledge of Plato and of the Stoic philosophers; he was well read in the medical writers of his time. But, having once made up his mind to become a Christian, he rejected secular knowledge as vain—even though he continued to use it. His best remembered paradox to express his faith in Christ alone comes from a later book— 'The Son of God was born, I am not ashamed of it because it is shameful; the Son of God died, it is credible for the very reason that it is silly; and, having been buried, he rose again, it is certain because it is impossible.' But already at the beginning of his career as a Christian he had reached virtually the same position as these extracts show. Mark the contrast to Clement of Alexandria.

Sources: A: Tertullian, *On the Objections of the Heretics* 7; B: Tertullian, *Apology* 46; C: Tertullian, *On the Evidence of the Soul* 1 and 5.

A.   ATHENS AND JERUSALEM

What has Athens to do with Jerusalem, the Academy with the Church? ... We have no need for curiosity since Jesus Christ, nor for inquiry since the Gospel ... Tell me what is the sense of this itch for idle speculation? What does it prove, this useless affectation of a fastidious curiosity, notwithstanding the strong confidence of its assertions? It was highly appropriate that Thales,[1]

[1] Greek philosopher, 6th century B.C.

while his eyes were roaming the heavens in astronomical observation, should have tumbled into a well. This mishap may well serve to illustrate the fate of all who occupy themselves with the stupidities of philosophy.

This is the substance of secular wisdom that it rashly undertakes to explain the nature and dispensation of God. . . . Heretics and philosophers deal with similar material, and their arguments are largely the same. It is the Platonic ideas which have supplied the Gnostics with their aeons, the Marcionite deity (the ideal of tranquillity) comes from the Stoics, the identification of God with matter is a doctrine of Zeno, with fire, of Heraclitus,[1] . . . the Epicureans supply the notion of the annihilation of the soul; and all alike are agreed in denying any possibility of regeneration for the flesh. . . . And unhappy Aristotle supplies them with a logic evasive in its propositions, far-fetched in its conclusions, disputatious in its arguments, burdensome even to itself, settling everything in order to settle nothing.

To know nothing against the rule of faith is to know everything.

B.   HELLAS AND HEAVEN

What is there in common between the philosopher and the Christian, the pupil of Hellas and the pupil of Heaven, the worker for reputation and for salvation, the manufacturer of words and of deeds, the builder and the destroyer, the interpolator of error and the artificer of truth, the thief of truth and its custodian?

C.   THE MAN IN THE STREET

It is not to thee that I address myself, the soul which, formed in the schools, trained in the libraries, belches forth a fund of academic wisdom, but thee, the simple and uncultivated soul, such as they have who have nothing else, whose whole experience has been gained on street-corners and cross-roads and in the industrial plant. I need thine inexperience since in thy little store of experience nobody believes. . . . The soul comes before letters, words before books, and man himself before the philosopher and the poet.

---

[1] A Greek philosopher of the same period as Thales; Zeno lived *c.* 300 B.C.

25. DISADVANTAGES OF BEING A CHRISTIAN   *c.* 190

In the time of Tertullian, and possibly influenced by his *Apology*, Minucius Felix produced an early piece of Christian apologetics in Latin. This took the form of a conversation between Octavius, a Christian after whom the book is called, and Caecilius, a pagan, with the author making a third in the talk. In this extract Caecilius is speaking and putting forward as objections to Christianity things which Christians actually did which appeared nonsense to ordinary people. Some of the things which Caecilius says here are repeated from the opposite angle by Tertullian on page 98.

Source: The *Octavius* of Minucius Felix.

Look: some of you—the greater, the better part, as you assert—suffer from want, cold, toil and hunger; and your God permits it, or pretends not to see it; he either will not or cannot help his people; hence he is either powerless or unjust. You, who dream of immortality after death, when unnerved by severe illness, consumed by fever, racked by pain, can you not yet understand your condition? Do you not yet recognize your frailty? Against your will, miserable wretch, you are convicted of weakness, but will not admit it.

But to pass over things common to all, consider again what awaits you—threats, punishment, torture, crosses no longer objects of worship but instruments of suffering, fires which you both anticipate and dread. Where is that God of yours, who is able to help those who come to life again, but not the living? Do not the Romans, without the help of your God, rule, govern, and possess the whole world, and hold sway over yourselves? But you, in the meantime, in your suspense and anxiety, abstain from legitimate amusements; you never visit the shows, never join the processions, never attend the public banquets. You express abhorrence of the sacred games, of meat already offered in sacrifice, of libations poured upon the altars. Thus you show your fear of the very gods whom you deny! You never crown your heads with garlands, nor grace your bodies with perfumes; you reserve unguents for funerals, you even refuse to lay wreaths on the graves, pale and trembling wretches, who deserve to be pitied—but by our gods.

Therefore, if you have any sense, any feeling of shame, give up prying into the quarters of the sky, the destinies and secrets of the universe. For ignorant, uneducated, rude, uncultivated people, to whom it has not been given to understand human affairs and who are still less qualified to discuss things divine—for such it is sufficient to look at what is before their eyes.

26. TERTULLIAN ON ENTERTAINMENTS

There was a strong strain of what we should now call Puritanism in Tertullian from the beginning of his Christian life. The book from which this extract is taken is another of his early works written before the persecution at Carthage under Septimus Severus. He writes clearly of things which he must have experienced before his conversion in middle life. Obviously there were some forms of entertainment which no Christian ought to attend, but Tertullian makes no distinction. The greatest tragedy is lumped together with the gladiatorial contest in one condemnation. Just to sit at a public spectacle would contaminate a Christian.

Source: Tertullian, *Of Spectacles* 25.

Seated where there is nothing of God, will he be thinking of his Maker? Will there be peace in his soul when there is eager strife for the charioteer? Wrought up into frenzied excitement, will he learn to be modest? Nay, in the whole thing he will meet with no greater temptation than that provided by the gay clothing of the men and women. The very intermingling of emotions, the very agreements and disagreements with each other in the bestowing of their favours, where you have such close communion, blow up the sparks of passion. And then there is scarce any other object in going to the show, but to see and to be seen. When a tragic actor is declaiming will one be giving thought to prophetic appeals? Amid the measures of the effeminate player, will he call up to himself a psalm? And when the athletes are hard at struggle, will he be ready to proclaim that there must be no striking again? And with his eye fixed on the bites of bears, and the sponge-nets of the net-fighters, can he be moved by compassion? May God avert from his people any such passionate eagerness for a cruel enjoyment!

27. THE SLAVE WHO BECAME BISHOP OF ROME   *c.* 190–195

Callistus (or Calixtus) was his name and this account of his early career was written by his chief enemy among his fellow Christians. What happened to Callistus is one thing; why it happened is another—and one on which one would not want to depend on the reasons given by Hippolytus.

The 'Cemetery of Callistus' on the Appian Way contains a fine collection of the tombs of the bishops of Rome of his time. Callistus succeeded his friend Zephyrinus as bishop in 217. Hippolytus refused to accept him and may have set himself up as a kind of anti-Pope—his own career is exceedingly obscure though his writings were widely known throughout the Christian world. He continued to attack Urban and Pontianus, the successors of Callistus. In the persecution of 235 he and Pontianus were both exiled to Sardinia, a notoriously pestilential place, and there they both died. Their bodies were brought back to Rome.

Both Callistus and Hippolytus were recognized by the Roman church as saints.

Apart from the personal vendetta, the chief complaint made by Hippolytus against Callistus was that he was lax in allowing Christians who had committed grave sins to be restored to full membership of the Church. This was now an important issue: there were by this time many born Christians as well as converted ones, and many of the converts were themselves, so to speak, only half-converted.

This extract comes from the book called *The Refutation of All Heresies* 9, 12. His other major work, *The Apostolic Tradition*, has been drawn on in chapter 4. There is a contemporary statue of Hippolytus in the Vatican Library in Rome (Plate 7) on which are recorded the names of his books. It is known to be contemporary because the table for finding the date of Easter, which he had worked out, is shown on it. This table was found to be inaccurate within a dozen years of his death.

In later times, when scholarship was at a low ebb, he was muddled up with the ancient Greek Hippolytus, the son of Theseus, who was said to have been killed through being thrown from his chariot and dragged along the shore by his horses, who were frightened by a bull sent out of the sea by Poseidon for that purpose.

Callistus was a slave to Carpophorus, a Christian in the household of Caesar, and because he was of the same faith, his master committed to him a large sum of money and asked him to make it yield profit through banking. Callistus tried opening a bank in the Fish Market. In course of time many widows and brethren trusted him with their money, but he got into difficulties. Someone informed Carpophorus, who demanded an account, but Callistus, expecting trouble, stole away from his master and made for the coast.

He found a ship in Portus ready to sail and got on board, determined to go wherever the ship was bound. But he could not escape detection even in this way, for someone informed Carpophorus, who hurried to the harbour and tried to board the ship, which was anchored in mid-water. The ferryman, however, was slow in his movements and Callistus had time to recognize his master. Knowing he would be captured and that his affairs were desperate, he recklessly threw himself overboard. But the sailors leapt into boats and drew him out against his will, to the shouts of those on the shore. So he was handed over to his master, who brought him to Rome and lodged him in the Pistrinum.[1]

After a time brethren entreated Carpophorus to release Callistus, as he admitted that he had money deposited with certain persons . . . And Carpophorus yielded and ordered him to be set free, but Callistus had no such money and could not try to abscond again because he was watched. So he planned a way to get himself killed. Pretending to be meeting his creditors, he hurried on their Sabbath-day to the synagogue of the Jews and made a disturbance. The Jews abused him, beat him, and dragged him before Fuscianus, the prefect of the city . . . And someone informed Carpophorus of these events, and he hurried to the judgment-seat and said:

'I implore you, my lord Fuscianus, to believe that he has done this not because he is a Christian, but because he seeks a way to die, having embezzled a lot of my money, as I shall prove.'

The Jews, however, thought this was a ruse to free Callistus and they made such a clamour that the prefect gave way to them, had Callistus flogged and sent to a mine in Sardinia.

There were other Christian martyrs there and after some time

[1] Treadmill used by slave-owners for punishing their slaves.

Marcia, the mistress of the emperor Commodus and a God-loving woman, anxious to do some good, summoned the blessed bishop Victor and asked him what martyrs were in Sardinia. He gave her the names of all, but not that of Callistus, knowing his evil deeds. Marcia obtained the permission of Commodus and entrusted the letter of emancipation to Hyacinthus, an aged presbyter, though a eunuch. He sailed to Sardinia and delivered it to the governor of the country, and all the martyrs were released, but not Callistus. He fell on his knees, weeping, and begged also to be freed. Hyacinthus was moved by his pleading and asked the governor to release him, alleging that Marcia had given permission, and promising that he would make sure the governor suffered no censure. So, thus persuaded, the governor released Callistus also.

On their return, Victor was very grieved at what had happened, but because he was a compassionate man, he did nothing about it except ... that he sent him to live in Antium, and gave him a certain monthly allowance for food. And after Victor's death Zephyrinus ... put him in charge of the cemetery.

28. HONOURING ABRAHAM, CHRIST AND ORPHEUS

Extracts 10 from Justin and Clement and 32 from Origen show the influence of the Greek pre-Christian philosophers on men who became Christians without rejecting what was good in their earlier experiences. In an age of syncretism[1] clearly many other men, who did not become Christians, were profoundly influenced by that religion. Among them was the young emperor Alexander Severus, who ruled from 222 to 235. The following extract is from Lampridius who wrote, in the next century, an idealized account of the good pagan emperor. He quotes a contemporary writer for his description of the emperor's private chapel. The emperor's mother exercised much influence over him. She was certainly keenly interested in the Christian religion and summoned Origen to Rome to tell her about it.

The reign of Alexander Severus was a period of peace and growth for the Church. Excavations at Dura-Europos in Syria have discovered a house, built early in the second century, which had in it a room used and decorated for Christian worship. Towards the end of the reign of Severus the whole house was altered for use as a church, witnessing to

---

[1] The attempt to combine beliefs and practices from different religions.

the growth in the number of Christians and the end, for the time being, of the need for secrecy. See Plate 6.

Source: Aelius Lampridius: *Alexander Severus* 30, 31.

Before I write about the wars, expeditions and victories of Alexander Severus, I will say a little about his daily life at home. His usual custom was this. First, if it was correct to do so—if he had not slept with his wife—he used to worship in the early morning in his private shrine. In this he kept images of the previous rulers (a selection of the best among them) and of such major saints and sages as Apollonius and, going by a writer of his own time, of Christ, Abraham and Orpheus, and others of this kind; and also of his ancestors. . . . After public affairs, whether military or civil, he gave more attention to reading Greek, especially Plato's book *On the Republic*. When he was reading Latin he read nothing but the *Duties* and the *Republic* of Cicero—not his speeches—and the poets, among them Serenus Summonicus, whom he himself had known and loved, and Horace. He also read the life of Alexander, whom he particularly imitated, even if he disapproved of his heavy drinking and cruelty towards his friends. Vergil and Plato he reckoned among the poets and kept their busts with that of Cicero in a minor shrine along with Achilles and other heroes. But Alexander the Great he commemorated in his major shrine with the gods.

29. ASPECTS OF CHRISTIAN LIFE:
Exorcism; Almsgiving; Traditional Ceremonies

These short extracts, mainly from the second century, bring together references to a variety of Christian practices at that time. Some are still familiar; others now strange.

Until recently many forms of madness have been almost universally attributed to 'possession' by spirits; in some parts of the world they still are. There is, of course, nothing exclusively Christian in this belief. 'Casting out devils' has been practised by men of many religions in different ways. We know that it was done by Christians in New Testament times—see Matt. 12. 22–7; Mark 9. 14–29; Acts 19. 11–16. This is how it was done round about the second century.

A.   EXORCISM

I. From Justin (*Second Apology*, A.D. 161).

And now you may learn from what goes on under your own eyes. For many devil-possessed all over the world and in your own city, many of our men, the Christians, have exorcized in the name of Jesus Christ, who was crucified under Pontius Pilate. When all other exorcists and sayers of charms and sellers of drugs failed, they have healed them, and still do heal, sapping the power of the demons who hold men, and driving them out.

II. From Irenaeus (*Against Heresies*, c. 185).

Some do, really and truly, cast out demons, so that those very ones who have been cleansed from evil spirits often believe, and are in the Church . . . Nor does the Church do anything by angelic invocations, nor incantations, nor other perverse meddling. It directs prayers in a manner clean, pure, and open, to the Lord who made all things, and calls upon the name of our Lord Jesus Christ.

III. From Tertullian (*Apology*, 197).

Now for a test case. Let someone be brought here before your judgment-seats who is clearly demon-possessed. Bidden to speak by any Christian you like, this spirit, so surely as he pretends to deity elsewhere, will truly own himself a demon . . . Mock as you will at our Christ and his 'fables'—his resurrection, his ascension, his coming again to judge the world; mock as you will—but get the demons to mock with you! . . . Get them to deny that they are bound for that same judgment day with all their worshippers and works! Why, all the authority and power we have over them is from naming the name of Christ, and reminding them of what threatens them from God at the hands of Christ. So, at our touch and insufflation[1] . . . they come out of bodies as we command, unwilling and distressed, and shamed before your eyes.

IV. From Origen (*Contra Celsum* III, 24, c. 250).

Some there are who show signs of having received through this Faith something the more incredible: I mean the cures which they perform. Over those who need their healing they call only upon

---

[1] Breathing, as a sign of giving the Holy Spirit; see John 20, 22.

the God who is over all and the name of Jesus, along with the account concerning him. For by these means we ourselves have seen many set free from grievous symptoms and distractions and madness, and ten thousand things beside, which neither men nor demons had cured.

V. From Cyprian (To Demetrianus 15, c. 255).

Oh, would you but hear and see them ['your gods', whom Cyprian equates with demons] when charged by us, cut with spiritual scourges, cast out from possessed bodies by torture of our words. As they feel the lashings and floggings they howl and groan at the voice of man and the power of God, and they confess that judgment is to come. Come and see that what we say is true. And since yourselves say that such are the gods you worship, believe what they say! . . . You will see that we are besought by those whom you beseech, we are feared by those whom you fear, whom you adore. You will see that under our hand they stand bound and tremble as captives, whom you admire and venerate as lords.

B.   ALMSGIVING

Source: Tertullian, *Apology* 39.   197

Even if there be with us a sort of treasury, no sum is therein collected which is descreditable to Religion, as though she could be bought. Every man places there a small gift on one day in each month, or when ever he will, so he do but will, and so he be but able; for no man is constrained, but contributes willingly. These are as it were the deposits of piety; for afterwards they are not disbursed in feasting and in drinking, and in disgusting haunts of gluttony, but for feeding and burying the poor, for boys and girls without money and without parents, and for old men now house-ridden, for the shipwrecked also, and for any who in the mines, or in the islands, or in the prisons, become their Creed's pensioners, so that it be only for the sake of the way of God. But it is the exercise of this sort of love which does, with some, chiefly brand us with a mark of evil. 'See,' they say, 'how they love each other'; for they themselves hate each other: and 'see how ready they are to die for each other'; for they themselves are more ready to slay each other.

C.   TRADITIONAL CEREMONIES

Source: Tertullian, *Of the Soldiers' Crown* 3 and 4.   211

For Baptism, when we are about to come to the water, in the same place, but at a somewhat earlier time, we do in the Church testify, under the hand of a chief minister, that we renounce the devil and his pomp and his angels. Then we are thrice dipped, pledging ourselves to something more than the Lord hath prescribed in the Gospel; then, some undertaking the charge of us, we first taste a mixture of milk and honey, and from that day we abstain for a whole week from our daily washing.

The Sacrament of the Eucharist commanded by the Lord at the time of supper and to all, we receive even at our meetings before daybreak, and from the hands of no others than the heads of the Church.

We offer on one day every year oblations for the dead as birthday honours. On the Lord's Day we account it unlawful to fast, or to worship upon the knees. We enjoy the same freedom from Easter Day even to Pentecost. We feel pained if any of the wine, or even of our bread, be spilled on the ground. In all our travels and movements, in all our coming in and going out, in putting on our shoes, at the bath, at the table, in lighting our candles, in lying down, in sitting down, whatever employment occupies us, we mark our forehead with the sign of the cross.

For these, and such-like rules, if thou requirest a law in the Scriptures, thou shalt find none. Tradition will be pleaded to thee as originating them, custom as confirming them, and faith as observing them.

30. PERPETUA AND FELICITY   March 7th, 203

'There were arrested the young catechumens Revocatus and his fellow slave Felicity, Saturninus and Secundulus; and among these also Vivia Perpetua, honourably born, liberally educated, a freeborn matron, married according to the most honourable rites; having a father and a mother and two brothers, one of these a catechumen like herself; and also an infant son at the breast. Her age was about twenty-two.'

This is the beginning of the narrative of the martyrdom of Perpetua, Felicity and her companions which took place at Carthage on March 7, 203. Note that the martyrs at the time of their arrest were not baptized Christians, only catechumens or learners. These martyrs of Carthage suffered under a new regulation enforced by the emperor Septimus Severus. His object was not to wipe out Christianity but to prevent its spread by forbidding conversions. Five years earlier Tertullian had closed his *Apology* with the words: 'The oftener we are cut down by you, the more in number we grow; the blood of Christians is seed.' Perpetua and her companions were fruitful seed.

It is probable that the narrative of their sufferings was edited by Tertullian. He was at the time, though not the bishop, undoubtedly the leading figure in the church at Carthage. Moreover he seems to have stood in a close relation to the group of which Perpetua was a member. In prison Perpetua and her brother, Saturus, both had visions. Saturus had a vision of heaven in which his sister and he stood before the throne of God and then, as they left, they saw Optatus, the bishop of Carthage, standing outside, on the left, looking sad. The bishop urged Perpetua and Saturus to stay with him. They began an argument in Greek until angels told the bishop to leave Perpetua and Saturus alone, to stop bickering, and to control his followers. The division in the church at Carthage to which this refers was an offshoot of the same New Prophecy or Montanism which had its origin in Asia Minor and was the subject of Extract 23. Perpetua and Saturus were members of what we might call a Montanist cell in the Christian community at Carthage.

It is from this time on that Tertullian began his defence of Montanism with which his naturally strict Puritan views made him temperamentally sympathetic. When he finally failed to secure for Montanism a place in the Church, he threw in his lot with the ejected and became the leader of a Montanist denomination in North Africa which survived in gradually diminishing strength for two hundred years after his death. This African Montanism differed from the Phrygian in being more orthodox in its beliefs, less given to ecstatic prophecy, and more rigorist in its moral teaching.

Because of his love for me [Perpetua], my father wishes to turn me from my purpose and tried to break down my faith.

'Father', I said, 'do you see this vessel lying here, a waterpot, or whatever it is?'

'I see it,' he said.

'Can it be called by any other name than what it is?'

'No.'

'So neither can I call myself anything else than what I am, a Christian.'

Angered by this word, my father flew at me as if to tear out my eyes, but he only shook me and was defeated, along with the devil's arguments. For a few days, then, I was separated from my father ... and in that interval we were baptized. When I was in the water the Spirit prompted me to ask only for patience to suffer in the flesh.

After a few days we were cast into prison and I was terrified, for I had never known such darkness. What a day of horror! The stifling heat of the crowds there, the rough handling of the soldiers! Worst of all, I was tortured with anxiety for my baby. But then Tertius and Pomponius, the good deacons who ministered to us, managed, at a price, to have us sent to better quarters of the prison for a few hours every day, and there I could suckle my baby, already weak for want of food ... and at last I got leave to have my baby with me in the prison. Immediately, I regained my strength and stopped fretting about the child, and the prison became a palace to me, and I would rather be here than anywhere else.

[While waiting in prison for her trial, Perpetua had a number of visions, which she describes. In one of them she sees herself and her brother Saturus, who shared her sufferings, mounting a brazen ladder into heaven. 'And I saw a vast stretch of garden and a man with white hair sitting in the middle of it, dressed as a shepherd, a tall man milking sheep; and round about were many thousands clothed in white.' Such a picture of Christ as the Good Shepherd occurs constantly in the catacombs at Rome. (See Plates 7, 12, 13.)

The story of Perpetua's 'Passion' is continued by some eye-witness, perhaps Tertullian. We select here those passages which deal chiefly with the patrician lady Perpetua and her companion, the slave Felicity. Only Saturus was actually killed by the animals; the rest

had their throats cut at the end of the games and Perpetua had to
guide the hand of the nervous gladiator.]

Felicity the slave was in great grief as the day of the spectacles
drew near, for she was eight months pregnant and she was afraid
that the day of her own conflict would be postponed, because it
was against the law for pregnant women to appear in the arena;
then she would have to die among common criminals.

And her fellow martyrs also grieved with her, not wishing to
leave so dear a comrade behind, her hope unattained. So with one
united cry of entreaty they prayed fervently to the Lord, and
immediately her travail came upon her. She was suffering agonies
from her premature labour, and one of the keepers of the iron
gates of the prison said to her,

'If you are suffering like this now, what will you do when you
are thrown to the wild beasts, which you have scorned, refusing to
sacrifice?'

'Now it is only I who suffer what I suffer,' Felicity answered.
'Then, another will be in me who will suffer for me, because I also
shall be suffering for him.'

So she began to be in labour and gave birth to her child, whom
a certain sister reared as her own daughter ...

The day of their victory dawned and they left the prison to go
to the arena as if to heaven, joyfully, with radiant faces, trembling
perhaps, but with happiness not fear. Perpetua moved serenely, as
a beloved bride of Christ, daunting the staring crowds with the
flash of her eyes. Felicity also, happy that her baby had been born,
went from her travail to the gladiatorial combat as if to be purified
by a second baptism ...

Eager to make them suffer by a creature of their own sex, the
devil had provided a wild cow for the women. So they were
stripped and brought out wrapped only in a net. Then the people
were horrified, seeing one in the tenderness of youth and the
other so recently a mother, and they were recalled and lightly
clothed.

Perpetua was first brought in and tossed by the cow. She fell on
her back, but sat up and straightened the tunic that had been torn

from her side, and tied up her disordered hair, for it was not becoming in a martyr to suffer with dishevelled hair, as though she were mourning on her day of glory. Then she arose and, seeing Felicity tossed, she went to her, gave her a hand and raised her up. Both stood firm and the cruelty of the crowd was checked, and they were recalled to the Sanivivaria Gate. There Perpetua was received by a certain catechumen, Rusticus, who was devoted to her and as if waking from a sleep—so completely was she in the Spirit and in ecstasy—she began to look around. Then, to the utter astonishment of them all, she said,

'I wonder when we are going to be brought out to that cow.'

31. A BISHOP ORDERS HIS TOMB   *c.* 190

Abercius was not only bishop of Hieropolis in Phrygia, Montanist country as Extract 23 told us, but also a much travelled man. He had been westward to Rome and eastward as far as Nisibis, a frontier town in Mesopotamia which was sometimes Roman, sometimes not.

The bishop was proud of his travels and ordered them to be recorded on his tombstone which he had carved during his lifetime. This stone was discovered by Sir William Ramsay in 1883 and is now in the Lateran Museum in Rome. Its symbolism is obscure to us, and would probably have been equally so to most men in the second century. But Christians would understand it perfectly. Christ is the shepherd and the fish. For his eyes, see Revelation 5. 6, and for the seal, Rev. 7. 2, 3. The Church, the bride of the Lamb (Rev. 21. 9), is the golden-robed Queen—here especially the Church at Rome. Everywhere, he records, he found the spiritual food of the Eucharist.

The citizen of a notable city I made this tomb in my lifetime, that in due season I might have here a resting place for my body. Abercius by name, I am a disciple of the pure Shepherd, who feedeth his flocks of sheep on mountains and plains, who hath great eyes looking on all sides; for he taught me faithful writings. He also sent me to royal Rome to behold it and to see the golden-robed, golden-slippered Queen. And there I saw a people bearing the splendid seal. And I saw the plain of Syria and all the cities, even Nisibis, crossing over the Euphrates. And everywhere I had

I

associates. In company with Paul, I followed, while everywhere faith led the way, and set before me for food the fish from the fountain, mighty and stainless (whom a pure virgin grasped), and gave this to friends to eat always, having good wine and giving the mixed cup with bread.

These words I, Abercius, standing by, ordered to be inscribed. In sooth I was in the course of my 72nd year. Let every friend who observeth this pray for me. But no man shall place another tomb above mine. If otherwise, then he shall pay 2,000 pieces of gold to the treasury of the Romans, and a 1,000 pieces of gold to my good fatherland Hieropolis.

32. ORIGEN, THE BELOVED SCHOLAR   *c.* 185–*c.* 254

Origen was a second generation Christian. His father was killed in the persecution of 202 and he only escaped because his mother hid his clothes to keep him at home. He lived on to witness the great Decian persecution during which he was imprisoned and tortured. He was a pupil of Clement, succeeded him as head of the Christian Academy at Alexandria and then moved to Caesarea where he undertook a similar job in 231. He visited Rome at the request of the mother of Alexander Severus and heard Hippolytus preach there (Extracts 15, 23c, 27). He was both a philosopher of religion and a great biblical scholar. Jerome used his Hexapla, his edition of the Old Testament giving six different versions in six parallel columns.

The first extract is from a farewell speech made on behalf of the graduating class of 238, as we should say, by Gregory 'Thaumaturgus' (the miracle worker) who had been converted by Origen. Gregory went back to his native Pontus on the Black Sea and became such a notable missionary bishop there that innumerable legends grew up about him—hence his posthumous nickname. Extract B is Origen's reply.

The third extract comes from the pagan writer Porphyry, a disciple of Plotinus the Neoplatonist, a strong opponent of Christianity—and an instructed one. He was, for instance, right about the date of Daniel and the orthodox of those days wrong. His picture of Origen is a fair counterpart to Gregory Thaumaturgus. They are describing recognizably the same man.

Origen was the greatest member of the Alexandrian school. Unfortunately we have fewer of his works than we deserve because well after his death influential churchmen by hindsight thought him heretical, so that many of his books have disappeared.

Sources: A: and B: Gregory Thaumaturgus, *To Origen*; C: Euesbius, *Church History* 6, 19; quoting Porphyry, *Against the Christians* 3.

A.   GREGORY THAUMATURGUS ON ORIGEN   238

... He took us over, and from the first day, veritably the first day, began by using every device to bind us firmly, us who were like some wild beasts, or fishes, or birds, fallen into snares or nets, trying to struggle out and escape away, and wishful to depart from him to Berytus [Beirut, where Gregory was to study law] or our fatherland. He used every turn of language, pulled every string as they say, employed every resource of his abilities, praised philosophy and those enamoured of philosophy in long, numerous and apt eulogies, insisting that they only lived the life befitting the reasonable beings who studied to live rightly, who 'knew themselves', firstly their own nature, and secondly the things essentially good which a human being ought to follow after, and the really evil things which he ought to avoid. . . .

Something else was striking the goad of friendship unto us, no easily resisted thing; that was the keenness and great urgency of his ability and good disposition, which shone so benevolently upon us as he discoursed or talked, trying not to get an easy victory over us in argument . . . I was led to neglect all that seemed to concern me: affairs, studies, even my favourite law, home and kindred there, no less than those among whom I was sojourning. One thing only was dear and affected by me: philosophy and its teacher, this divine man—and the soul of Jonathan was knit with David (1 Sam. 18. 1).

Gregory describes Origen's training in Dialectic:

He taught us to consider not only obvious and evident arguments, but sometimes erroneous and sophisticated ones, to probe each and sound it to see whether it gave any echo of unsoundness. In this manner he gave us a reasonable training for the critical part of our soul . . .

Science:

He also raised up the humility of our souls, amazed by the great and marvellous and manifold and all-wise workmanship of the universe . . . by Physics . . . He established a reasonable, in place of an unreasoning wonder in our souls. This divine and lofty science is taught by the study of Nature, most delectable to all. What need to mention the sacred studies, Geometry dear to all and irrefragable, and Astronomy whose path is on high? . . . He made heaven accessible to us by 'the ladder reaching up to heaven' of either study.   .

Philosophy, Ethics:

He was the first and only one to direct me to Greek philosophy, persuading me by his own manner of life to listen and adhere to the study of ethics.

Theology:

He thought it right that we should philosophize, and collate with all our powers every one of the writings of the ancients, whether philosophers or poets, excepting and rejecting nothing save only those of the atheists . . . lest some one argument in these teachers should be heard and approved by itself as the only true one, though it might as a matter of fact be unsound . . .

Scripture:

He himself would interpret and make clear whatever was dark and enigmatical, such as are many utterances of the sacred voices, whether because it is God's wont to speak thus to man, that the divine word may not enter in bare and unveiled to some soul unworthy, as most are; or else, although every oracle of God is naturally most clear and simple, yet by reason of time and antiquity it has come to seem indistinct and dark to us . . . But he made them clear and brought them into the light. This gift was his alone of all men whom I have known personally.

Do thou, dear Head, rise and bless us as thou sendest us forth. Thou hast been our salvation while we frequented thy holy instruction. Save us with thy prayers also when we are gone.

B.   ORIGEN TO GREGORY: 238

Greeting in God, sir, my most excellent and reverend son Gregory, from Origen.

... Thine ability is fit to make thee an accomplished Roman lawyer, or a Greek philosopher in some one of the schools esteemed reputable. But my desire has been that thou shouldest employ all the force of thine ability on Christianity as thine end, and to effect this I would beseech thee to draw from Greek philosophy such things as are capable of being made encyclic or preparatory studies to Christianity, and from geometry and astronomy such things as will be useful for the exposition of Holy Scripture, in order that what the sons of the philosophers said about geometry and music and grammar and rhetoric and astronomy, that they are the handmaidens of philosophy, we may say of philosophy in relation to Christianity.

Possibly something of this sort is hinted in Exodus (11. 2–35) which was written from the mouth of God, saying that the sons of Israel were to ask from their neighbours and fellow-residents vessels of silver and of gold, and raiment, that having spoiled the Egyptians, they might have material for the construction of the things . . . in the Holy of Holies, the ark with its crown, and the cherubim, and the mercy seat, and the golden pot in which was stored the manna, the bread of angels.

But do thou, sir my son, first and foremost attend to the reading of the Holy Scriptures, yes attend. For we need great attention in reading the Scriptures, that we may not speak or think too rashly about them . . .

Be not content with knocking and seeking; for most essential is the prayer to understand divine things.

| c. | ORIGEN BY AN OPPONENT | *c.* 275 |

'Enigmas' is the pompous name they give to the perfectly plain statements of Moses, glorifying them as oracles full of hidden mysteries, and bewitching the critical faculty by their extravagant nonsense. . . . This absurd nonsense must be attributed to a man whom I met while I was still quite young, who enjoyed a great reputation and thanks to the works he has left behind him enjoys it still. I refer to Origen, whose fame among teachers of these theories is widespread. He was a pupil of Ammonius, the most distinguished philosopher of our time. Theoretical knowledge in plenty he acquired with the help of his master, but in choosing the right way to live he went in the opposite direction. For Ammonius was a Christian, brought up in Christian ways by his parents, but when he began to think philosophically he promptly chagned to a law-abiding way of life. Origen on the other hand, a Greek schooled in Greek thought, plunged headlong into un-Greek recklessness; immersed in this, he peddled himself and his skill in argument. In his life he behaved like a Christian, defying the law: in his metaphysical and theological ideas he played the Greek, giving a Greek twist to foreign tales. He associated himself at all times with Plato, and was at home among the writings of Numenius and Cronius, Apollophanes, Longinus, and Moderatus, Nicomachus, and the more eminent followers of Pythagoras. He made use, too, of the books of Chaeremon the Stoic and Cornutus, which taught him the allegorical method of interpreting the Greek mysteries, a method he applied to the Jewish Scriptures.

ϮABIANO C✶Є ΠI ✦

Bishop Fabian's name in the burial vault of the third century Bishops of Rome discovered in the catacomb of Callistus in 1854

CHAPTER SEVEN

THE FIRST SYSTEMATIC PERSECUTIONS

249–60

The fifties of the third century were a time of great empire-wide difficulty for Christians. The familiar paradox of Roman history repeated itself—a good emperor meant hard times. Decius, who became emperor in 249, was bent, in Gibbon's words, on 'restoring public virtue, ancient principles and manners, and the oppressed majesty of the laws'. That meant in one small sector of public life insisting on conformity to the State religion, whatever other religion a citizen might privately follow in addition. Nearly two years followed in which this policy was enforced. What might have happened to the Church had not Decius been killed in a battle on the empire's Danubian frontier is not difficult to imagine.

An interval of peace under two bad emperors, both of whom were murdered, was followed by renewed, though less complete persecution under an emperor of whom Gibbon remarked that 'if mankind (according to the observation of an ancient writer) had been left at liberty to choose a master, their choice would most assuredly have fallen on Valerian'. The first half of his reign was peaceful enough for Christians, but its second half was another matter. In 260, however, Valerian was taken prisoner by the king of Persia and his effeminate and dissolute son was left as sole emperor. Once again Christians were left alone. They enjoyed more than forty years of peace.

33. CARTHAGE: ON THE EVE c. 249

Cyprian, bishop of Carthage, who wrote this sad account of the state of affairs in the church at Carthage, was looking back in 251 from the other side of the great persecution under the emperor Decius. He had only been a Christian for three years and bishop for one when the persecution began. Cyprian was a lawyer, a rich man, a quiet man who loved his garden, and a popular man. He became bishop because the laity insisted, besieging him in his house until he agreed to be consecrated.

The condition of the church in Carthage was probably typical of its condition in most parts of the empire. It reflects what might have been expected to happen at the end of the Long Peace. Probably things were not as bad as Cyprian paints them—clergy and converts are given to looking at the world through dark glasses—but one would not expect much heroism or widespread other-worldliness. After all Tertullian had failed in his immediate objectives, however influential his writings may still be. And Tertullian had been dead for a quarter of a century.

Source: Cyprian, *Of the Lapsed* 6.

Everyone was striving to get rich. Forgetting how the faithful lived in Apostolic times and how they ought to behave in every age, they devoted themselves with insatiable greed to the increase of possessions. The priests lacked spiritual devotion, the ministers were deficient in faith. There was no mercy in works of charity, no discipline in manners. Men trimmed their beards, and women stained their faces. The eyes were altered from what God made them, and a false colour was given to the hair. The hearts of the simple were led astray by deceitful devices and brethren were caught in seductive snares. Marriages were made with unbelievers and members of Christ abandoned to the heathen. Not only rash swearing was heard, but even false.

Prominent people were swollen with pride, poisonous reproaches fell from their lips, and endless quarrels divided men. Many bishops, who ought to have been an inspiration and example to others, despised their sacred calling and engaged in secular pursuits, abandoned their thrones, deserted their people, travelled in foreign provinces and hunted the markets for business profits. They tried to amass large sums of money, while they had starving brethren within the Church. They got hold of estates by fraud, and increased their gains through usury.

34. ROME FIRST   250

The persecution started in Rome. Its first victim was the bishop, Fabian, who had held office for sixteen years when he was executed on January 20. He was buried first in the catacomb of Callistus on the Appian Way, and later re-buried in the church of St. Sebastian. His grave in the catacomb has a rough inscription: 'Fabian, Bishop and

Martyr' which is reproduced on page 114. The 'martyr' seems to have been added by a different hand.

The Roman church sent the news and an account of his death to the Church at Carthage, and doubtless to other churches as well. Bishop Cyprian's reply survives and is given in this extract in a translation by Dr Pusey, the great leader of the Oxford Movement.

During his long episcopate Fabian had overhauled the organization and administration of the Christian community. He divided the city into seven regions with a deacon in each responsible for welfare and community work. These were the offices which in later times grew into the body of Cardinal Deacons forming, with the Cardinal Priests of the Roman parishes and Cardinal Bishops of the suburban sees, the Sacred College which elects the Pope.

Source: Cyprian, *Letters* 9.

TO THE PRESBYTERS AND DEACONS ABIDING IN ROME

When there was an uncertain rumour among us, dearest brethren, of the departure of that good man my colleague [Fabian], and I was in suspense what to think, I received an epistle from you, sent me by Crementius the subdeacon, wherein I was fully informed of his glorious departure: and I rejoiced that he had gone on to his consummation with honour, suited to the integrity of his administration. Wherein I heartily congratulate you also that you honour his memory with a testimony so public and illustrious; so as to make known to me what is both so glorious to yourselves as regards the memory of your bishop, and may give me too an example of faith and virtue. For, in how much the fall of a bishop is pernicious in leading to the lapse of his followers, in so much, contrariwise, is it useful and salutary, when a bishop by the constancy of his faith makes himself an example to be imitated by his brethren.

35. ALEXANDRIA: MOB RULE, OFFICIAL PERSECUTION   250

The first extract is part of a letter from Dionysius, bishop of Alexandria, to the bishop of Antioch describing what happened to Christians in his city during the reign of Decius. Dionysius had become head of the Christian Academy there in 233 in succession to Origen. Fourteen years later he became bishop of Alexandria. During the events

described in this letter he went underground, was caught, but escaped·
He tells how in the second extract.

Note that the riots against the Christians must have started in 249 at
the very beginning of the reign of Decius. The emperor's order that
all citizens should secure an official certificate that they had sacrificed
to the gods was not issued until June 250.

Source: Eusebius, *Church History* 6, 41; quoting a letter of Dionysius.

A.   RIOTS, MURDERS, EXECUTIONS

It was not the imperial edict that started the persecution against us;
it had already been going on for a whole year. Some prophet and
author of evils for this city had already roused and incited the
heathen masses against us, setting the local superstitions aflame
again. Roused to riot, they seized every chance of mischief,
thinking that the holiest service of their demons was to slaughter
us.

First they seized an old man named Metras and ordered him to
utter blasphemous words. Because he refused, they beat him with
clubs, drove sharpened sticks into his face and eyes, dragged him
out of the city and stoned him to death. Then they took a woman,
a believer named Quinta, to the temple of their idol and tried to
force her to worship. When she turned away in disgust, they tied
her feet and dragged her right through the city over the cobbled
streets, banging her against the stones and beating her as they went;
and, taking her to the same place, stoned her to death.

Then all with one accord rushed to the houses of Christians,
breaking in on those who were known as neighbours, and looted
and plundered. The more valuable property they stole; the cheaper
wooden articles were strewn about the streets and burnt, so that
the city looked as if it had been taken by an enemy. But the
believers withdrew and went away, and like those to whom Paul
bore witness 'took joyfully the spoiling of their goods' (Hebrews
10, 34). I do not know of anyone, except possibly one who fell
into their clutches, who has denied the Lord as yet.

Next they seized that most admirable virgin Apollonia, an old
woman, kept hitting her on the jaws till they had broken all her
teeth, built a pyre outside the city and threatened to burn her alive

if she would not repeat with them their heathen incantations. She asked for a moment's respite and, when she was released, leapt eagerly into the fire and was consumed,

They seized Serapion in his own house, put him to the cruellest tortures and, when they had broken all his limbs, threw him head-first from an upper storey.

No street, highway or lane was open to us, by night or day; always and everywhere, everybody was shouting that anyone failing to repeat their blasphemies should immediately be dragged away and burnt.

Matters continued like this for a considerable time, and then the wretched people were caught up in factions and civil war, and turned the cruelty they had shown against us against one another. So for a little while we breathed again as they ceased to rage against us.

Soon, however, we heard the news of the change from that kinder reign, and we were very afraid of what was in store for us. And the edict arrived and it was almost like that terrible time foretold by our Lord which, if it were possible, would offend even the elect (see Matt. 24. 24). Everyone was terrified, and many prominent people, through fear, came forward immediately (to sacrifice); others, in public employment, were led to do so by their official duties, and yet others were urged on by their neighbours. As their names were called out, they approached the foul, profane sacrifices. Some were pale and trembling as if they were going, not to sacrifice, but to be sacrificed, to be offered themselves to the idols; so the great crowd of spectators jeered at them, as it was obvious that they were terrified either to die or to sacrifice.

Others came to the altars more readily, as showing by their boldness, that they had never been Christians. These, as our Lord truly foretold, shall 'hardly' be saved (see Matt. 19, 23). Of the rest, some followed each of these groups, some fled and some were caught. Of the latter, some continued faithful for many days while chained and imprisoned, but renounced their faith before they were brought to trial. Others endured great tortures for a while and then gave in. But the firm and blessed pillars of the Lord, strengthened by him and given power in proportion to the greatness of their faith, became wonderful witnesses (martyrs) of his kingdom.

The first of these was Julian, who suffered so much from gout that he could not walk or even stand. He was brought to trial with two others who carried him. One of these immediately denied the Lord; the other, named Cronian and nicknamed Goodfellow, with the aged Julian himself, confessed the Lord and were taken through the whole city, which, as you know, is a vast one, perched up on camels, and beaten as they went. Finally they were burnt up in quicklime, the crowd surging around them.

But a soldier called Besas, who was standing by as they were led past, protested against those who were insulting them. This roused the mob against him too, and he was put on trial, this heroic warrior of God, and having fought nobly in the great battle for the faith, he was beheaded.

Another man, a Libyan by birth, was true both to his name Macar ('blessed') and to the Beatitude (Matt. 5, 10); though strongly urged by the judge to recant, he stood firm and was burnt alive. After these Epimachus and Alexander, who had been in prison a long time enduring countless agonies from iron scrapers and whips, were also consumed in quicklime.

With them were four women. Ammonarium, a holy virgin, was tortured mercilessly and excessively by the judge because she declared beforehand that she would say none of the things he ordered her to say. She kept her promise faithfully and was dragged away. The others were Mercuria, a very distinguished old lady, and Dionysia, the mother of many children, who did not love them more than the Lord (Matt. 10, 37). As the governor was ashamed to go on torturing so ineffectually and be always defeated by women, they were killed by a sword without testing by torture. Ammonarium, the champion, had endured that for all of them.

Certain Egyptians—Hero, Ater, Isidore, and a boy about fifteen called Dioscorus—were delivered up. At first the judge tried to trick the lad with fair words, and then to break him down by tortures, thinking that he would easily be brought over or made to yield. But Dioscorus yielded neither to blandishments nor force. The others also stood firm, and they were beaten up and sent to the flames. But Dioscorus so impressed the judge with his behaviour in public, and his wise answers during private examination, that that judge dismissed him, saying that because he was so young he would be given time to change his mind. And this most holy Dioscorus is with us now, awaiting an even longer and severer trial.

Another Egyptian, Nemesion, was accused of being one of a gang of robbers, but when he had cleared himself of this grossly false accusation before the centurion, he was denounced as a Christian and taken in chains before the governor. Most unjustly, he inflicted twice the tortures and floggings meted out to the robbers, and then burnt him between them, thus honouring that blessed man with a likeness to Christ.

A group of soldiers, Ammon, Zeno, Ptolemy, Ingenes, and an old man called Theophilus, were standing close together in the court. And when a certain person, on trial as a Christian, seemed about to deny it, they ground their teeth, grimaced, stretched out their hands and made angry gestures with their bodies. All eyes were turned to them, and then, before anyone could stop them, they dashed to the dock saying that they were Christians. The governor and the members of his council were terrified and while they trembled the accused showed complete courage in the face of the suffering to come. Jubilantly they left the court, proud of their witness, for God had made them to 'triumph gloriously' (see Exod. 15, 1).

Many others, in cities and villages, were torn in pieces by the heathen . . . Need I tell of the numbers that 'wandered in deserts and in mountains' (Hebrews 11, 38), and perished of hunger, and thirst, and cold, and sickness, and robbers, and wild beasts? Those who survived are witnesses of the victory of these elect. But I will describe one case as characteristic. Chaeremon, the aged bishop of Nilopolis, fled with his wife to the Arabian mountains and never returned. Though the brethren made a thorough search they could not find either them or their bodies. And many who fled to the same mountains were enslaved by the barbarous

Saracens.[1] Some were ransomed—with difficulty and at great cost—others never to this day.

B.   THE BISHOP'S ESCAPE   250

About sunset, I and the lads with me were seized by soldiers and taken to Taposiris, but by the providence of God Timothy was absent and was not caught. When he arrived later he found the house deserted, guarded, and ourselves beyond hope of freedom . . . As he fled, distraught, Timothy met one of the country folk who asked him why he was in such a hurry. He told him the truth. The man was on his way to a wedding feast which customarily lasted all night, and as soon as he heard the news he went in and told it to those reclining at the table.

With one accord, as if at a prearranged signal, they leapt to their feet, rushed out quickly and came and burst in upon us with shouts. The soldiers guarding us fled immediately. The men came to us as we lay on the bare mattresses and at first, God knows, I thought they were robbers looking for spoil and plunder. So I stayed on the bed. I had only a linen shirt on me and I offered them the rest of my clothes, which were lying beside me. But they told me to get up and escape . . . and they seized me by the hands and feet . . . set me on an ass without a saddle and carried me away.

36. THOSE WHO GAVE IN: The Aftermath of Persecution

The method which Decius used to enforce his will was simple. He ordered that on a given day everybody should offer sacrifice to the gods and obtain an official certificate that he had done so. This order applied everywhere—not only in the great cities, but in little villages. The first extract is a translation of one of these certificates issued in the village of Alexander's Island in Egypt which had been preserved in the sand and was discovered at Faiyum in 1893.

Some of the people who got certificates sacrificed; others managed— presumably by bribery or influence—to get certificates without sacrificing. Both alike were guilty in the eyes of their fellow Christians who resisted or somehow or other missed the parade. But they were not equally guilty. What was to be done about them? This provoked a

---

[1] This is the first mention of these people in surviving records.

heated argument after the persecution was over, and led in the end to a schism, or split, in the Church which lasted for over 150 years.

Some wanted to be merciful and allow those who repented of their weakness to return to the Church; others wanted to take a stern line and leave them out. Dionysius, bishop of Alexandria, took the former view as the second extract shows. So, too, did Cyprian and his fellow African bishops (see the third extract). But Novatian in Rome after some hesitation felt that this would not do. He had been perhaps the leader in the Roman church in the long gap when there was no bishop and had been in close touch with Cyprian in those days. But when it became possible to elect another bishop Novatian had been passed over and one of the more charitable school elected. Novatian did not give in. He had supporters and found three bishops to consecrate him. He was executed in the renewed persecution under the emperor Valerian in 257 or 258.

The fourth extract shows that, though the official bishop, Cornelius, might be charitable to those who had sacrificed and got their certificates, he was the reverse to his rival.

Sources: A: Inscription found at Fayum, Egypt; B: A letter of Dionysius, bishop of Alexandria, quoted by Eusebius in *Church History* 6, 42; C: Cyprian, *Letters* No. 55; D: A letter of Cornelius, bishop of Rome, quoted by Eusebius 6, 43.

A. A CERTIFICATE OF CONFORMITY June 26, 250

To those who have been elected to preside over the sacrifices in the village of Alexander's Island [comes this petition] from Aurelius Diogenes, son of Satabus, of the village of Alexander's Island, aged seventy-two, with a scar on his right eyebrow. I have always sacrificed to the gods; and now, in your presence, and according to the terms of the edict, I have sacrificed and [poured libations?] and [tasted] the sacrificial victims, and I ask you to append your signature. Farewell. Presented by Aurelius Diogenes.

I, Mys . . . the son of . . . non, [saw him] sacrificing, and have subscribed. In the first year of Imperator Caesar Gaius Messius Quintus Trajanus Decius Pius Felix Augustus, on Epiphi 2 (June 26, 250).

B. SHOULD THOSE WHO GAVE IN BE BROUGHT BACK?

Thus even the divine martyrs among us, who now sit by Christ's side as partners in his kingdom, share his authority, and are his fellow judges, opened their arms to their fallen brethren who faced the charge of sacrificing. Seeing their conversion and repentance, they were sure that it would be acceptable to him who does not in the least desire the death of a sinner, but rather his repentance; so they received them, admitted them to the congregation as 'bystanders', and allowed them to take part in services and feasts. What then, brothers, is your advice to us in this matter? What must we do? Shall we take our stand in full agreement with them, uphold their merciful decision, and deal gently with those they pitied? Or shall we condemn their decision as improper . . . and turn their practice upside down?

C.   THE TREATMENT OF THE LAPSED   June 251

When persecution ceased, and assemblies were permitted, many bishops, whom their own faith and the Lord's protection had kept safe and sound, met together. We tempered firmness with moderation, supporting both attitudes by reference to the holy Scriptures. In this way the hope of communion and of peace was not denied to the lapsed, lest they should fall away even further in despair and, with the Church shut against them, follow the world into heathenism. On the other hand we decided that Gospel strictness was not to be relaxed to let them rush in haste to communion. Penance should be long drawn out; the mercy of the Father entreated with tears, and all the circumstances of each case carefully examined.

This is set out in a tract (*On the Lapsed*) which I hope has reached you, where our decisions are shown.

And lest the African bishops should seem insufficient (to make such a decision by themselves), we wrote about this to our colleague Cornelius at Rome who, in a council with many of our brother bishops, agreed with us in favour of a solemn and salutary moderation.

D.   NOVATIAN BY HIS ENEMY

The occasion of his becoming a believer came from Satan, who entered into him and stayed within him a considerable time.

While the exorcists were trying to help him he fell desperately ill, and since he was thought to be on the point of death, there as he lay in bed he received baptism by affusion[1]—if it can be called baptism in the case of such a man. And when he recovered he did not receive the other things of which one should partake according to the rule of the Church, in particular the sealing by a bishop (confirmation) . . .

The man who through cowardice and love of life at the time of the persecution denied that he was a presbyter! The deacons begged and besought him to come out of the chamber in which he had shut himself, and to help his brothers, in danger and in need of assistance, in every way right and possible for a presbyter; but so far was he from answering the deacons' appeal that he actually went right away in a rage, declaring that he did not want to be a presbyter any longer . . .

37. THE TRIAL AND LAST HOURS OF CYPRIAN   257–8

At Carthage in 257 even persecution was conducted with courtesy and decorum. When Valerian launched his attack on the Church, Cyprian bishop of Carthage was banished by the proconsul, Paternus, to the quiet little seaside resort of Carubis fifty miles from the city. His deacon, Pontius, went with him. This action was part of the first stage of the persecution when the emperor banned Christian meetings and had many bishops arrested. The Proconsular Acts survive, giving details of the trial. The following year Valerian issued a further order for the execution of clergy and laymen of high rank who would not abjure. Cyprian came back to Carthage determined to die among his people.

Sources: A and c: *The Proconsular Acts*; B: Pontius, *Life and Suffering of St Cyprian.*

A.   THE TRIAL, AUGUST 30, 257

When the Emperor Valerian was consul for the fourth, and Gallienus for the third time . . . Paternus, proconsul at Carthage, in his council-chamber thus spoke to Cyprian, bishop:

P. The most sacred emperors Valerian and Gallienus have

---

[1] Sprinkling.

K

honoured me with letters, wherein they enjoin that all those who do not use the religion of Rome shall formally make profession of their return to the use of Roman rites. I have accordingly made enquiry of your name; what answer do you make to me?

C. I am a Christian, and bishop. I know no other gods beside the one and true God, who made heaven and earth, the sea, and all things therein. This God we Christians serve, to him we pray day and night, for ourselves, for all mankind, for the health of the emperors themselves.

P. Do you persist in this purpose?

C. That good purpose, which hath once acknowledged God, cannot be changed.

P. Will you then, obeying the mandate of the emperors, depart into exile to the city of Curubis?

C. I go.

P. The letters I have been honoured with by the emperors speak of presbyters as well as of bishops. I would know of you therefore who they are; who are presbyters in this city?

C. By your laws you have righteously and with great benefit forbidden any to be informers, therefore they cannot be discovered and denounced by me; but they will be found in their own cities . . .

P. They shall be discovered by me. The emperors further ordain that no assemblies be held in any place, and that the Christians shall not enter their cemeteries. Any who disobey this wholesome order shall be put to death.

C. Do as you have been instructed.

Then Paternus the proconsul bade them lead Cyprian away into exile. During his abode in that place Aspasius Paternus was succeeded by Galerius Maximus, who bade the bishop Cyprian be recalled from exile and brought before him . . .

B.   THE LAST HOURS   258

On an order from the proconsul, an officer with his soldiers came suddenly and unexpectedly (or so he thought) upon Cyprian in his garden, the garden which he had sold when he accepted the faith and which, restored by God's mercy, he would certainly have sold again for the use of the poor, if he had not wished to avoid ill-will from the persecutors. But when can a mind ever prepared be taken unawares, as if by an unforeseen attack? So now, confident that what had been long delayed was to be concluded, he came forward proudly, with cheerfulness in his face and courage in his heart.

But his case was postponed to the morrow and he returned from the praetorium to the officer's own house, where he was held for that night in a gentle custody, so that we, his comrades and friends, were as usual in his company. And meanwhile, the people kept watch before the officer's door, anxious that nothing should be done in the night without their knowledge.

At last there dawned the destined holy day, which the tyrant had no power to put off, even if he wished to do so. The day shone with a brilliant sun. Cyprian left the house, walled in on all sides by a mighty throng. He, having finished his course, running for the crown of righteousness, most appropriately, as though it had been arranged on purpose, had to pass the race-course.

But when he reached the praetorium, the proconsul had not yet emerged, and he was taken to a place of retirement. The seat happened to be covered with linen, so that even in the moment of his passion he might enjoy the honour of a bishop. As he sat there, soaked in sweat after his long journey, the officer of the watchword (Tessararius), who had formerly been a Christian, offered him his own clothes, so that he could change his wet garments for drier ones. Doubtless all he desired by this kind offer was to possess the blood-stained sweat of the martyr going to God. Cyprian answered,

'We apply medicines to plagues, but these are likely to end today.'

What more should we tell? He is suddenly announced to the proconsul. He is brought forward. He is placed before him. He is asked his name. He answers who he is, and nothing more.

C.   **THE EXECUTION**   258

So, on September 14, a great crowd was collected early at Sexti, as the proconsul commanded. And the same day Cyprian was brought before him as he sat for judgment in the court called Sauciolum.

Galerius Maximus. Are you Thascius Cyprianus?

C. I am he.

G.M. The most sacred emperors have commanded you to conform to the Roman rites.

C. I refuse to do so.

G.M. Take heed for yourself.

C. Execute the emperors' orders; in a matter so manifest I may not deliberate.

Galerius, after briefly conferring with his judicial council, with much reluctance . . . read the sentence of the court from a written tablet: 'It is the will of this court that Thascius Cyprianus be immediately beheaded.'

C. Thanks be to God.

38. PLAGUE AT EASTER   *c.* 260

Dionysius, bishop of Alexandria, not only survived the Decian persecution but came safely through the Valerian, though he was banished from his diocese. He came back to find the city still in the grip of an appalling plague that raged throughout the Mediterranean world from about 250 to 268. He wrote this letter to his people one Easter at about this time. Dionysius died, an old man, about 264.

Source: Dionysius, *Festival Letters*, quoted by Eusebius, *Church History* 7, 22.

Other people would not think this a time for festival . . . Now, alas! all is lamentation, everyone in mourning, and the city resounds with weeping because of the numbers that have died and are dying every day. As Scripture says of the firstborn of the Egyptians, so now there has been a great cry: there is not a house in which there is not one dead—how I wish it had been only one!

Many terrible things had happened to us even before this. First we were set on and surrounded by persecutors and murderers, yet we were the only ones to keep festival even then. Every spot where we were attacked became for us a place for celebrations, whether field, desert, ship, inn, or prison. The most brilliant festival of all was kept by the fulfilled martyrs, who were feasted in heaven.

After that came war and famine, which struck at Christian and heathen alike . . . Then out of the blue came this disease, a thing more terrifying to them than any terror, more frightful than any disaster whatever, and as a historian of their own once wrote: 'the only thing of all that surpassed expectation'. To us it was not that, but a schooling and testing as valuable as all our earlier trials; for it did not pass over us, though its full impact fell on the heathen. . . .

Most of our brother-Christians showed unbounded love and loyalty, never sparing themselves and thinking only of one another. Heedless of the danger, they took charge of the sick, attending to their every need and ministering to them in Christ, and with them departed this life serenely happy; for they were infected by others with the disease, drawing on themselves the sickness of their neighbours and cheerfully accepting their pains. Many, in nursing and curing others, transferred their death to themselves and died in their stead, turning the common formula that is normally an empty courtesy into a reality: 'Your humble servant bids you good-bye.' The best of our brothers lost their lives in this manner, a number of presbyters, deacons, and laymen winning high commendation, so that death in this form, the result of great piety and strong faith, seems in every way the equal of martyrdom. With willing hands they raised the bodies of the saints to their bosoms; they closed their eyes and mouths, carried them on their shoulders, and laid them out; they clung to them, embraced them, washed them, and wrapped them in grave-clothes. Very soon the same services were done for them, since those left behind were constantly following those gone before.

The heathen behaved in the very opposite way. At the first on-set of the disease, they pushed the sufferers away and fled from their dearest, throwing them into the roads before they were dead and treating unburied corpses as dirt, hoping thereby to avert the spread and contagion of the fatal disease; but do what they might, they found it difficult to escape.

CHAPTER EIGHT

THE FINAL STRUGGLE
Diocletian and Galerius

The forty-three years of toleration after the captivity of Valerian (p. 115) was a time of very rapid growth for the Church. Christians were to be found in high government positions; their bishops began to be people of high status in civil society. The last eighteen years of this period of calm were in the reign of Diocletian. But then there was once again a reversal of fortune: Diocletian turned persecutor, and the last two years of his reign were grim for Christians. So were the next six.

'Like Augustus, Diocletian may be considered the founder of a new empire. Like the adopted son of Caesar, he was distinguished as a statesman rather than a warrior; nor did either of those princes employ force, whenever their policy could be effected by policy.' So Gibbon described the man who restored peace to the Roman world and nearly destroyed the Christian church. What Diocletian did for the empire was to recognize that it could only be defended from the barbarians and given internal good government if there was an orderly devolution of power. The problem was too big for one man. Diocletian, the son of a slave, kept control of the East, with Galerius, the son of a herdsman, in charge under him of the Danube frontier provinces. The supreme control in the West went to his fellow Maximian, the son of a peasant, with Constantius, the only aristocrat among them, in command under him of Gaul and Britain. The four men together formed a college, cabinet or in Gibbon's phrase, 'a chorus of music, whose harmony was regulated and maintained by the skilful hand of the first artist'. See Plates 14A, 15.

Why did Diocletian turn against the Christians? One reason, no doubt, was a series of incidents which suggested that Christians could not be relied on as soldiers. A young man called Maximilianus was executed for refusing to serve in the army on grounds of conscience. In 298 a more serious incident occurred. A centurion of the Theban legion called Marcellus suddenly at the emperor's birthday parade threw away his badges of rank, refused to offer sacrifice, saying 'I serve

Jesus Christ, the eternal King.' He was court-martialled and executed. When the death sentence was passed, the court secretary, Cassian, protested that the sentence was unjust and said that he too was a Christian. Naturally he too was arrested, tried and executed.

It is unlikely that isolated incidents like these would have weighed sufficiently heavily with Diocletian to make him change the whole policy of his reign towards Christians. But they would have infuriated the quick-tempered soldier Maximian in whose part of the empire both the incidents happened, and would equally have angered Galerius, who 'entertained the most implacable aversion for the name and religion of the Christians'. So did his wife. Galerius, another rough soldier, spent the winter of 302–3 with Diocletian in the imperial palace at Nicomedia on the Asiatic coast of the Sea of Marmora. There they decided to put down Christianity once for all.

39. DIOCLETIAN STARTS IT OFF:
The Church at Nicomedia Destroyed   February 23, 303

In the imperial palace at Nicomedia Diocletian and Galerius made their plans. The senior civil magistrate and high civil servants directed operations; the Praetorian Guard, the emperor's household troops, were called out. The two rulers looked on.

Lactantius, the writer of this account, had been a professor of rhetoric at Nicomedia until he lost his job on becoming a Christian about the year 300—a sign that Diocletian, who had appointed him, was changing his attitude to Christians. Rhetoric—oratory, the art of public speaking —was an important part of training for the law and public life. The emperor Constantine made Lactantius tutor to his son. Lactantius died about 320. Besides a number of theological works he wrote a book *On the Deaths of the Persecutors*, from which this account is taken.

Notice the surprise that there was no 'image of the Divinity' to be found. Even the Cross was not directly employed in church decoration, though the anchor and the Chi-Rho symbol were freely used by Christians and their suggestion of the Cross understood. In the West the crucifixion was not represented before the fifth century. The earliest symbol of Christ was a fish (second century); on the earliest carved tombs he is represented as the Good Shepherd (third century).[1]

Notice also that the Christians now possess a church, a tall building, within sight of the imperial palace.

[1] For Chi-Rho see page 143. For pictures of symbols see Plates 8, 9, 12, 13, 17, and drawings on page 157.

A fit and auspicious day was sought for the accomplishment of this undertaking, and the festival of the god Terminus, celebrated on the seventh of the kalends of March (Feb. 23), was chosen, in preference to all others, to terminate, as it were, the Christian religion . . .

When that day dawned, in the eighth consulship of Diocletian and seventh of Maximian, suddenly, while it was yet hardly light, the prefect, together with chief commanders, tribunes and officers of the treasury, came to the church in Nicomedia, and the gates having been forced open, they searched everywhere for an image of the Divinity. The books of the Holy Scriptures were found, and they were committed to the flames; the utensils and furniture of the church were abandoned to pillage: all was rapine, confusion, tumult.

That church, situated on rising ground, was within view of the palace, and Diocletian and Galerius stood as if on a watch-tower, disputing long whether it ought to be set on fire.

The sentiment of Diocletian prevailed, who dreaded lest so great a fire, being once kindled, some part of the city might be burnt; for there were many and large buildings that surrounded the church.

Then the Praetorian Guards came in battle array, with axes and other iron instruments, and having been let loose everywhere, they, in a few hours, levelled that very lofty edifice with the ground.

40. THE BURNING OF THE BOOKS 303

The day after the destruction of the church at Nicomedia a notice setting out the full terms of Diocletian's orders was posted in the capital. A Christian tore it down and said what he thought of it. He was arrested, tortured and burnt to death. During the next fortnight there were two mysterious fires in the palace at Nicomedia. Diocletian was frightened. There were many arrests and executions. The persecution was well begun.

The method of repression which Diocletian and Galerius had agreed was this:

a. all churches were to be demolished;

b. death was to be the penalty for holding services;

   c. all Christian books were to be handed in and burnt;

   d. all Church property was confiscated;

   e. all Christians who were free men were deprived of all public employment;

   f. Christian slaves lost the right of becoming free men;

   g. Christians could not be plaintiffs in any legal action, but they could be sued.

There were a few disturbances and in 304 further, more severe orders were issued with the result that there were more executions.

The persecution varied greatly in duration and intensity in different parts of the empire. Gaul and Britain under Constantius, the father of Constantine, escaped lightly—tradition gives Britain its first martyr, Alban, in this persecution, but there is no written authority until late in the sixth century. Italy and North Africa had a relatively short but severe terror. The eastern provinces suffered worst and longest.

Two incidents from Africa are worth giving. Felix, bishop of Thibiuca, maintained: 'It is better for me to be burned than the divine Scriptures.' Anulinus, the proconsul, tried to save him: 'Why don't you give up some spare and useless books?' It was no good. He was forced to send him in chains to Rome where the prefect of Italy also tried to persuade him, but in vain. 'I have books, but I give them not,' was all Felix would say. He was condemned and executed.

At Abithinae forty-nine Christians met secretly to celebrate the Eucharist—'as if a Christian could exist without the Eucharist,' the owner of the house told Anulinus. Saturninus, the presbyter, and his four children were among the martyrs. The proconsul tried to frighten the youngest, Hilarian, out of his faith after the others had been beaten to death. 'I will cut off your hair, your nose and your ears, and then let you go,' he said. 'Do as you please. I am a Christian,' Hilarian answered and went to his prison saying 'Thanks be to God.'

This extract is from the official record of the search for books at Cirta in Numidia, the province immediately to the west of Carthage. The inventory of the property confiscated shows that the church there possessed two gold chalices; six silver chalices; six urns, one kettle, and seven lamps, all of silver; and a large quantity of brass utensils, and vestments. Some bishops hid their most precious manuscripts and handed over only heretical books. The bishop of Carthage was said to have done this, and the local Senate complained but the proconsul took no further action. (See also p. 297).

Source: *Gesta apud Zenophilus.*

When they reached the library the bookshelves were empty. Felix, the Perpetual Flamen,[1] curator of the republic, said,

'Bring out what Scriptures you have, that you may be able to obey the precepts and bidding of the emperors.'

Catulinus produced one roll of an extremely large size.

'Why have you given me but one? Bring out all you have.'

'We have no more, because we are sub-deacons. The readers have the books.'

'Point us out the readers.'

'We do not know where they live.'

'You do not know where they live. Then tell us their names.'

'We are not going to betray people. Here we are. Order us to be executed.'

'Take them to jail,' Felix said.

And when they reached the house of Eugenius, Felix said to him, 'Bring out your Scriptures,' and he brought four manuscripts. Felix said to Silvanus and Carosus,

'Show us the rest of the readers.'

They said, 'The bishop has told you already that Edusius and Junius, your secretaries, know them all. Let *them* show you the way to their houses.'

Edusius and Junius said, 'We will show you them, my Lord.'

And when they came to the house of Victorinus, he brought eight. And when they came to the house of Projectus, he brought five big and two little books. And when they came to the house of Victor, the grammar-master, he brought out two codices, and four books in five volumes each. Felix said to him,

'Bring your Scriptures out. You have more.'

'If I had more I should have brought them.'

When they came to Eutychius' house, the flamen said,

'Bring out your books, that you may obey the order.'

---

[1] Flamen, a priest.

'I have none.'

'Your answer is taken down.'

When they came to the house of Coddes, Coddes' wife brought out six codices. Felix said,

'Look and see if you have not some more. Bring them out.'

'I have no more.'

Felix said to Bos the policeman, 'Go in and look if she has no more.'

'I have looked and found none,' said Bos.

41. TYRE AND EGYPT: UNBRIDLED PERSECUTION 310–11

These two extracts refer to the last and bitterest stage of the last persecution. Diocletian had retired in May, 305 to spend the last twelve years of his life in his great palace at Split in Dalmatia, his own home country. When pressed to return to the throne he merely remarked that if his friends could but see the cabbages he had planted with his own hands they would not press him 'to relinquish the enjoyment of happiness for the pursuit of power'. Under Diocletian persecution followed the rule of law; it was indeed strictly law enforcement often by reluctant officials. When Galerius was alone things were different.

The writer of these two extracts was Eusebius. We have quoted frequently from his book in previous chapters, but this is the first extract from his own writings: previous extracts have been from the collection of older authors that he made. He was himself involved in this persecution. He lived at Caesarea where he was under the influence of Pamphilus, the pupil of Origen. Pamphilus was martyred in 309 and Eusebius wisely moved on. He went first to the north to Tyre, then south into Egypt. There he was himself arrested and spent some time in prison. These two extracts refer to what happened, some of which he saw for himself, in these two places. The second extract refers to the persecution in the Thebaid in Upper Egypt about 500 miles upstream from the Nile delta.

Source: Eusebius, *Church History* 8, 7 and 9.

A.   AT TYRE

We know those who became shining lights in Palestine, and we know those at Tyre in Phoenicia. Did any man see them without being amazed at the merciless floggings and the endurance displayed under them by these truly astounding champions of pure religion; at the ordeal with man-eating beasts which came directly after the floggings, when they were attacked by panthers, bears of different kinds, wild boars, and bulls goaded with red-hot irons; at the unflinching courage of these noble people in the face of every one of the beasts? When these things were going on I was there myself, and there I witnessed the ever-present divine power of him to whom they testified, our Saviour Jesus Christ himself, visibly manifesting itself to the martyrs.

For some time the man-eaters did not dare to touch or even approach the bodies of God's beloved, but rushed at the others who apparently were irritating them from outside; only the holy champions, as they stood naked, and in accordance with their instructions waved their hands to attract the animals to themselves, were left quite unmolested. Sometimes when the beasts did start towards them, they were stopped short as if by some divine power, and retreated to their starting-point. When this went on for a long time it astounded the spectators, so that, in view of the ineffectiveness of the first, a second and third beast were set on to one and the same martyr.

Nothing could be more amazing than the fearless courage of these saints under such duress, the stubborn, inflexible endurance in youthful bodies. You would see a youngster not yet twenty standing without fetters, spreading out his arms in the form of a cross, and with a mind unafraid and unshakable, occupying himself in the most unhurried prayers to the Almighty, not budging in the least and not retreating an inch from the spot where he stood, though bears and panthers breathing fury and death almost touched his very flesh. Yet by some supernatural, mysterious power their mouths were stopped, and they ran back again to the rear.

Again you would have seen others—there were five altogether —thrown to an infuriated bull. When others approached from outside he tossed them into the air with his horns and mangled them, leaving them to be picked up half-dead; but when in his fury he rushed head down at the lonely group of holy martyrs, he could not get near them, but stamped his feet and pushed with his horns in all directions. Provoked by the hot irons, he breathed rage and threats, but divine providence dragged him back. So, as he too did his intended victims no harm whatever, other beasts were set on them. At last, when these animals had launched their terrible varied assaults, the martyrs were one and all butchered with the sword, and instead of being buried in the earth were given to the waves of the sea.

B.   IN EGYPT

Words cannot describe the outrageous agonies endured by the martyrs in the Thebaid. They were torn to bits from head to foot with potsherds like claws, till death released them. Women were tied by one foot and hoisted high in the air, head downwards, their bodies completely naked without a morsel of clothing, presenting thus the most shameful, brutal, and inhuman of all spectacles to everyone watching. Others again were tied to trees and stumps and died horribly; for with the aid of machinery they drew together the very stoughtest boughs, fastened one of the martyr's legs to each, and then let the boughs fly back to their normal position; thus they managed to tear apart the limbs of their victims in a moment.

In this way they carried on, not for a few days or weeks, but year after year. Sometimes ten or more, sometimes over twenty, at other times at least thirty, and at yet others not far short of sixty; and there were occasions when on a single day a hundred men as well as women and little children were killed, condemned to a succession of ever-changing punishments.

I was in these places, and saw many of the executions myself. Some of the victims suffered death by beheading, others punishment by fire. So many were killed on a single day that the axe, blunted and worn out by the slaughter, was broken in pieces, while the exhausted executioners had to be periodically relieved. All the time I observed a most wonderful eagerness and a truly divine power and enthusiasm in those who had put their trust in the Christ of God. No sooner had the first batch been sentenced, than others from every side would jump on to the platform in front of the judge and proclaim themselves Christians. They paid no heed to torture in all its terrifying forms, but undaunted spoke boldly of their devotion to the God of the universe, and with joy, laughter, and gaiety received the final sentence of death; they sang and sent up hymns of thanksgiving to the God of the universe till their very last breath.

42. THE PERSECUTORS LOSE THEIR NERVE   311–13

There was, as we have seen, disagreement among the emperors and their associates about the persecution. By 311 even Galerius, the prime instigator of the terror, had doubts which may well have been inspired by a mixture of policy and superstition. He lay dying of a painful disease. He issued a strangely worded rescript, or decree, of toleration. He spoke for himself and two of his associates, but not for Maximin who was in power in Egypt and Syria. Gibbon's eighteenth-century version, Extract A, catches the imperial flavour.

Maximin indeed at first allowed a considerable relaxation of the persecution. The Christian prisoners were released and their friends demonstrated. But he soon followed this up by an attempt to organize the worship of the many pagan gods in a single unitary system—to set up an Established (pagan) Church in opposition to the organized Christian Church. He supported this with forged anti-Christian documents, and with a renewal of persecution. This is illustrated by the second of these extracts.

But in the end, as he was dying, he too gave way. He extended toleration to Christians in his part of the empire, put the blame for what had happened on subordinate officials, and restored confiscated property. The third extract, taken from his decree, contains the first use of the word 'kyriakon' (kirk, church) for the building in which Christians worship—the Lord's house is its meaning. Before this 'ekklesia' was used to cover both church and people.

Sources: A: Lactantius, *On the Deaths of the Persecutors* 100, 34; B and C: Eusebius, *Church History* 9, 4 and 5; 9, 10.

A.   GALERIUS GRANTS TOLERATION   April 30, 311

Among the important cares which occupied our mind for the utility and preservation of the empire, it was our intention to correct and re-establish all things according to the ancient laws and public discipline of the Romans. We were particularly desirous of reclaiming, into the way of reason and nature, the

deluded Christians, who had renounced the religion and ceremonies instituted by their fathers, and, presumptuously despising
the practice of antiquity, had invented extravagant laws and
opinions, according to the dictates of their fancy, and had collected
a various society from the different provinces of our empire. The
edicts which we have published to enforce the worship of the
gods, having exposed many of the Christians to danger and distress,
many having suffered death, and many more, who still persist
in their impious folly, being left destitute of *any* public exercise
of religion, we are disposed to extend to those unhappy men the
effects of our wonted clemency.

We permit them, therefore, freely to profess their private
opinions, and to assemble in their conventicles without fear or
molestation, provided always that they preserve a due respect to
the established laws and government. By another rescript we shall
signify our intentions to the judges and magistrates; and we hope
that our indulgence will engage the Christians to offer up their
prayers to the Deity whom they adore, for our safety and prosperity, for their own, and for that of the republic.[1]

[1] 'Republic' here means State.

B.   MAXIMIN'S PAGAN CHURCH

Priests, if you please, were appointed in every town by Maximin
himself—priests of the images and high priests too—men of the
greatest note in political life and continuously in the public eye,
who were filled with enthusiasm for the gods they served. The
absurd superstition of the emperor, in short, was inducing all
under him, rulers and ruled alike, to seek his favour by an all-out
attack on us ... They actually forged Memoranda of Pilate and
our Saviour, full of every kind of blasphemy against Christ. These
with the approval of their superior, they sent to every district
under his command, announcing in edicts that they were to be
publicly displayed in every place, whether hamlet or city, for all
to see, and that they should be given to children by their teachers
instead of lessons, to study and learn by heart.

C.   REBUILDING THE KIRK

The Emperor Caesar Gaius Valerius Maximinus, Germanicus
Sarmaticus, Pius Felix Invictus Augustus . . . we have decreed . . .
that everyone who chooses to follow this sect and form of worship may, in accordance with this our indulgence and in fulfilment
of his own choice and desire, participate in such acts of worship
as he was accustomed and wishful to practise. Permission to build
the 'Lord's houses' (kirks), as they call them, has also been
accorded. . . .

CHAPTER NINE

THE EMPIRE BECOMES CHRISTIAN

The co-emperor Constantius, who had been only a reluctant and mild persecutor, died at York on his return from a war in Scotland. He was succeeded by his son, Constantine, who was with him. That was in 306. He continued his father's policy of toleration and in 312 he went further and aligned himself definitely with the Christians. But the imperial power was still divided between co-emperors and it was by no means certain that Constantine would prevail and with him Christianity. But in 323 Constantine fought his last battle, took Byzantium by siege, defeated his co-emperor just across the Bosphorus where Scutari now stands, and reigned alone. The Christian empire had begun. All government influence was put behind the new imperial faith, but persecution was not put into reverse. There was toleration for the worshippers of the old gods.

During his reign the first general council of the church was held, and a creed was agreed and promulgated under imperial supervision and consent. A great period of church building began. Special reverence was paid to the holy places in Jerusalem and Bethlehem. The age of pilgrimages had begun.

What is one to make of Constantine himself? One thing is certain. He thoroughly deserves his title of 'the Great'. Was he the Christian hero whom Eusebius painted? Was he, as Jacob Burckhardt thought, 'the murderous egoist who possessed the great merit of having conceived of Christianity as a world power and of having acted accordingly?' (*The Age of Constantine the Great.*) See Plate 16.

43. IN THIS SIGN HE CONQUERED 312

The critical year for Constantine's relation to Christianity was 312. He was engaged in civil war with his co-emperor, Maxentius. Their armies met outside Rome. Constantine's troops apparently already bore the Chi-Rho sign on their shields—to the Christians among them the initial letters of the word 'Christ' in which they could see the Cross suggested. Constantine's troops were victorious and Maxentius was drowned in the Tiber as he fled towards Rome. In the city Constantine erected his statue with his 'labarum', the standard with the Chi-Rho sign, in his hand. Constantine had committed himself to the Christian cause. He won enthusiastic, disciplined, invaluable support. But he was careful to provide an inter-faith form of worship for his troops to use on Sundays, which he made festival days. It was a form which soldier followers of Mithras could use without objection. (Extract B.)

Years later Constantine told bishop Eusebius a story of two visions which he swore he had seen before the battle of the Milvian Bridge. Eusebius included them in the life he wrote of his master. His account (Extract A) is first-rate evidence of what Constantine by then wanted people to believe. The hold which it has had ever since on the Christian imagination is proof of how sound Constantine's instinct was. But the passage in Eusebius is much less good evidence for what actually happened in 312.

Sources: A and B: Eusebius, *Life of Constantine*.

A.   CONSTANTINE'S VISION

When Constantine realized that he was in need of some better help beyond troops of soldiers, because of the wicked and magical enchantments so assiduously practised by the tyrant (Maxentius), he tried to win God to his side. Arms and soldiers took second place in his plan, and he believed divine assistance would render him unconquered and invincible.

Accordingly he began to pray earnestly that God would make himself known to him and in this immediate need stretch out the right hand of help. While he was thus engaged there appeared to him a wonderful sign sent by God. Now to hear this at second hand must tax believing, but I can assure you that the victorious emperor told it to the author of this history, long after, when he was honoured with his acquaintance and companionship. He told me these things and confirmed them with a sacred oath, in the light of which one cannot but believe his account, especially since subsequent events have borne out its truth.

He said that early in the afternoon, when the sun was past its zenith, he saw in the sky the trophy of a cross, composed of light, standing above the sun. He swore that he saw it with his own eyes, and that it bore this inscription:

'By this you shall conquer!'

He and his whole army—for he was out on some expedition—likewise witnesses to the miracle, were utterly amazed.

He admitted that he began to doubt within himself concerning the meaning of this apparition. He was still pondering in his mind when night fell. While he slept the Christ of God appeared with the same sign that he had been shown in the sky, and he commanded him to have a standard made in the same form, and to use it as a protection in battle.

He rose very early and revealed all this to his friends. Then he collected together craftsmen in gold and precious stones and, sitting down in the middle, painted as it were a picture in words of the sign that he had seen, ordering its likeness to be made in gold and precious stones. This we remember having seen ourselves more than once.

It was composed after this manner. A long spear, plated with gold, was given a transverse arm to make the form of a cross. At the top of the spear was fixed a crown of gold and precious stones. On this was placed the badge of our salvation, that is to say, the first two letters of the name Christ, Chi and Rho, the X intersecting the P in the middle.[1] Afterwards the emperor used to wear this monogram on his helmet. From the crossbar on the spear was suspended a kind of pennant of purple cloth, embroidered with precious stones of dazzling brilliance, and so richly interwoven with gold thread that the general effect was one of indescribable beauty. This pennant was square in form. The upright staff, of which the greater length by far was below the crossbar, had, just below that trophy of the cross and at the top of the embroidered pennant, a half-length portrait in gold of the divinely favoured emperor and his children.

The emperor never failed to use this saving sign as a defence against any adverse or hostile army, and commanded that replicas of the trophy should be carried at the head of all his armies.

At last Constantine entered Rome in triumph. The Senate, nobility, the entire Roman population came out like prisoners released from jail, smiling and acclaiming him from the bottom

---

[1] Chi is written X in Greek, P is Rho. See Plate 17.

of their hearts with unbounded joy. This great crowd of men, women, children, and slaves welcomed him as liberator, the author and preserver of better times, with an unbelievable clamour which no one was able to restrain. Acclamation and praise, however, did not go to his head, but he preserved his new-found piety in God as one born thereto. On the contrary, he fully acknowledged himself to have been aided by divine assistance, and humbly paid thanks to the true author of victory.

By many means, especially by public inscriptions, he made this sign of our salvation known to all men, setting it up as the trophy that subdued enemies in the midst of the imperial city. In letters that can never fade he had that saving sign proclaimed as the protection of the Roman empire and of the whole world. Then he ordered a long spear in the form of the Cross to be placed in the hand of his statue which stands in the most important place in the city, and had this inscription added beneath in Latin:

'By this saving sign, which is the token of true strength, I have kept your city free from the yoke of tyrannical oppression. To the free Roman Senate and people I confirm their former rank of nobility and I restore their ancient splendour.'

B.   CHURCH PARADE

Constantine taught all armies zealously to honour the Lord's Day, which is also called the day of light and of the sun. . . . The pagans too were required to go forth into an open field on Sunday, and together to raise their hands, and recite a prayer learned by heart to God as giver of all victory: 'Thee alone we acknowledge as God and King, Thee we invoke as our helper. From Thee we have obtained our victories, through Thee conquered our enemies. Thee we thank for past favours, from Thee we hope for future favours. Thee we all beseech, and we pray Thee that Thou long preserve to us unharmed and victorious our Emperor Constantine and his God-loving sons.'

44. THE COUNCIL OF NICAEA   325

No sooner was Constantine sole emperor than he was asked, or thought it wise, to call a general council of the whole Church—the first ever held unless one were to reckon the council or consultation at Jerusalem described in Acts 15. The first extract is from the *Life of Constantine* by bishop Eusebius. It underlines the importance attached by the emperor to the council, and the importance of the part he played. Remember that Constantine, though he had thrown in his lot for good with the Christians, was not yet baptized. Like many adult converts he preferred to delay baptism until death was near since baptism remits all sins but cannot be repeated.

Unlike some of his successors Constantine was not himself excited about theological niceties. But he was concerned to see that the empire had the support of a united Church, and not one divided by bitter controversies which in the climate of the times could hardly fail to have political consequences. The council was called to deal with the greatest of these disputes—that about the relation of Jesus to God the Father. In what sense was he God? The leaders of the two sides, Arius and Athanasius, both came from Alexandria. Arius did not deny that the Son was God: 'His point was that as any son must be posterior to his father, so the name Son, applied to our Lord, indicated that he was not like the Father from all eternity; but that there was—he would not say *a time* when the Son was not, for he owned him to be anterior to all time—but at least there *was* when the Son was not.'[1]

Most of the bishops thought Arius was wrong. Some wanted a solution which would avoid a split. Many thought that at all costs the council must define the doctrine in such a way that it ruled Arius out. This was the view of Athanasius, who in 325 was only a deacon but went to the council as secretary to the bishop of Alexandria. Their difficulty was to find a term which the Arians could not accept. Athanasius recorded how the Arians were overheard consulting with each other and then agreeing that they could accept each successively proposed title of honour for the Son because they could find a text of Scripture in which it was also used of a creature. But at last the Athanasian party found what they were looking for in 'homoousion' ('of one substance') which leading Arians had already rejected. So it came about that the creed which bishop Eusebius suggested, that of his own church at Caesarea, was rejected because the Arians might have accepted it although it said nothing that was not orthodox.

The council produced a creed, given in the second extract, and Constantine backed it with all his influence. But it did not do what

[1] Salmon, *The Infallibility of the Church*. Note reference on p. 148.

Constantine wanted. The Church was no nearer peace. The creed of 325 was, for the orthodox, only one victory in a campaign in which there were to be many battles, some of them lost.

Sources: A: Eusebius, Life of Constantine 3; 6, 7, 10; B: Eusebius, Epistle I; C: Socrates, Church History I. 9.

A.   THE EMPEROR AND THE COUNCIL

(The emperor Constantine) convoked a general council, and invited the speedy attendance of bishops from all quarters... Nor was this merely the issuing of a bare command, but the emperor's goodwill contributed much to its being carried into effect: for he allowed some the use of the public means of conveyance, while he afforded to others an ample supply of horses for their transport. The place, too, selected for the synod, the city of Nicaea in Bithynia (named from 'victory'), was appropriate to the occasion. As soon as the imperial injunction was generally made known, all with the utmost willingness hastened thither, as though they would outstrip one another in a race; for they were impelled by the anticipation of a happy result to the conference, by the hope of enjoying present peace, and the desire of beholding something new and strange in the person of so admirable an emperor. ...

In effect, the most distinguished of God's ministers from all the churches which abounded in Europe, Libya, and Asia were here assembled. And a single house of prayer, as though divinely enlarged, sufficed to contain at once Syrians and Cilicians, Phoenicians and Arabians, delegates from Palestine and others from Egypt; Thebans and Libyans, with those who came from the region of Mesopotamia. A Persian bishop too was present at this conference, nor was even a Scythian found wanting to the number. Pontus, Galatia, and Pamphylia, Cappadocia, Asia and Phrygia, furnished their most distinguished prelates; while those who dwelt in the remotest districts of Thrace and Macedonia, of Achaia and Epirus, were notwithstanding in attendance. Even from Spain itself, one whose fame was widely spread took his seat as an individual in the great assembly. ...

Now when the appointed day arrived on which the council met for the final solution of the questions in dispute, each member was present for this in the central building of the palace, which appeared to exceed the rest in magnitude. On each side of the interior of this were many seats disposed in order, which were occupied by those who had been invited to attend, according to their rank. As soon, then, as the whole assembly had seated themselves with becoming orderliness, a general silence prevailed, in expectation of the emperor's arrival. And, first of all, three of his immediate family entered in succession, then others also preceded his approach, not of the soldiers or guards who usually accompanied him, but only friends in the faith. And now, all rising at the signal which indicated the emperor's entrance, at last he himself proceeded through the midst of the assembly, like some heavenly messenger of God, clothed in raiment which glittered as it were with rays of light, reflecting the glowing radiance of a purple robe, and adorned with the brilliant splendour of gold and precious stones. Such was the external appearance of his person; and with regard to his mind, it was evident that he was distinguished by piety and godly fear. This was indicated by his downcast eyes, the blush on his countenance and his gait. For the rest of his personal excellences, he surpassed all present in height of stature and beauty of form, as well as in majestic dignity of mien, and invincible strength and vigour. All these graces, united to a suavity of manner, and a serenity becoming his imperial station, declared the excellence of his mental qualities to be above all praise. As soon as he had advanced to the upper end of the seats, at first he remained standing, and when a low chair of wrought gold had been set for him, he waited until the bishops had beckoned to him, and then sat down, and after him the whole assembly did the same.

B.   THE NICENE CREED AS AGREED AT THE COUNCIL

We believe in One God, the Father, Almighty, Maker of all things visible and invisible.

And in One Lord Jesus Christ, the Son of God, begotten of the Father, Only-begotten, that is, from the essence of the Father; God from God, Light from Light, Very God from Very God, begotten not made, of one substance with the Father, by whom all things were made, both things in heaven and things in earth;

who for us men and for our salvation came down and was made flesh, was made man, suffered, and rose again the third day, ascended into heaven, and cometh to judge quick and dead.

And in the Holy Ghost.

C.   THE SYNODAL LETTER

To the Church of the Alexandrians, holy, by the grace of God, and great, and to our beloved brethren throughout Egypt, Libya, and Pentapolis, the bishops assembled at Nicaea, constituting the great and holy synod, send greeting in the Lord.

Since, by the grace of God, a great and holy synod has been convened at Nicaea, our most God-beloved sovereign Constantine having summoned us out of various cities and provinces, it seemed to us essential to send you a letter from the sacred synod, that you may know what was discussed, what closely examined, and what finally decided and decreed.

Firstly then, the impiety and illegality of Arius and his followers were examined in the presence of our most God-beloved sovereign Constantine; and it was unanimously decided that his impious opinion should be anathematized with all the blasphemous expressions he has uttered in affirming that 'the Son of God is from nothing' and 'there *was* when he was not'; saying also that the Son of God, being possessed of free-will, is capable of evil and good, and calling him a creature and a work. All these assertions have been anathematized by the holy synod, which could scarcely endure to hear such impious, or rather insensate opinions and such abominable blasphemies.

45. CONSTANTINE, HELENA, AND THE HOLY PLACES   *c.* 326

Now that the empire was Christian it was natural that attention and devotion should turn to Jerusalem. Two hundred years earlier Rome had tried to rob the city of all religious significance to Jews and, incidentally, to Christians. The old city was destroyed; a new Roman city—Aelia Capitolina—took its place. A temple of Venus rose where Jesus was crucified. It was all but inevitable that Constantine should honour what his predecessors had dishonoured. Eusebius in his life of Constantine tells the story of how he and his mother, Helena, built and endowed churches which made Jerusalem for the first time the goal of Christian pilgrims from all over the empire. See Plates 14B: 18–20.

In the Book of Common Prayer May 3 is marked in the calendar as the feast of The Invention of the Cross ('invention' here means finding). This refers to the legend that Helena on her visit to Jerusalem found the remains of the cross on which Jesus was crucified. This story first appears fifty years after Helena's visit. If she had found it, Eusebius would certainly have known and recorded it. There is one other reference to the cross in the Prayer Book calendar. September 14 is Holy Cross Day. In the eastern church this festival is associated with the vision of Constantine; in the west it is connected with the recovery in 629 by the emperor Heraclius of a relic of the Cross which had been carried off from Jerusalem by the Persian king.

Source: Eusebius, *Life of Constantine* III, 25–8, 33, 35–6, 42–3; IV, 45.

After these things, the pious emperor addressed himself to another work truly worthy of record, in the province of Palestine. What then was this work? He judged it incumbent on him to render the blessed locality of our Saviour's resurrection an object of attraction and veneration to all. . . .

This sacred cave . . . certain impious and godless persons had thought to remove entirely from the eyes of men, supposing in their folly that they thus should be able effectually to obscure the truth. Accordingly they brought a quantity of earth from a distance with much labour, and covered the entire spot. . . . Then . . . they prepared on this foundation a truly dreadful sepulchre of souls, by building a gloomy shrine of lifeless idols to the impure spirit whom they call Venus. . . . As soon as his commands were issued, these engines of deceit were cast down from their proud eminence to the very ground, and the dwelling-places of error, with the statues and the evil spirits which they represented, were overthrown and utterly destroyed.

. . . He gave further orders that the materials of what was thus destroyed, both stone and timber, should be removed and thrown as far from the spot as possible . . . once more, fired with holy ardour, he directed that the ground itself should be dug up to a considerable depth, and the soil which had been polluted by the foul impurities of demon worship transported to a far distant place.

. . . As soon as the original surface of the ground beneath the covering of earth appeared, immediately, and contrary to all expectation, the venerable and hallowed monument of our Saviour's resurrection was discovered. . . .

Accordingly, on the very spot which witnessed the Saviour's sufferings, a new Jerusalem was constructed, over against the one so celebrated of old, which, since the foul stain of guilt brought upon it by the murder of the Lord, had experienced the last extremity of desolation, the effect of Divine judgment on its impious people. It was opposite this city that the emperor now began to rear a monument to the Saviour's victory over death, with rich and lavish magnificence. And it may be that this was that second, and new, Jerusalem spoken of in the predictions of the prophets. . . . First of all, then, he adorned the sacred cave itself, as the chief part of the whole work, and the hallowed monument at which the angel radiant with light had once declared to all that regeneration was first manifested in the Saviour's person.

The next object of his attention was a space of ground of great extent, and open to the pure air of heaven. This he adorned with a pavement of finely polished stone, and enclosed it on three sides with porticos of great length.

For at the side opposite to the cave, which was the eastern side, the church itself was erected; a noble work rising to a vast height, and of great extent both in length and breadth. The interior of this structure was floored with marble slabs of various colours; while the external surface of the walls, which shone with polished stones exactly fitted together, exhibited a degree of splendour in no respect inferior to that of marble. With regard to the roof, it was covered outside with lead as a protection against the rains of winter. But the inner part of the roof, which was finished with sculptured panel work, extended in a series of connected compartments like a vast sea over the whole church; and, being overlaid with the purest gold, caused the entire building to glitter as it were with rays of light.

[The empress Helena] having resolved to discharge the duties of pious devotion to God, the King of kings, and feeling it incumbent on her to render thanksgivings with prayers on behalf both of her own son, now so mighty an emperor, and of his sons, her own grandchildren, the divinely favoured Caesars, though now advanced in years, yet gifted with no common degree of wisdom, had hastened with youthful alacrity to survey this venerable land. As soon, then, as she had rendered due reverence to the ground which the Saviour's feet had trodden. . . . without delay she dedicated two churches to the God whom she adored, one at the grotto which had been the scene of the Saviour's birth; the other on the mount of his ascension. For he who was 'God with us' had submitted to be born even in a cave of the earth, and the place of his nativity was called Bethlehem by the Hebrews. Accordingly the pious empress honoured with rare memorials the scene of her travail who bore this heavenly child, and beautified the sacred cave with all possible splendour. The emperor himself soon after testified his reverence for the spot by princely offerings, and added to his mother's magnificence by costly presents of silver and gold, and embroidered hangings. And farther, the mother of the emperor raised a stately structure on the Mount of Olives also in memory of his ascent to heaven who is the Saviour of mankind, erecting a sacred church and temple on the very summit of the mount. . . . And here also the emperor testified his reverence for the King of kings by diverse and costly offerings.

[When the church of the Holy Sepulchre was ready for consecration Constantine called a synod of bishops from all over the empire to Jerusalem.] Meantime the festival derived additional lustre both from the prayers and discourses of the ministers of God, some of whom extolled the pious emperor's willing devotion to the Saviour of mankind, and dilated on the magnificence of the edifice which he had raised to his memory. Others afforded, as it were, an intellectual feast to the ears of all present, by public disquisitions on the sacred doctrines of our religion. Others interpreted passages of holy Scripture, and unfolded their hidden meaning; while such as were unequal to these efforts presented a bloodless sacrifice and mystical service to God in the prayers which they offered. . . . I myself, too, unworthy as I was of such a privilege, pronounced various public orations in honour of this solemnity, wherein I partly explained by a written description the details of the imperial edifice, and partly endeavoured to gather from the prophetic visions apt illustrations of the symbols it displayed.

46. A LADY PILGRIM AT JERUSALEM   *c.* 395

First identified as Silvia, this pilgrim is now believed to have been an abbess or nun, Etheria, 'from the furthest shore of the western sea, the Ocean', in north-west Spain. She went to Egypt and followed the accepted track of the Hebrews' exodus, finding a monastery at the foot of Mount Sinai and climbing to the chapel on the summit. She gives a full account of the services, held in and around Jerusalem from Epiphany to Whitsuntide, in the fine new churches built by Constantine and his mother Helena on the sacred sites, and from this our extracts are taken. See Plates 18–20.

The Anastasis was the basilica built over 'the cave' where Christ's body was laid; it is the Greek word for 'resurrection'. We find that the feast of the Nativity was held on January 6th (though observed in Rome on December 25th for more than half a century). Etheria's account gives us the first reference to the feast of the Purification (here February 14th), the use of incense, the children's procession of palms on Palm Sunday, and the many choir boys, singing the *Kyrie* (Lord, have mercy) at Vespers.

The daily offices described were Matins, Sext, Nones, and Vespers. The Ascension was commemorated at the church at Bethlehem. Note the orgy of sermons on Sundays, the division between the faithful (baptized Christians) and catechumens (those being instructed for baptism). A puzzle is the often repeated description of how each person 'came to the bishops' hand' as he filed out. Apparently he or she did not kiss the bishop's hand; an ancient Coptic custom suggests that the bishop touched the cheek of each one.

Source: Peregrinatio Silviae.

DAILY OFFICES: VESPERS

Now at the tenth hour . . . all the people assemble at the Anastasis . . . and all the candles and tapers are lit, making a very great light. Now the light is not introduced from outside, but it is brought from within the cave, that is from within the rails, where a lamp is always burning day and night; and the vesper psalms and antiphons are said, lasting for a considerable time. Then the bishop is summoned, and he comes and takes a raised seat, and likewise the priests sit in their proper places, and hymns and antiphons are said.[1]

And when all these have been recited according to custom, the bishop rises and stands before the rails . . . and one of the deacons makes the customary commemoration of individuals one by one. And as the deacon pronounces each name the many little boys who are always standing by answer with countless voices, *Kyrie eleison*, or as we say, *Miserere Domine*.

And when the deacon has finished all that he has to say, first the bishop says a prayer for all, then they all pray, both the faithful and catechumens together. Again the deacon raises his voice, bidding each catechumen to bow his head where he stands, and the bishop stands and says the blessing over the catechumens. Again prayer is made and again the deacon bids the faithful, each where he stands, to bow the head, and the bishop likewise blesses the faithful. Thus the dismissal takes place at the Anastasis, and one by one all draw near to the bishop's hand.

SUNDAY OFFICES: VIGIL

On the Lord's Day, the whole multitude assembles before cock-crow, in as great numbers as the place can hold, as at Easter, in the basilica which is near the Anastasis, but outside the doors, where lights are hanging for the purpose. And for fear that they should not be there at cockcrow, they come beforehand and sit down there. Hymns as well as antiphons are said, and prayers are made between the several hymns and antiphons; for at the vigils there are always both priests and deacons ready there for the assembling of the multitude, the custom being that the holy places are not opened before cockcrow.

Now as soon as the first cock has crowed, the bishop arrives and enters the cave at the Anastasis; all the doors are opened and the whole multitude enters the Anastasis, where countless lights are already burning. And when the people have entered, one of the

---

[1] Antiphons: sung responses such as, *O Lord open thou our lips: And our mouth shall show forth thy praise*. Etheria always uses the word 'said' (dicitur) instead of 'sung', for hymns, psalms, and antiphons.

priests says a psalm to which all respond, and afterwards prayer is made; then one of the deacons says a psalm and prayer is again made, a third psalm is said by one of the clergy, prayer is made for the third time and there is a commemoration of all.

After these three psalms and three prayers are ended, lo! censers are brought into the cave of the Anastasis so that the whole basilica of the Anastasis is filled with odours. And then the bishop, standing within the rails, takes the book of the Gospel, and proceeding to the door, himself reads the story of the Resurrection of the Lord. And when the reading is begun, there is so great a moaning and groaning among all, with so many tears, that the hardest of hearts might be moved to tears for that the Lord had borne such things for us.

After the reading of the Gospel, the bishop goes out, and is accompanied to the Cross by all the people with hymns, where again a psalm is said and prayer is made, after which he blesses the faithful and the dismissal takes place; and as he comes out all approach to his hand. And forthwith the bishop betakes himself to his house, and from that hour all the monks return to the Anastasis, where psalms and antiphons, with prayer after each psalm or antiphon, are said until daylight; the priests and deacons also keep watch in turn daily at the Anastasis with the people, but of the lay people, whether men or women, those who are so minded remain in the place until daybreak, and those who are not return to their houses and betake themselves to sleep.

MORNING SERVICE

Now at daybreak because it is the Lord's Day every one proceeds to the greater church, built by Constantine, which is situated in Golgotha behind the Cross, where all things are done which are customary everywhere on the Lord's Day. But the custom here is that of all the priests who take their seats, as many as are willing, preach, and after them all the bishop preaches, and these sermons are always on the Lord's Day, in order that the people may always be instructed in the Scriptures and in the love of God. The delivery of these sermons greatly delays the dismissal from the church, so that the dismissal does (not) take place before the fourth or perhaps the fifth hour.

PALM SUNDAY

At the seventh hour all the people and the bishop with them go up to the Mount of Olives, that is, to the church Eleona, where hymns and antiphons suitable to the day and place are said, and lessons similarly. And when the ninth hour approaches they go up with hymns to the Imbomon whence the Lord ascended into heaven, and there they sit down, for all are always told to sit when the bishop is present; the deacons alone stand. Hymns and antiphons suitable to the day are said, interspersed with readings and prayers.

And as the eleventh hour approaches, that passage from the gospel is read, where the children, carrying branches and palms, met the Lord, saying: *'Blessed is he that cometh in the name of the Lord'*; and the bishop immediately rises and all the people with him, and they all go on foot from the top of the Mount of Olives, all going before him with hymns and antiphons, answering one another: *'Blessed is he that cometh in the name of the Lord'*.

And all the children of the neighbourhood, even those who are too young to walk, are carried by their parents on their shoulders, all of them bearing branches, some of palms and some of olives; and thus the bishop is escorted as the Lord was of old. For all, even those of rank, both matrons and men, accompany the bishop all the way on foot in this manner, making these responses, from the top of the mount to the city, and thence through the whole city to the Anastasis, going very slowly lest the people should be wearied; and thus they arrive at the Anastasis at a late hour. [Then Vespers follow.]

GOOD FRIDAY: VENERATION OF THE CROSS

Then a chair is placed for the bishop in Golgotha behind the Cross, which is now standing; the bishop duly takes his seat in the chair, and a table covered with a linen cloth is placed before him; the deacons stand round the table, and a silver-gilt casket is brought, in which is the holy wood of the Cross. The casket is opened and (the wood) is taken out, and both the wood of the Cross and the title (John 19, 19. A.V.) are placed upon the table.

Now when it has been put upon the table, the bishop, as he sits, holds the extremities of the sacred wood firmly in his hands, while the deacons who stand around guard it. It is guarded thus because the custom is that the people, both faithful and catechumens, come one by one and, bowing down at the table, kiss the sacred wood and pass through. And because, I know not when, someone is said to have bitten off and stolen a portion of the sacred wood, it is thus guarded by the deacons . . .

And as all the people pass by one by one, all bowing themselves, they touch the Cross and the title, first with their foreheads and then with their eyes; then they kiss the Cross and pass through, but none lays his hand upon it to touch it.

STATION BEFORE THE CROSS: THE THREE HOURS

And when the sixth hour has come, they go before the Cross, whether it be in rain or in heat, the place being open to the air, as it were, a court of great size and of some beauty between the Cross and the Anastasis; here all the people assemble in such great numbers that there is no thoroughfare. The chair is placed for the bishop before the Cross, and from the sixth to the ninth hour nothing else is done but the reading of lessons, which are read thus: first from the psalms wherever the Passion is spoken of, then from the Apostles, either from the Epistles or from their Acts, wherever they have spoken of the Lord's Passion; then the passages from the Gospels, where he suffered, are read. Then the readings from the prophets where they foretold that the Lord should suffer, then from the Gospels where he mentions his Passion.

Thus from the sixth to the ninth hours the lessons are so read and the hymns said, that it may be shown to all the people . . . that nothing was done which had not been foretold, and that nothing was foretold which was not wholly fulfilled. Prayers also suitable to the day are interspersed throughout. The emotion shown and the mourning by all the people at every lesson and prayer is wonderful; for there is none, either great or small, who, on that day during those three hours, does not lament more than can be conceived that the Lord had suffered those things for us.

Afterwards, at the beginning of the ninth hour, there is read that passage from the gospel according to John where he gave up the ghost. This read, prayer and dismissal follow.

Roman Catacomb inscriptions

1. '*Demetris and Leontia to darling Siricia the well deserving.*
Remember Jesus O Lord our child'.

2. '*Fish of the Living*'.

CHAPTER TEN

MEN OF FAITH; AND POWER POLITICS

'We must not forget that alongside a Church rapidly disintegrating in victory, there was also a religion.' So Burckhardt wrote in his study of the age of Constantine. That religion found its most characteristic expression in the withdrawal from ordinary life of innumerable men and women who for a time or a lifetime went out into the desert to give themselves completely to God. It was a positive reaction to the rich but disintegrating world of the Roman State. It was not negative or escapist. For, if the hermits and monks withdrew, they could also emerge. They were perhaps the most vital and influential force in the fourth century. Men whose souls are well formed have power though they do not seek it.

But there was also the world of the clerical diplomats, rushing from council to council, arguing over the wording of documents as if the bottom would fall out of their very material world if the other side won—as indeed it did fall out for each in turn when first one side and then the other was ejected from their churches and their endowments. But all of them had one eye on the desert. For many it was a wistful eye.

And then there were the politicians—the emperors and their government officials. They had three pre-occupations. First, and always, there was the preservation of the State—there was constant frontier trouble, and the frontier was not far away. Secondly, and usually, there was the preservation of the emperor's own life from rivals. Political life was a struggle, as it always is, but in those days defeat meant death. Thirdly, and surprisingly, there is the intellectual and emotional involvement of the emperors who followed Constantine in the theological issues. They took a hand themselves not only in the interests of the State, as Constantine had done, but because it mattered to them who won.

The extracts in this chapter illustrate these interweaving forces as they are found up to the end of the first Council of Constantinople, in the second year of the reign of Theodosius (381).

47. THE DESERT EXTREMISTS   c. 330–430

Even before the persecution under Diocletian some dauntless men

turned their backs on the world and took to the desert in this spirit:
'Let no one who hath renounced the world think that he hath given
up some great thing ... the whole earth set against heaven's infinite
is scant and poor.' Antony, the greatest of them, took to the desert
as early as 285 and lived there until his death in 356. The sentence just
quoted is from his life by his friend Athanasius. The movement gained
impetus as the growing worldliness of the Church after persecution was
over led thousands of unsatisfied idealists to follow his example. For 150
years the desert was a magnet to Christians.

In this sense the desert was any place where a man could be alone
with his soul and God. Most commonly it was either the desert of the
Thebaid in Upper Egypt, the Libyan desert west of the Nile delta, or
the Gaza desert in Palestine. But remote islands, formerly used only as
penal settlements, also attracted solitaries. Sometimes the solitaries
could be absolutely alone; more often they lived in widely scattered
collections of individual cells—in some settlements they were just in
sight of one another's camp fires; in others they were further apart.
Inevitably a rough rule of life was established. The monk in the original
sense (the Greek 'monos' means 'alone') had become something like the
monk in the familiar sense. See Plate 23.

What is to be said about their ascetic practices? Lecky, the nineteenth-
century rationalist historian, was disgusted by 'the hideous, distorted
and emaciated maniac, without knowledge, without patriotism, without natural affection, spending his life in a long routine of useless and
atrocious self-torture, and quailing before the ghastly phantoms of
his delirious brain'. No doubt some of their contemporaries would
have agreed—Eusebius has virtually nothing to say about them, which
suggests that he disapproved. But more of their Christian contemporaries looked on them as 'athletes of God', men in training for a
purpose, not masochists.

The first extract is from a letter of Basil, whose writings fill much of
this chapter. The second extract is from *The Lausiac History* of bishop
Palladius who as a young man had spent several years in the desert.
Here he recounts his meeting, when he was a young man, with old
Isidore, the desert monk who accompanied Athanasius to Rome in
340. The third extract is from the *History of the Monks of Egypt* by
Rufinus, a North Italian from Aquileia, who visited Egypt and Palestine about 371, went out into the desert and met Macarius. The fourth
comes from the *Sayings of the Fathers*, the collection of anecdotes and
oracles which in Helen Waddell's judgment best enshrine the quality of

these men of God. The fifth comes from Jerome's *Life of Paul* the hermit. Jerome, too, had visited and for a time lived in the desert but this was a whole generation after the death of Paul which took place about 340. The close friendship between the Desert Fathers and wild animals is a constantly recurring theme. The sixth extract comes from a contemporary life of Simeon 'Stylites' by Theodoret, bishop of Cyrrhus in Syria, written about 435.

Sources: A: Basil, *Letters* 223; B: Palladius, *The Lausiac History* 100, 1; C: Rufinus, *History of the Monks of Egypt* 29; D: *Sayings of the Fathers* 9, 4; E: Jerome, *Life of Paul*; F: Theodoret, *Religious History* 26.

A.   BASIL VISITS THE DESERTS   *c.* 360

Having read the gospel, and having perceived therein that the greatest incentive to perfection is the selling of one's goods and the sharing of them with the needy of the brethren, and the being entirely without thought of this life, and that the soul should have no sympathetic concern with the things of this world, I prayed that I might find someone of the brethren who had taken this way of life, so as to traverse with him his life's brief flood.

And indeed I found many men in Alexandria, and many throughout the rest of Egypt, and others in Palestine, and in Coele-Syria and Mesopotamia, at whose continence in living I marvelled, and I marvelled at their steadfastness in sufferings, I was amazed at their vigour in prayers, at how they gained the mastery over sleep, being bowed down by no necessity of nature, ever preserving exalted and unshackled the purpose of their soul, in hunger and thirst, in cold and nakedness, not concerning themselves with the body, nor deigning to waste a thought upon it, but as if passing their lives in alien flesh, they showed in deed what it is to sojourn here below, and what to have citizenship in heaven. Having marvelled at all this and deemed the lives of these men blessed, because by deed they show that they bear about in their body the mortification[1] of Jesus, I prayed that I myself also, in so far as was attainable by me, might be an imitator of these men.

---

[1] A Pauline term. See Col. 3, 5. A.V.

B.   PALLADIUS MEETS THE MONK ISIDORE   *c.* 370

The first time that I set foot in the city of the Alexandrians, in the second consulate of the great Emperor Theodosius, who now lives with the angels because of his faith in Christ, I met in the city a wonderful man, distinguished in every respect, both as regards character and knowledge, Isidore the priest, hospitaller of the Church of Alexandria. He was said to have fought successfully his first youthful contests in the desert, and I actually saw his cell in the mountain of Nitria. But when I met him, he was an old man seventy years of age, who lived another fifteen years and then died in peace. I visited him as a young man and besought that I might be trained in the solitary life, since I was in the full vigour of my age and needed, not discourse, but bodily hardships. Like a good tamer of colts he led me out from the city to the so-called Solitudes five miles away (and handed me over to Dorotheus).

Up to the very end of his life he wore no linen except a head-band, never had a bath, nor partook of meat. His slender frame was so well-knit by grace that all who did not know his manner of life expected that he lived in luxury. Time would fail me if I were to tell in detail the virtues of his soul. He was so benevolent and peaceable that even his enemies the unbelievers themselves reverenced his shadow because of his exceeding kindliness.

So great a knowledge had he of the holy scriptures and the divine precepts that even at the very meals of the brethren he would have periods of absent-mindedness and remain silent. And being urged to tell the details of his ecstasy he would say: 'I went away in thought on a journey, seized by contemplation.' For my part I often knew him weep at table, and when I asked the cause of the tears I heard him say: 'I shrink from partaking of irrational food, being myself rational and destined to live in a paradise of delight owing to the power given us by Christ.'

He became known to all the Senate at Rome and to the wives of the nobles, when he paid his first visit in company with Athanasius the bishop, and on a second occasion with Demetrius the bishop; a man of great wealth and extensive property, he wrote no will when he came to die, and left neither money nor goods to his sisters, who were virgins. But he commended them to Christ, saying: 'He that created you will provide for your life, as he has done for me.'

C.   MACARIUS AND THE BUNCH OF GRAPES   c. 370

He was a lover beyond all other men of the desert, and had explored its ultimate and inaccessible wastes . . . The place in which the holy Macarius lived was called Scete. It is set in a vast desert, a day and a night's journey from the monasteries on Nitria, and the way is to be found or shown by no track and no landmarks of earth, but one journeys by the signs and courses of the stars. Water is hard to find, and when it is found it is of a dire odour and as it might be bituminous yet inoffensive in taste. Here therefore are men made perfect in holiness (for so terrible a post could be endured by none save those of austere resolve and supreme constancy), yet their chief concern is the love which they show to one another and towards such as by chance reach that spot.

They tell that once a brother brought a bunch of grapes to the holy Macarius: but he who for love's sake thought not on his own things but on the things of others, carried it to another brother, who seemed more feeble. And the sick man gave thanks to God for the kindness of his brother, but he too thinking more of his neighbour than of himself, brought it to another, and he again to another, and so that same bunch of grapes was carried round all the cells, scattered as they were far over the desert, and no one knowing who first had sent it, it was brought at last to the first giver. But the holy Macarius gave thanks that he had seen in the brethren such abstinence and such loving-kindness and did himself reach after still sterner discipline of the life of the spirit.

D.   MOSES AND THE RUNNING SAND

Once a brother in Scete was found guilty, and the older brethren came in assembly and sent to the abbot Moses, asking him to come: but he would not. Then the priest sent to him, saying, 'Come: for the assembly of the brethren awaits thee.' And he rose up and came. But taking with him a very old basket, he filled it with sand

and carried it behind him. And they went out to meet him, asking, 'Father, what is this?' And the old man said to them, 'My sins are running behind me and I do not see them, and I am come to-day to judge the sins of another man.' And they heard him, and said naught to the brother, but forgave him.

E.   PAUL, ANTONY AND THE LIONS   *c.* 340

Paul of Thebes, the first hermit, had just died; but Antony had no spade to dig a grave:

'But even as he pondered, behold two lions came coursing, their manes flying, from the inner desert, and made towards him. At sight of them, he was at first in dread: then, turning his mind to God, he waited undismayed, as though he looked on doves. They came straight to the body of the holy dead, and halted by it wagging their tails, then couched themselves at his feet, roaring mightily; and Antony well knew they were lamenting him, as best they could. Then going a little way off, they began to scratch up the ground with their paws, vying with one another in throwing up the sand, till they had dug a grave roomy enough for a man: and thereupon, as though to ask the reward of their work, they came up to Antony, with drooping ears and downbent heads, licking his hands and his feet. He saw that they were begging for his blessing; and pouring out his soul in praise to Christ for that even the dumb beasts feel that there is God, "Lord," he said, "without whom no leaf lights from the tree, nor a single sparrow falls upon the ground, give unto these even as thou knowest."

'Then, motioning with his hand, he signed to them to depart. And when they had gone away, he bowed his aged shoulders under the weight of the holy body: and laying it in the grave, he gathered the earth above it . . .'

F.   SIMEON AND HIS PILLAR   *c.* 390–459

Always ambitious to increase his wealth of virtue, Simeon wanted to go for forty days without food like Moses and Elias. He therefore urged the venerable Bassus, who was then going round individual settlements supervising the priests, to seal up his door with clay, leaving nothing inside. Bassus warned him of the difficulty of the business and advised him not to think a violent death was a virtue, for this was the first and greatest crime.

'Well, Father,' said Simeon, 'set aside ten loaves and a jar of water for me, and if I see my body needs nourishment I will partake of them.'

It was done as he asked; the food was set out, and the clay was applied to the door. When the days were completed, the venerable Bassus, that man of God, came and removed the clay from the door, and going inside found the number of the loaves the same and the jar of water full. Simeon was prostrate on the ground unable to breathe, speak, or move. Bassus asked for a sponge, moistened and wiped his mouth, and applied the symbols of the divine mysteries. Strengthened by them in this way, he rose up and received a little nourishment in the form of lettuces and endive . . .

Having completed three years in that cell, he came to this celebrated mountain-top, and ordered a circular wall to be built. He had an iron chain made, thirty feet long, and fastened one end to an enormous rock, the other to his right foot, so that even if he wanted to he could not leave these limits. He then remained inside, continually contemplating heaven and physically forced to look at what was above the sky. For the iron fetter did not hinder the soaring of his mind.

But when the venerable Meletius (who had then been appointed bishop of the territory of Antioch, and who was a man shining with wisdom and judgment and rich in intelligence) said that the iron was superfluous, his mind being sufficient to apply the bonds of reason to his body, Simeon yielded and readily accepted the advice. He ordered a blacksmith to be summoned and told him to strike off the chain. A piece of leather had been fitted to his leg so that his flesh should not be injured by the iron, and this too, being sewn together, had to be severed. More than twenty enormous bugs were found to have made their home in it, and the venerable Meletius said he had actually seen this. I mention the remarkable power of endurance in him which this shows. For though he could easily have squashed the leather and killed them all, he resolutely endured the painful bites, welcoming the training in small matters as practice for greater trials.

As his fame spread everywhere, everyone flocked to him, not only those living near but also those living many days' journey away. Some brought men paralysed in body, some sought health for the sick, others wanted to become fathers and besought him to give them what nature had denied. When they had been granted their requests and enjoyed the benefits, they returned home joyfully, and as they proclaimed the blessings they had received, even more people came forward, seeking similar benefits.

In this way, as vast numbers come from all parts, and every road is like a river, one can see an ocean of people gathered in that spot, receiving the rivers from all directions. For not only the dwellers in our part of the world flock together, but Ishmaelites, Persians, Armenians, Iberians, Homerites,[1] and even remoter peoples. And many come from the furthest parts of the West, Spaniards, Britons, and Gauls who live between them. No need to speak of Italy! For they say that in the mighty city of Rome he has become so celebrated that in the doorways of all the workshops they have set up small images of him to provide in this way a kind of protection and safeguard for themselves.

Thus the visitors became innumerable, and they all tried to touch him and reap some blessing from those leather garments. It was firstly because he thought this excess of honour monstrous, and secondly because he found the labour involved troublesome, that he devised his station on the pillar. First he ordered one to be made 9 feet high, then 18 feet, afterwards 33, and now 54. For he desires to soar into heaven and to be quit of this life on earth . . .[2]

More than anything else I admire his endurance. Night and day he stands in full view of all. For having taken away the doors and broken down a considerable part of the enclosure, he is exposed to all as an unprecedented and remarkable spectacle, now standing for a long time, now making many prostrations and offering worship to God. Many of the bystanders count these acts of worship. Once a man with me counted 1,244, and then got

[1] From the Yemen.   [2] See Plate 24.

tired and stopped counting. When bending down he always touches his toes with his forehead. His stomach accepts nourishment only once a week, and not much then, and this makes it easy for his back to bend.

They say that, owing to his standing, a persistent sore has developed in one of his feet, and a great deal of matter continually oozes from it ... He was once forced to show this sore ... A man came from Rabaena, a good man, and one honoured in the service of Christ. Arriving at this mountain he said,

'Tell me in the name of truth which sways the race of men, are you a man or a bodiless essence?'

The bystanders were indignant at the question, but Simeon bade them all be quiet and said to the man,

'Why have you brought this enquiry?'

'Because I hear it everywhere noised abroad that you neither eat nor sleep, yet each of these things is natural to man; for no one having a human nature could live without nourishment and sleep.'

Simeon had a ladder put against the pillar and told him to come up. First he told him to feel his hands, then to put his hand inside his leather garment, and to inspect not only his feet but also the horrible sore. When he had seen and marvelled at the extent of the wound, and learnt from Simeon how he took food, the man descended, came to me and told me the whole story ...

In spite of the majesty of his achievements and the number of his miracles, he is as modest in his nature as if he were the lowest of men in reputation. In addition to his modesty he is excessively approachable, pleasant and agreeable. He answers every one who talks to him, workman, beggar, or peasant.

He received the gift of teaching from our generous Lord. Twice every day he gives exhortations, washing out the ears of his hearers, speaking with grace, showing forth the instructions of the divine Spirit, and urging man to look up and soar up heavenwards, get quit of earth, form a picture of the expected heaven, fear the threat of hell, despise things earthly and await the future. It is also possible to see him acting as judge and bringing forth just and upright decisions. He transacts this and similar business after the ninth hour, for he spends the whole of the night and the day up to that point in prayer.

48. THE MODERATE SOLUTION

Basil spent two years in the desert but he settled down in a rural paradise. He modified the extreme and unlimited privations of the hermits and established a way of life which combined withdrawal from the secular world with life in a community of Christians where each had his or her appointed work and all shared in daily worship. He drew up a rule for his monks which is still the basis of monastic life in the east. The practice of the Desert Fathers died out though their inspiration lived on. But before the desert lost its magnetic power, there was an institution ready to take its place and provide for the same spiritual need in a modified and less heroic form. That this was so is Basil's claim to the title of 'the Great'.

The first extract is from a letter of Basil to his friend Gregory Nazianzus with whom he had been a fellow student at Athens, along with the emperor's cousin Julian (the Apostate). It was written soon after Basil's return from the desert when he was about to settle down to a monastic life of prayer and study. Contrast his description of the ideal monastic site with that given by Rufinus in Extract 47c.

The second extract comes from a book written by Basil's brother Gregory, of Nyssa, about his sister Macrina. They belonged to an old and wealthy Cappadocian family and were at least third generation Christians. One grandfather was a martyr, one grandmother was a saint. Macrina established a household that was virtually a monastery for monks and nuns. It was on the opposite bank of the river Iris to Basil's first community.

From 364 onwards Basil took a prominent part in anti-Arian propaganda, and in 370 he became bishop of Caesarea, the capital of the province of Cappadocia with several subordinate sees under it. He continued to foster monastic communities. The third and fourth extracts, from his letters, refer to the 'Basileum' he established at Caesarea.

Sources: A: Basil, *Letters* 14; B: Gregory of Nyssa, *Life of Macrina*; c and D: Basil, *Letters* 94 and 207.

A.   THE RIGHT PLACE

Basil to Gregory of Nazianzus

My brother Gregory (of Nyssa) writes to tell me that he has long been wanting to join me, and adds that you are of the same mind.

However I could not wait ... I must make for Pontus at once.
... There God revealed to me a spot so exactly suiting my taste,
that it was like seeing before my eyes what I had often imagined
in idle fancy.

There is a high mountain, clad in thick woods, and on its north
flank watered with cool and limpid streams. Beneath, a plain,
enriched by the waters ever draining off upon it, and skirted by a
dense belt of trees that serve it as a fence. Thus it even improves on
Calypso's island, which Homer seems to have considered the
most beautiful place on earth. In fact that is what it resembles—an
island—being closed in on every side. On two sides it is cut off
by deep ravines. A river, cascading over a precipice, runs along
the front, impassable as a wall. Behind, the mountain forms a
crescent which meets the ravines, and stops up the path at its roots.
There is only one entrance, and I am the master of it!

Behind my dwelling there is another ravine, which rises up to a
ledge, from which one commands a view of the entire plain and
of the river which bounds it ... mine is the fastest water that I
know, and even turbid in its upper course among the rocks. It
shoots over them, eddying into a deep pool, a most pleasant scene
for myself or anyone to contemplate, and in its depths an inex-
haustible supply of fish for the local countryfolk.

What need to tell of the scents of the earth, or the breezes from
the river? Another might admire the multitude of flowers and
song-birds, but my leisure is not for such thoughts. The highest
praise to pay this place is that ... it nurtures in me the sweetest
produce of all—quiet! Not only is it rid of the city's bustle, but
even, apart from a chance huntsman, unfrequented by travellers.
In game it does in fact abound, as in other things, but not, I am
glad to say, in bears and wolves, such as you have, but in deer,
wild goats, hares, and the like.

B.   A FAMILY OF SAINTS

When our mother had arranged excellent marriages for our other
sisters, the best possible, Macrina's brother, the great Basil, came
home from his long schooling, already a practised public speaker.
He was conceited beyond measure with his ability and looked

down on all our local dignitaries, thinking himself better than all the men of leading and position. But Macrina took him in hand, and with such speed that she drew him too towards the pursuit of philosophy; Basil forsook the glory of this world and despised fame gained by public speaking. He renounced it for a busy life of manual labour. He gave up all his property, so that nothing should hinder a life of virtue. But all he did afterwards, his world-famous life which put into the shade everyone else renowned for holiness, would need a long description and take too much time.

The second of the four brothers, next after great Basil, was Naucratius. In natural gifts, physical beauty, strength, speed, and an ability to turn his hand to anything, he surpassed the others. At the age of twenty-one he gave such a demonstration of public speaking that the entire audience was thrilled, but divine providence led him to give up fortune already in his grasp and, following an irresistible impulse, he went off to a life of solitude and poverty. He took nothing with him but himself, except that one of the servants, Chrysapius, followed him, because he loved him so and had decided to lead the same sort of life. So, having found a suitable place on the banks of the Iris, well wooded, and with a hill nestling under the mass of an overhanging mountain, Naucratius lived alone, far removed from city noise and the distractions that surround the lives of soldiers and lawyers.

Freed from the din of worldly cares that distract a man from the higher life, Naucratius, with the work of his own hands, looked after some poor, frail old people, as a task more suited to his new way of life. The generous youth would go out on fishing expeditions from which, as he was expert in every sport, he provided food for these grateful dependants.

After five years there fell on our mother a grievous, a tragic affliction. Naucratius was suddenly snatched away from this life. No sickness prepared the family for this blow, nor did any ordinary misfortune bring death upon the young man. Along with Chrysapius, he started off on one of those expeditions by which he provided for the old people under his care, but both were brought home dead.

Then the virtue of the great Macrina, our sister, was displayed.

Calmly facing the disaster, she not only preserved herself from collapse but became the prop of her mother's weakness; she lifted her up out of her grief, and by the example of her own unshaken purpose taught her mother's soul to be brave. She persuaded her to give up the luxuries she was used to, and to share her own standard of humility, to live with her servants as equals, sharing the same food, the same kind of bed, the same necessaries of life, without any regard to differences of rank. Their manner of life, the height of their philosophy, the holiness of their conduct by day and by night, were more than words of mine can tell.

Macrina was helped most of all in her great aims by her brother Peter, the youngest of the family. He was naturally clever at every sort of handicraft, so that even without any training he acquired a mastery of things that other people only learn by time and trouble. He scorned giving up time to worldly studies, and as he had in nature a competent instructor in all good knowledge, and in his sister a constant model of all good conduct, he advanced to such a height of virtue that eventually he seemed in no way less than the great Basil. Once, when there was a severe famine, crowds gathered at their retreat, drawn by his reputation for generosity. Peter's kindness supplied such an abundance of food that the desert seemed transformed into a city.

C. THE BASILEUM

Basil to the Governor of Cappadocia, 372

I wish, however, that those who keep annoying your honest ears be asked what harm the state receives at our hands; or what, either small or great, of the public interests has suffered injury through our government of the churches; unless, indeed, someone may say that it inflicts injury upon the state to raise in honour of our God a house of prayer built in magnificent fashion, and, grouped about it, a residence, one portion being a generous home reserved for the bishop, and the rest subordinate quarters for the servants of God's worship arranged in order—access to all of which is alike free to you magistrates yourselves and to your retinue. And whom do we wrong when we build hospices for strangers, for those who visit us while on a journey, for those who require some care because of sickness, and when we extend to the latter the necessary comforts, such as nurses, physicians, beasts for travelling and attendants? There must also be occupations to go with these men, both those that are necessary for gaining a livelihood, and also such as have been discovered for a decorous manner of living. And, again, they need still other buildings equipped for their pursuits, all of which are an ornament to the locality, and a source of pride to our governor, since their fame redounds to your credit.

D. MUSIC AT THE BASILEUM

Basil to the Clergy of Neocaesarea, 375

Among us the people rise early at night to go to the house of prayer, and in labour and affliction and continuous tears confessing to God, finally rise from their prayers and enter upon the singing of psalms. And now indeed divided into two groups they sing antiphonally,[1] thereby both strengthening their practice in reciting the Scriptures and securing both their close attention and means of keeping their hearts from distraction. Then again after entrusting to one person to lead the chant, the rest sing the response; and so having passed the night in a variety of psalm-singing, and praying in the meantime, as the day begins to dawn, all in common, as of one voice and one heart, intone the psalm of confession to the Lord, each one forming his own expressions of repentance.

49. THE DEACON AND THE DANCERS   *c.* 373

The next three letters tell a mild ecclesiastical atrocity story, and illustrate the process by which some pagan festivals were being christianized in the fourth century. At Venasa there had long been a great sanctuary of Zeus, the king of the gods, with many temple servants and endowed with large estates. The god's annual festival was attended by great crowds. Religious dancing played a large part. It continued when Venasa became a Christian shrine.

Sir William Ramsay explains: 'Basil is giving us a picture, coloured to his view, of a naïve and quaint ceremony of early Cappodocian

---

[1] Each half of the choir sings alternate verses or half-verses with the other half, a practice still maintained in many cathedrals and colleges.

Christianity, which he regarded with horror, and was resolved to stamp out. One of the most striking features in the whole incident is the important part played by women. Now this is the most striking feature also in the native religion and society of Asia Minor. . . . Probably the dancing of the great dervish establishments of Kara Hissar and Iconium at the present day (1893) would give the best idea of the festival at Venasa in the time of Basil, though the solemnity and iconoclastic spirit of Mohammedanism have still further toned down the ecstasy and enthusiastic *abandon* of the old ritual. But the strange, weird music of the flute and cymbals, and the excited yet always orderly dancing, make the ceremony even yet the most entrancing and intoxicating that I have ever witnessed. . . . In the old pagan festival the leader of the festival wore the dress and bore the name of the deity whom he represented. . . . Glycerius, as Basil tells us, assumed the name and the dress of a 'patriarch'. The meaning of this seems to be that the director of ceremonies (who, like the modern dervish sheikh, never danced himself) was equipped in a style corresponding to the pagan priest, and assumed the character of the highest religious official, the patriarch.' (*The Church in the Roman Empire*, pp. 456–9.)

Source: The Letters of Basil, Nos. 169–71.

Basil to Bishop Gregory of Nazianzus

You have taken a reasonable and kindly and compassionate course in showing hospitality to the captives of the mutineer Glycerius (I assume the epithet for the moment) and in veiling our common disgrace so far as possible. But when your discretion[1] has learned the facts with regard to him, you ought to put an end to the scandal. This Glycerius who now parades among you with such respectability was consecrated by ourselves as deacon of the church of Venasa, to be a minister to the presbyter there and to attend to the work of the church; for though he is in other respects unmanageable, yet he is clever in doing whatever comes to his hand. But when he was appointed, he neglected the work as completely as if it had never existed. Gathering together a number of poor girls, on his own authority and responsibility, some of them flocking voluntarily around him (for you know the flightiness of young people in such matters), and some of them unwillingly, he

---

[1] A conventional courtesy.

set about making himself the leader of a company; and taking to himself the name and garb of a patriarch, he of a sudden paraded as a great power, not reaching this position by a course of obedience and piety, but making it a livelihood, as one might take up any trade. He has almost upturned the whole Church, disregarding his own presbyter, and disregarding the village-bishop and ourselves too, as of no account, and ever filling the civil community and the clergy with riot and disorder. And at last, when a slight rebuke was given by ourselves and the village-bishop, with the intent that he should cease his mutinous conduct (for he was exciting young men to the same courses), he conceives a thing very audacious and unnatural. Impiously carrying off as many young women as he could, he runs away under the cover of night. This must seem quite horrible to you.

Think too what the occasion was. The festival of Venasa was being celebrated, and as usual a vast crowd was flocking there from all quarters. He led forth his chorus, marshalled by young men and circling in the dance, making the pious cast down their eyes, and rousing the ridicule of the ribald and loose-tongued. Nor is this all, serious as it is. But further, as I am informed, when the parents could not endure to be orphaned of their children, and wished to bring them home from the dispersion, and came as weeping suppliants to their own daughters, he insults and scandalizes them, this admirable young fellow with his piratical discipline.

This ought to appear intolerable to your discretion, for it brings us all into ridicule. The best thing would be for you to order him to return with the young women, for he would meet with allowance if he comes with letters from you. If that be impossible, the young women, at any rate, you should send back to their mother the Church. Or, in the third place, do not allow those who are willing to return to be kept under compulsion, but persuade them to come back to us.

Otherwise we testify to you, as we do to God and men, that this is a wrong thing, and against the rules of the Church. If Glycerius returns with a spirit of wisdom and orderliness, that would be best; but, if not, he must be removed from the ministry.

Basil to Glycerius

How far will you carry your madness, working evil for yourself and disturbance for us, and outraging the common order of monks? Return then, trusting in God and in us, who imitate the compassion of God. For, though like a father we have chidden you, yet we will pardon you like a father. Such are our words to you, for many intercede for you, and before all your presbyter, whose grey hairs and kindly spirit we respect. But if you continue to stay away from us, you are altogether cast out from your office; and you shall be cast out from God with your songs and your raiment by which you lead the young women, not towards God, but into the pit.

Basil to Gregory

I wrote to you already before this about Glycerius and the maidens. Yet to this day they have not returned, but are still delaying. Nor do I know why and how; for I would not accuse you of doing this in order to cause slander against us, either because you yourself are annoyed with us or to do a favour to others. Let them come then without fear; you may guarantee this. For we are afflicted when the members of the Church are cut off, even though they deserve to be. But if they resist, the responsibility must rest on others, and we wash our hands of it.

50. THE THEOLOGIAN EMPERORS

It would have been impossible for the emperors who succeeded Constantine to pay no attention to the theological disputes which split the Church that had just been established as the State religion. They need not, however, have taken as partisan a line as they did. Between the death of Constantine and the accession of Theodosius, a period of forty-two years, there were on two occasions brothers as co-emperors. On both occasions they followed different parties, one orthodox, the other Arian. As it happened the Arian emperors were in power at Constantinople, New Rome, now the main administrative capital of the empire. Thus the cause which triumphed at Nicaea was under a cloud from 337 to 378.

The first extract shows how dangerous it was to be emperor—something which was in everybody's mind, and which helps to explain why an opposition party was liable to persecution. It was written by Chrysostom not long after the end of this period.

The second extract, from a pagan writer (*c.* 385), expresses his contempt for an emperor who took part in what he regarded as ecclesiastical squabbles. Valens did indeed revel in councils almost for their own sake. During his reign councils were held at Antioch, Tyre, Sardica, Arles, Rimini and Constantinople.

These were, of course, for the most part, councils with a built-in Arian majority. But there were protests from the orthodox. The third extract is a letter from one important protester, bishop Hosius of Cordova who had been a principal theological adviser to Constantine. At the time he wrote this letter he was ninety-eight, an exile at Sirmium near Belgrade. The letter may well have reached Constantius at Milan where he forced a condemnation of Athanasius with a high hand—'Let my will be deemed a canon among you, as it is among the Syrian bishops.' At this juncture Hosius gave way, signed a document arising out of a council called by Constantius and was allowed to return to Cordova. There he withdrew his signature, put his affairs in order and died.

The fourth group of extracts all come from the letters of the emperor Julian, called the Apostate because he threw over Christianity, in which he had been brought up, and tried to restore paganism. The first action of his predecessor Constantius had been to insure himself by having all Julian's male relations, except his half-brother Gallus, murdered. Julian escaped thanks to the bishop of Arethusa. At Athens, he was a fellow-student with Gregory Nazianzus and Basil (whom he tried to bring into his court circle). There he was initiated into the Eleusinian Mystery—Christianity was established but paganism was not prohibited. Julian succeeded his cousin Constantius in 361. In 363 he was killed by an arrow, fighting the Persians. His attempts to re-animate paganism were sincere, vigorous, civilized—but rather pathetic. Christianity had triumphed partly at least because the gods of Olympus had died. Julian urged pagan priests to live respectable lives and imitate the active charity of the Galileans, his name for Christians. His rules for teachers are enlightened; his appeal to the Alexandrians to return to their ancient worship of the sun is eloquent. But, he adds, if they persist in studying the Scriptures, let them find another teacher than the crafty Athanasius—in this judgment at least he agreed with Constantius.

Julian's short reign was followed by fifteen years of Valens, another strongly Arian emperor. He, however, having decided his line, was content to leave theology to bishops, unlike his predecessor Constantius. They took, perhaps, stronger anti-Arian action than he might himself have done. At any rate, rather surprisingly, he gave Basil, now the chief orthodox leader, money for the Basileum and left him undisturbed in his diocese.

Sources: A: Chrysostom, *Letters*; B: Ammianus Marcellinus, quoted by Gibbon; C: Athanasius, *History of Arianism* 42 f.; D: Julian, *Letters* 52, 7, 49, 42, *Fragments* and 51.

A.   THE DANGER OF BEING EMPEROR

Chrysostom to a young widow, c. 381

And to leave old matters, of those who have reigned over our generation, nine in all, two only have died by a common death (Constantine and Constantius). But of the rest, one by an usurper (Constans), one in a war (Constantine II), one by a conspiracy of his household guards (Jovian), one by the very man who raised him to the imperial throne and put the purple robe upon him (Gallus) . . . Julian fell in battle with the Persians, Valentinian died in a fit of rage, and Valens, together with his retinue, was burnt in a house to which the Goths set fire.

Of the wives whom these emperors married, some, they say, died of poison, and others of very despair. And of those widows who yet survive, one, having an orphan child, fears and trembles lest any of the rulers through fear of the future should destroy it; and the other, with difficulty, by the entreaty of many persons, has been recalled from the banishment to which the former emperor had sentenced her.

Of the wives of the reigning emperors, one is racked by constant anxiety on account of the youth and inexperience of her husband [Gratian was in fact murdered in 383]; the other is subject to no less anxiety for her husband's safety, inasmuch as ever since his elevation to the throne he has been engaged in constant warfare with the Goths [but Theodosius lived on and died a natural death in 395].

B. CONSTANTIUS AND HIS ARIAN COUNCILS

The Christian religion, which, in itself, is plain and simple, he confounded by the dotage of superstition. Instead of reconciling the parties by the weight of his authority, he cherished and propagated, by verbal disputes, the differences which his vain curiosity had excited. The highways were covered with troops of bishops, galloping from every side to the assemblies, which they call synods; and, while they laboured to reduce the whole sect to their own particular opinions, the public establishment of the posts was almost ruined by their hasty and repeated journeys.

C. A BISHOP WARNS THE EMPEROR

Hosius, bishop of Cordova, to Constantius, 355

I was at first a confessor when persecution arose in the time of your Maximian, and if you persecute me now I am prepared to endure anything rather than shed innocent blood or betray the truth. But I cannot approve of your behaviour in writing so threateningly. Stop it; don't champion the cause of Arius, nor listen to those in the East, nor believe Ursacius and Valens.[1] Whatever they say, they are interested not in Athanasius but their own heresy. Believe me, O Constantius, me, old enough to be your grandfather.

I was present at the Council of Sardica, when you and your brother Constans of blessed memory assembled us all together. By myself I challenged the enemies of Athanasius when they came to the church where I was staying: 'if you have anything against him, declare it. You can be sure that only a right judgment will be passed in all cases'.

I did this twice and asked them, if they were unwilling to appear before the whole Council, to come to me alone, promising them that Athanasius should certainly be rejected by us if he were proved guilty. If, however, he should be found innocent and they

---

[1] The two chief leaders of the Arians in the West. Ursacius was bishop of Singidunum, now Belgrade, Valens, bishop of Mursa, 90 miles to the west. Sirmium, where Hosius was exiled, was about midway between them.

shown to be slanderers then, if they still refused to hold communion with Athanasius, I would persuade him to come to Spain with me. Athanasius agreed to these conditions and made no objection to my plan, but they, having no confidence in their cause, would not consent.

Stop these proceedings, I implore you. Remember that you are but mortal. Be afraid of the day of judgment and keep yourself pure for it. Do not interfere in church matters, nor give us orders about them; but learn them from us. For God has put the kingdom into your hands, and the affairs of his Church he has committed to us. Should anyone steal the Empire from you he would be going against the law of God, and similarly you ought to be afraid of incurring the guilt of a grave offence by taking upon yourself the government of the Church. 'Render unto Caesar the things that are Caesar's, and unto God the things that are God's.'[1] So we are not allowed to exercise an earthly rule, and you, Sire, are not authorized to burn incense. I write these things out of concern for your salvation.

As for the subject of your letter: I will not write to the Arians. I anathematize their heresy. Neither will I sign the indictment of Athanasius, whom we and the Church of Rome and the whole Council acquitted.

D.   JULIAN TRIES TO PUT THE CLOCK BACK

I

Men should be taught and persuaded by reason, not by blows, invectives and corporal punishments. I therefore again and again admonish those who embrace the true religion in no respect to injure or insult the Galilaeans, neither by attacks nor reproaches. We should rather pity than hate those who in the most important concerns act ill. For as piety is the greatest of blessings, impiety, certainly, is the greatest of evils. Such is their fate who turn from the immortal gods to dead men and their relics. With those who are thus unhappy we condole, but them who are freed and delivered by the gods we congratulate.

Given at Antioch on the calends of August (362).

[1] Matt. 22, 21.

II

By the gods, I would neither have the Galilaeans put to death, nor scourged, unjustly, nor in any other manner ill-treated. I think it, nevertheless, highly proper that the worshippers of the gods should be preferred to them. By the madness of the Galilaeans, the empire was almost ruined, but by the goodness of the gods we are now preserved.

III

That Hellenism [traditional Greek religion] does not succeed as we wish is owning to its professors . . .

It is not sufficient for you only to be blameless. Intreat or compel all the priests that are in Galatia to be also virtuous. If they do not, with their wives, children, and servants, attend the worship of the gods, expel them from the priestly function; and also forbear to converse with the servants, children and wives of the Galilaeans, who are impious towards the gods, and prefer impiety to religion. Admonish also every priest, not to frequent the theatre, nor to drink in taverns, nor to exercise any trade or employment that is mean or disgraceful. Those who obey you, honour; and those who disobey you, expel. Erect also hospitals in every city, that strangers may partake our benevolence; and not only those of our own religion but, if they are indigent, others also.

How these expenses are to be defrayed must now be considered. I have ordered Galatia to supply you with thirty thousand bushels of wheat every year. Of which the fifth part is to be given to the poor who attend on the priests, and the remainder to be distributed amongst strangers and our own beggars. For when none of the Jews beg, and the impious Galilaeans relieve both their own poor and ours, it is shameful that ours should be destitute of our assistance.

IV

Whoever thinks one thing but teaches his scholars another, falls short from an educational no less than from a moral point of view. If the difference between the mind and the tongue of the teacher extended only to trifles, his dishonesty, though objectionable, might yet be tolerated. But where the subject is all-important and the teacher instills the exact contrary of his own convictions, it becomes nothing less than intellectual huckstering . . .

Homer, Hesiod, Demosthenes, Herodotus, Thucydides, Isocrates, Lysias found in the gods the source of all learning. Some esteemed themselves priests of Hermes, others of the Muses. I hold it absurd and improper for those who undertake to expound these authors to dishonour the gods whom they honoured. I do not say —it would be absurd to do so—that they are bound to reform their opinions and remain instructors of the young. I leave them the option of not teaching what they consider vicious; or else, if anxious to continue teaching, of primarily and bona fide impressing upon their scholars, that neither Homer nor Hesiod nor any other author, whom in their teaching they have charged with irreligion and theological folly and error, is such as they have represented.

v

Now it would perhaps have been well to say earlier from what class of men and by what method priests must be appointed; but it is quite appropriate that my remarks should end with this. I say that the most upright men in every city, by preference those who show most love for the gods, and next those who show most love for their fellowmen, must be appointed, whether they be poor or rich. And in this matter let there be no distinction whatever whether they are unknown or well known. For the man who by reason of his gentleness has not won notice ought not to be barred by reason of his want of fame. Even though he be poor and a man of the people, if he possess within himself these two things, love for God and love for his fellowmen, let him be appointed priest. And a proof of his love for God is his inducing his own people to show reverence to the gods; a proof of his love for his fellows is his sharing cheerfully, even from a small store, with those in need, and his giving willingly thereof, and trying to do good to as many men as he is able.

We must pay special attention to this point and by this means effect a cure. For when it came about that the poor were neglected and overlooked by the priests, then I think the impious Galilaeans observed this fact and devoted themselves to philanthropy. And they have gained ascendancy in the worst of their deeds through the credit they win for such practices. For just as those who entice children with a cake, and by throwing it to them two or three times induce them to follow them, and then, when they are far away from their friends, cast them on board a ship and sell them as slaves, and that which for the moment seemed sweet, proves to be bitter for all the rest of their lives—by the same method, I say, the Galilaeans also begin with their so-called love-feast, or hospitality, or service of tables—for they have many ways of carrying it out, and hence call it by many names—and the result is that they have led very many into atheism.

VI

By the gods, men of Alexandria, I am ashamed that any of you should avow himself a Galilaean. The ancestors of the Hebrews were formerly slaves to the Egyptians. But now, men of Alexandria, you, the conquerors of Egypt (for Egypt was conquered by your founder), sustain a voluntary servitude to the despisers of your national rites, in opposition to your ancient laws; not recollecting your former happiness, when all Egypt held communion with the gods, and enjoyed many blessings . . .

Are you alone insensible of the splendour that flows from the sun? Are you alone ignorant that summer and winter are produced by him, and that to him all things owe their life and origin? Do you not also perceive the great advantages that accrue to your city from the moon, from him and by him the disposer of all things? Yet you dare not worship either of these deities; and this Jesus, whom neither you nor your fathers have seen, you think must necessarily be God the Word; while you despise him whom, from eternity, every generation of mankind has seen and worships, and by worshipping, lives happily, the great Sun, I mean, a living, animated, rational, and beneficent image of the intelligible Father . . .

If you will follow my advice, my joy will be exuberant. But if you will still persevere in that superstitious institution of designing men, agree, however, among yourselves, and do not desire Athanasius. There are many of his disciples who are abundantly able to please your itching ears, desirous as they are of such impious discourses. I wish that this wickedness were confined to Athanasius and his irreligious school. But you have among you many, not ignoble, of the same sect, and the business is easily done. For any one whom you may select from the people, in what relates to expounding the Scriptures, will be by no means inferior to him whom you solicit. But, if you are pleased with the shrewdness of Athanasius (for I hear the man is crafty) and therefore have petitioned, know that for this very reason he was banished. That such an intriguer should preside over the people is highly dangerous; one who is not a man, but a puny, contemptible mortal, one who prides himself on hazarding his life, cannot but create disturbances. That nothing of that kind might happen, I ordered him formerly to leave the city, but I now banish him from all Egypt.

51. ATHANASIUS CONTRA MUNDUM

Athanasius had his great triumph at the beginning of his career when at the Council of Nicaea in 325, at about the age of thirty, he managed to secure approval for the 'homoousion' formula (see page 145). The fighting came afterwards. He became bishop of Alexandria in 328. By then the official world was becoming pro-Arian. He was exiled to Trier in 336 for a year, and again in 339 to Rome. He was allowed back to Alexandria from 346 to 356. He spent the next five or six years in hiding, partly among the monks of the Delta and partly, when business took him there, in Alexandria in the house of the young woman who many years later told this story of his strange arrival to Palladius who recorded it in his *Lausiac History* from which this extract is taken.

The five years of underground work was followed by a brief return to authorized power. Two more short exiles were followed by a final seven years in his bishopric. But when he died in 373 it still looked as if the Arian party was likely to win the day.

In Alexandria I [Palladius] met a virgin when she was about 70 years old. All the clergy confirmed that when she was a young maiden of about 20 she was exceedingly pretty and really to be avoided because of her beauty, lest one should be suspected of having been with her.

Now it happened that the Arians were in conspiracy against Athanasius, the bishop of Alexandria, working through Eusebius[1] while Constantius was emperor. They were bringing false charges and accusing Athanasius of unlawful deeds, and he fled to avoid the risk of being judged by a corrupt court. He trusted his person to no one, not to relative, friend, cleric, or anyone else.

But when the prefects came suddenly into the bishop's palace looking for him, he fled in the middle of the night, taking only his tunic and cloak, and went to the maiden. She was astonished and frightened by this.

He told her, 'Since the Arians are searching for me and have informed on me unjustly, I made up my mind to flee, so that I might not get a bad reputation and be the cause of a crime by those who want to punish me. Just this night now God made it clear to me that I shall be saved by no one but you.'

With great joy then she cast all doubts to the wind and became the instrument of the Lord. She hid the most holy man for six years, until the death of Constantius. She washed his feet and cared for all his bodily needs and his personal affairs, obtaining the loan of books for his use. During these six years no one in Alexandria knew where Athanasius was spending his time.

When news of the death of Constantius reached him, he got dressed and appeared in the church at night (Feb. 22, 362). All were amazed and looked on him as one risen from the dead. Then he explained all to his dear friends.

'I did not flee to you, in order that you might be able to swear that you did not know of my whereabouts. It was the same in regard to the search for me. Now I took flight to one who would be the last to be suspected, she being so pretty and young. I paid court to her on two counts, really: her salvation—for it did help her—as well as my own good name.'

52. A GUARANTEE OF SACRED RELICS 375

Handkerchiefs that had touched St Paul's body were used for healing (Acts 19, 12). The earliest Christians of Rome held their services in the catacombs and by the fourth century the Eucharist was generally

[1] Bishop of Nicomedia (not the historian).

celebrated over the tombs of the martyrs. The Second Council of
Nicaea in 787 ordered that no new church should be consecrated without such relics. The Crusades brought a flood of relics back to Europe
from the Holy Land, many of them spurious. Chaucer's Pardoner had
a pillow-case which he said was Our Lady's veil, and a piece of sail-
cloth from Peter's fishing boat, and a glass full of pigs' bones. It is interesting that as early as 375 it was necessary to have written guarantees
of relics.

This is from a letter of Basil to bishop Ambrose of Milan in 375,
which accompanied the bones of Dionysius of Milan, who died in
Cappadocia. In the letter Basil describes Ambrose as 'a man eminent
for intellect, illustrious lineage, prominence in life, and power of speech,
an object of admiration to all of this world, a man who, having cast
aside all the advantages of life and having counted them as loss that he
may gain Christ, has been entrusted to receive the tiller of the great
ship famous for its faith in God, even the Church of Christ'. And he
urges him to 'fight the good fight and correct the infirmities of the
people in case the disease of the Arian madness has indeed touched any'.

Source: Basil, *Letters* 197.

Let no one stagger, let no one be uncertain: this is indeed that
unconquerable athlete. These bones the Lord recognizes, for they
shared in the contest along with the blessed departed's soul. Bones
and soul will he crown on the righteous day of his requital,
according to what is written: 'We must stand before the judgment
seat of Christ that everyone may receive according as he hath done
in the body.'[1] One coffin it was that received that honoured body:
no one lay beside him: glorious was his burial: worthy of a martyr
his honour. Christians, who had received him as a guest, with their
own hands laid him away then and have taken him up now. They
wept as though they were being bereft of a father and protector:
but they sent him on, considering your joy of greater worth than
their own consolation. Therefore, they who have surrendered him
are pious; they who have received him are scrupulously strict.
Nowhere has there been deceit, nowhere fraud, we ourselves bear
witness to this; let the truth be free from all calumny on your
part.

[1] 2 Cor. 5, 10.

53. BASIL AND GREGORY CARRY ON 372–81

After the death of Athanasius the leadership of the orthodox party passed first to Basil and then to his friend Gregory Nazianzus. This was natural for, though most of the western bishops including the bishop of Rome were orthodox, so was the co-emperor who ruled their part of the empire. The main struggle was an eastern one. Valens was quite willing to remove orthodox bishops to make room for Arians, and to divide the large province of Cappadocia, partly at least to reduce Basil's influence as Metropolitan (the name now being given to the leading bishops). Church organization followed the pattern of the civil government.

The first three extracts are from letters written by Basil to the West asking for support, which in the nature of things could only be moral. He was driven almost to regret the 'good old days of persecution', forgetting that heresy was not a new invention. In a letter (164) to bishop Ascholius of Thessalonica he wrote in 374: 'We thought we were back in the olden times, when the churches of God flourished, taking root in the faith, united by charity, there being, as in a single body, a single harmony of the various members; when the persecutors indeed were in the open, but in the open were also the persecuted . . . Then we Christians had peace among ourselves, that peace which the Lord left to us, of which now not even a trace remains to us, so utterly have we driven it away from one another.'

In 379, the year of Basil's death, Gregory moved to Constantinople and began to hold services for the orthodox party. Constantinople was the only great city of the empire which was overwhelmingly Christian. But it was one in which every heresy and sect flourished, and in which the Arians were well in the ascendant. At the beginning of the same year Theodosius became co-emperor with responsibility for the East. In 380 he was seriously ill in Thessalonica and was baptized by Ascholius, the orthodox bishop of that city. The fourth extract, with connecting narrative, is from the autobiography in verse which Gregory wrote in his retirement, translated by the Quaker historian Thomas Hodgkin in 1880.

Even before Theodosius arrived in Constantinople he issued orders that all should follow the orthodox faith. When he reached the capital he summoned the Arian bishop to his presence, and told him to conform. But he refused, went to the cathedral and spoke to his people: 'Brethren, it is written in the Gospel, "if they persecute you in one city flee ye to another".[1] The emperor excludes us from our churches: take notice therefore that we will henceforth hold our assemblies outside the city.' Theodosius appointed Gregory as the new bishop.

The next year there was a council in Constantinople, the second recognized throughout the Christian world as a General Council. Its president was old bishop Meletius of Antioch (see Extract A). Arianism in all its forms was condemned, and that, as far as the rules of the Church are concerned, was the end of that metaphysical argument.

Then Meletius died. Gregory became president in his place. But who was to be the new bishop of Antioch? There was now a chance of ending the existing schism. Meletius had been consecrated by an Arian bishop, but he himself was orthodox. No sooner had he been enthroned in Antioch than he was banished by Constantius. He got back under Julian, but was twice banished by Valens. And he had also had to face a schism. His rival, Paulinus, was equally orthodox. This, then, was a more than normally squalid struggle. Basil and all the Asian bishops had supported Meletius. Rome supported Paulinus; so, on the whole, did Alexandria. Gregory thought that the time had now come to end the split by recognizing Paulinus. What he said to the Council (Extract E) was badly received—the noise the angry bishops made was, he said, like the croak of jack-daws or wasps whose nest had been disturbed. Gregory retired to private life. Paulinus did not get his bishopric. The Church came out badly. The clash between Constantinople and Rome had been serious. It was the precursor of worse to come.

Sources: A, B and C: Basil, *Letters* 92, 242, and 243; D, and E: Gregory of Nazianzus, *On his Life*.

A.   AN APPEAL TO THE ITALIANS AND GAULS

[Basil writes on behalf of 32 Eastern bishops. Their sees,
when known, are given in brackets]

To our most God-beloved and holy brethren, co-workers in Italy and Gaul, bishops of like mind with us, we, Meletius (of Antioch), Eusebius (of Samosata), Basil (of Caesarea), Bassus (of Edessa), Gregory the elder (of Nazianzus), Pelagius (of Laodicea), Paul, Anthimus (of Tyana), Theodotus (of Nicopolis), Vitus (of Carrhae), Abraham (of Batnae), Jobinus (of Perrha), Zeno (of Tyre), Theodoretus, Marcianus, Barachus, Abraham (of Urimi in

---

[1] Matt. 10, 23.

Syria), Libanius, Thalassius, Joseph, Boethus, Iatrius (of Melitine), Theodotus, Eustathius (of Sebasteia), Barsumas, John, Chosroes, Iosaces (of Armenia Major), Narses, Maris, Gregory (of Nyssa), Daphnus, send you greetings in the Lord.

Even a groan repeatedly uttered from the depths of the heart brings some degree of consolation to souls in affliction, and doubt-less, too, a falling tear has swept away the greater portion of our anguish. But the telling of our woes to your charity[1] means for us, not consolation such as groans and tears may bring; nay, there is also hope for better things that warms us, a hope that perhaps, if we should announce to you the causes of our affliction, we might rouse you to take those measures for our relief which we have long been expecting would come from you to the churches in the East, but which we have not yet received. The reason surely is that God, who in his wisdom disposes our affairs, has ordained according to the inscrutable judgments of his justice that we should be racked in these trials for a still longer period. For you surely have not remained ignorant how affairs are amongst us, most honoured brethren, whereof the rumour has gone forth to the uttermost parts of the world.

For the danger is not confined to a single church, nor are there two or three only which have been overthrown by this fierce tempest. For we can almost say that the curse of this heresy is spreading out from the borders of Illyricum to the Thebaid; its baneful seeds were formerly scattered by the infamous Arius, and, taking deep root through the efforts of many who have cultivated them assiduously in the meantime, they have now produced their death-dealing fruits. For the teachings of the true faith have been overthrown and the ordinances of the Church have been set at naught.

The lust for office on the part of men who do not fear the Lord leaps upon the positions of high authority, and quite openly now the foremost place is offered as a prize for impiety; and conse-quently that man who has uttered the more horrible blasphemies is accounted the more worthy of the episcopal direction of the people. Gone is the dignity of the priesthood. None are left to

[1] A conventional courtesy.

tend the flock of the Lord with knowledge, while ambitious men ever squander the sums collected for the poor on their own pleasures and for the distribution of gifts.

B. TO THE WESTERNERS 376

The laity have abandoned the houses of prayer and are congregating in desert places, a pitiable sight—women, and children, and old men, and the otherwise infirm, in most furious rains, and in snowstorms, and in winds and frost of winter, and likewise also in summer suffering under the heat of the sun in the open air! And this they suffer for not consenting to become a part of the wicked leaven of Arius.

C. TO THE BISHOPS OF ITALY AND GAUL 376

Persecution has laid hold of us, most honoured brethren, and the most oppressive of persecutions. For shepherds are being persecuted that their flocks may be scattered. And the most oppressive part of this is, that neither do those who are being wronged accept their sufferings in the certainty of martyrdom, nor do the laity reverence their athletes (heroes) as being in the class of martyrs, because the persecutors are cloaked with the name of Christians . . .

The ears of the more simple-minded are being turned away; already they have become accustomed to the heretical impiety. The nurslings of the Church are being brought up in the doctrines of ungodliness. For what are they indeed to do? Baptisms are in the heretics' hands, attendance upon those who are departing this life, visits to the sick, the consolation of those who grieve, the assisting of those who are in distress, succour of all kinds, communion of the mysteries; all of these things, being performed by them, become a bond of agreement between them and the laity. Consequently, after a little time has passed (even if all fear should be removed), there can be no hope of recalling to the recognition of the truth those in thrall to a long-standing deception.

D. GREGORY'S VERSE AUTOBIOGRAPHY

[Gregory's friend, Basil, persuaded him (*c.* 372) to be bishop of Sasima, a dreary posting station on the highway from Ankara to Tarsus. He spent only a very short time there, if any, preferring to go home and help his father who was bishop of Nazianzus twenty-four miles away.]

> There is a posting-place for travellers planned
> Where three ways meet in Cappadocian land.
> This squalid hamlet is the home of slaves,
> No spring refreshes it, no foliage waves.
> There ever dust, and the car's rattle reigns,
> Wails, groans, the exactor's shout, the clank of chains.
> Its people—strangers who benighted roam:
> And this was Sasima, my church, my home.
> This in his goodness had to me assigned
> The Lord of fifty bishops: wondrous kind!
> To this new see, this fort must I repair
> That I might fight my patron's battle there.

[When Gregory came to Constantinople in 379 he was pelted in the streets by the mob who thought he was no better than a polytheist. He was looked down on by the upper classes.]

> For that 'the poorest of the poor,' said they,
> 'Wrinkled, with downcast look and mean array,
> Whose fasts, and tears, and fears had left their trace
> Deeply on what was ne'er a comely face,
> A wandering exile from earth's darkest nook,'
> That such should rule, no well-born souls could brook.

[But almost at once the Nicene faith became the rising cause when Theodosius was baptized by an orthodox bishop. An adventurer from Egypt, a Christian and a Cynic, arrived and set about getting himself consecrated as bishop of Constantinople secretly in Gregory's own church. They were interrupted before his long hair, dyed to resemble the fair hair of a Goth, had been cut off to give him the tonsure. He and his supporters fled and finished the service in the house of a band-master. The new bishop left the capital and went in search of Theodosius, who was fighting a frontier war, in the hope of getting his support]:

o

Gathering the refuse of the Egyptian crowd,
(Those 'neath whose shears his yellow ringlets bowed)
He hastens to the camp with nimble feet
By royal edict to reclaim his seat.
Ejected thence by Caesar's anger dread,
With fearful imprecations on his head,
(For Theodosius still to me was kind,
And none had poisoned yet the Imperial mind),
The pestilential creature seeks once more
(His wisest course) the Alexandrian shore.

[Next year Theodosius returned from the war and turned the Arians out of the churches they had held for forty years. Theodosius was not a mild man, but was he stern enough with the heretics? Gregory had his doubts]:

A man not evil is he, one whose rule
The simple-minded for the Faith may school;
A loyal servant of the One in Three,
So says my heart: and with its voice agree
All who hold fast Nicaea's great decree.
Yet zeal is not in him nor purpose high
To compensate the wrongs of years gone by
With answering sternness, nor the ruins raise;
Or was there zeal enough, but lacked he still
Courage? or rashness? Answer it, who will.
Haply 'twere better take a kindlier tone
And say the Prince's *forethought* here was shown.
For of a truth persuasion and not force
For us and ours I hold the worthier course.

E.   GREGORY OFFERS TO RETIRE   381

It would not be worth while to disturb the peace of the world, for which Christ died, even for the sake of two angels, much less on account of the rival claims of two bishops. During the lifetime of the venerable Meletius, it was perhaps right that we should stand up for his claims against the opposition of the West: but now that he is dead, let Paulinus take the vacant see. Soon will death cut the knot, for Paulinus is an aged man: and meanwhile we shall have regained the affections of the estranged churches of the West and restored peace to Antioch. Now the faith itself is in danger of perishing through our miserable squabbles: and rightly, for men may reasonably ask what the faith is worth which permits of our bearing such bitter fruits. If any one think that I am influenced by any fear or favour in giving this counsel, or that I have been prompted thereto by the rulers of the state, I can only appeal to the Judgment of Christ at the Last Day to disprove such a charge. For me, I care not for my episcopal dignity, and am quite ready, if you wish me to do so, to lead a throneless life, without glory but also without danger, in some retirement 'where the wicked cease from troubling and the weary are at rest' (Job 3, 17).

CHAPTER ELEVEN

JEROME AND THE BIBLE

Jerome (c. 342–420) was reckoned in later times to be one of the four Doctors (teachers) of the Latin Church along with Ambrose, Augustine and Gregory the Great. He was the greatest biblical scholar of the early Church and arguably of all time. He was also a great letter-writer—great in quality as well as quantity. In the strong language he used in theological controversy, words which severed precious friendships, he was typical of his age. Extracts 54–57 illustrate aspects of the man as well as of his work. Extracts 58 and 59 deal with other aspects of early biblical study.

54. MAKING HARD WORDS HARDER

The Bible contained much that, taken at face value, was either difficult to understand or to reconcile with Christian morality, or contemporary knowledge. So did Homer and other ancient writers, and pagans were as bothered as Christians. Thus Apollo was explained as the sun. He did not 'descend and shoot arrows at the Greeks for seven days'. What Homer meant was that the heat of the sun on the damp ground caused a sickness which affected the Greek army. That was an Alexandrian explanation. Philo followed a similar line of allegorizing the Old Testament. The Alexandrian Christian scholars, Clement and Origen, took naturally to this method. Origen distinguished three levels of meaning: the literal, the moral, and the mystical or allegorical. Ambrose and Augustine used the same allegorical method; so did Jerome, as Extract A illustrates.

Besides this ingenious Alexandrian method of interpretation, there was another school, associated with Antioch, which believed in discovering what the man who wrote the passage meant, and leaving it there without a superstructure of imported fancy. The great men of this school were Theodore, bishop of Mopsuestia (c. 350–428) and his friend John Chrysostom (c. 347–407). Extract B, a typical example of this expository method, is from a sermon preached by Chrysostom at Constantinople about the year 400. It illustrates the theoretical foundation of the growing anti-semitism which is seen in action in Extracts

63 and 69. It may be said that Chrysostom's language, though harsh, is relatively mild for fourth-century theological controversy.

Sources: A: Jerome, *Commentary on Ecclesiastes*; B: Chrysostom, 3rd Sermon on 1 Thessalonians.

A.   JEROME'S COMMENTARY ON ECCLESIASTES II, 2

'Give a portion to seven, and also to eight; for thou knowest not what evil shall be on the earth.' The number 7 denotes the Old Testament because of the Sabbath therein enjoined to be celebrated on the seventh day; the number 8 denotes the New Testament, because the Saviour rose on the eighth day. The text, then, directs us not to restrict our faith, as the Jews do, to the Old Testament; nor, as do the Marcionites,[1] Manichees,[2] and other heretics, to the New. We must believe both Testaments for 'we know not what evil shall be on the earth'; that is to say, we cannot comprehend now the merited tortures and punishments reserved for those who are upon earth, namely for the Jews and heretics who deny either Testament.

B.   CHRYSOSTOM ON 1 THESSALONIANS 2, 14–16

'For ye, brethren, became followers of the churches of God which in Judaea are in Christ Jesus: for ye also have suffered like things of your own countrymen, even as they have of the Jews: who both killed the Lord Jesus, and their own prophets, and have persecuted us; and they please not God, and are contrary to all men: forbidding us to speak to the Gentiles that they might be saved, to fill up their sins alway: for the wrath is come upon them to the uttermost.' '*Who both killed the Lord*', he says. But perhaps they did not know him. What then? Did they not slay and stone their own prophets, whose books even they carry about with them? And this they did not do for the sake of truth. There is therefore not only a consolation (for the Thessalonians) under their temptations, but they are reminded not to think that the Jews did it for the truth's sake, and be troubled on that account. '*And have persecuted us*', he says. We also, he says, have suffered numberless evils. '*And they please not God, and are contrary to all men, forbidding*

[1] See page 96.   [2] Pages 279–82.

us to speak to the Gentiles that they might be saved'. 'Contrary to all men', he says. How? Because if we ought to speak to the world and they forbid us, they are the common enemies of the world. They have slain Christ and the prophets, they insult God, they are the common enemies of the world, they banish us who come to them for their salvation.

55. CHRISTIAN OR CICERONIAN? 374

Jerome attached great importance to the spiritual experience (of the nature of a conversion) which he describes in this letter written ten years afterwards. It has an additional importance for us. It shows Jerome as the passionate Latin scholar whom in fact no number of dreams would have turned away from his beloved authors. It was on this foundation that he based the biblical scholarship to which bishop Damasus wisely directed his inquisitive, restless secretary in 382. He realized that Christ could make use of a good Ciceronian: it ought to be both, not, as Jerome had thought, 'either-or'.

Source: Jerome, *Letters* 22.

Many years ago when, for the kingdom of heaven's sake, I had cut myself off from home, parents, sister, relatives and—harder still—from the dainty food to which I had been accustomed, and when I was on my way to Jerusalem to wage my warfare, I still could not bring myself to forgo the library which I had formed for myself at Rome with great care and toil. And so, miserable man that I was, I would fast only that I might afterwards read Cicero. After many nights spent in vigil, after floods of tears called from my inmost heart, after the recollection of my past sins, I would once more take up Plautus. And when at times I returned to my right mind and began to read the prophets, their style seemed rude and repellent. I failed to see the light with my blinded eyes; but I attributed the fault not to them, but to the sun.

While the old serpent was thus making me his plaything, about the middle of Lent a deep-seated fever fell upon my weakened body, and while it destroyed my rest completely—the story seems hardly credible—it so wasted my unhappy frame that scarely anything was left of me but skin and bone. Meantime, preparations for my funeral went on; my body grew gradually colder, and the warmth of life lingered only in my throbbing breast. Suddenly I was caught up in the spirit and dragged before the judgment-seat of the Judge; and here the light was so bright, and those who stood around were so radiant, that I cast myself upon the ground and did not dare to look up. Asked who and what I was, I replied: 'I am a Christian.' But he who presided said: 'Thou liest, thou art a Ciceronian, not a Christian. For "where thy treasure is, there will thy heart be also" '(Matt. 6, 21).

Instantly, I became dumb, and amid the strokes of the lash—for he had ordered me to be scourged—I was tortured more severely still by the fire of conscience, considering that verse (Psalm 6, 5): 'In the grave who shall give thee thanks?' Yet, for all that, I began to cry and to bewail myself, saying; 'Have mercy upon me, O Lord: have mercy upon me.' Amid the sound of the scourges this cry still made itself heard. At last the bystanders, falling down before the knees of him who presided, prayed that he would have pity on my youth, and that he would give me space to repent of my error. He might still, they urged, inflict torture on me, should I ever again read the works of the Gentiles. Under the stress of that awful moment, I should have been ready to make even still larger promises than those. Accordingly I made oath and called upon his name, saying: 'Lord, if ever again I possess worldly books, or if ever again I read such, I have denied thee.' Dismissed then, on taking this oath, I returned to the upper world . . .

Thenceforth I read the books of God with a zeal greater than I had previously given to the books of men.

56. JEROME AS HERMIT AND MONK

These extracts show Jerome commending first the solitary life of the desert recluse, and secondly, nearly forty years later, the disciplined life of a regular religious community. He wrote with first-hand experience of both. He wrote the first letter very soon after the spiritual experience described in the last extract, at the beginning of the four or five years he spent as a hermit in the Syrian desert. While he was there he learned Hebrew. He was thus equipped for his life work, though he did not yet know what it was to be.

The second letter was written towards the end of his long life after he had finished his revision of the text of the Bible. He was then head of a monastery for men at Bethlehem. It was there that he had carried out the greater part of his life work, moving back from Rome to Palestine in 386.

A.   THE YOUNG JEROME PRAISES THE SOLITARY LIFE
Jerome to Heliodorus, 374

O wilderness, bright with Christ's spring flowers! O desert, rejoicing in God's familiar presence!

What are you doing in the world, brother, you who are more than the universe? How long is the shade of a roof going to confine you? How long shall the smoky prison of these cities shut you in? Believe me, I see something more of light than you behold. How sweet it is to fling off the burden of the flesh, and to fly aloft to the clear radiance of the sky! Are you afraid of poverty? Christ calls the poor blessed. Are you frightened by the thought of toil? No athlete gains his crown without sweat. Are you thinking about food? Faith feels not hunger. Do you dread bruising your limbs worn away with fasting on the bare ground? The Lord lies by your side. Is your rough head bristling with uncombed hair? Your head is Christ. Does the infinite vastness of the desert seem terrible? In spirit you may always stroll in paradise, and when in thought you have ascended there you will no longer be in the desert. Is your skin rough and scurfy without baths? He who has once washed in Christ needs not to wash again. Listen to the apostle's brief reply to all complaints: 'The sufferings of this present time are not worthy to be compared with the glory which shall come after them, which shall be revealed in us.' (Romans, 8. 18.) You are a pampered darling indeed, dearest brother, if you wish to rejoice here with this world and afterwards to reign with Christ.

B.   JEROME IN OLD AGE PREFERS A COMMUNITY LIFE
FOR MONKS
Jerome to Rusticus, 411

The first point with which I must deal is whether you ought to live alone or in a monastery with others. I would prefer you to have the society of holy men and not to be your own teacher. If you set out on a strange road without a guide you may easily at the start take a wrong turning and make a mistake, going too far or not far enough, running till you weary yourself or delaying your journey for a sleep. In solitude pride quickly creeps in, and when a man has fasted for a little while and has seen no one, he thinks himself a person of some account. He forgets who he is, whence he comes, and where he is going . . .

What then, you will say? Do I disapprove of the solitary life? Not at all: I have often commended it. But I wish the soldiers who march out from a monastery-school to be men who have not been frightened by their early training, who have given proof of a holy life for many months, who have made themselves last that they might be first, who have not been overcome by hunger or satiety, who take pleasure in poverty, whose garb, conversation, looks and gait all teach virtue, and who have no skill—as some foolish fellows have—in inventing monstrous stories of their struggles with demons, tales invented to excite the admiration of the ignorant mob and to extract money from their pockets . . .

Engage in some occupation, so that the devil may always find you busy. If the apostles who had the power to make the Gospel their livelihood still worked with their hands that they might not be a burden on any man, and gave relief to others whose carnal possessions they had a right to enjoy in return for their spiritual benefits, why should you not provide for your own future wants? Make creels of reeds or weave baskets of pliant osiers. Hoe the ground and mark it out into equal plots, and when you have sown cabbage seed or set out plants in rows, bring water down in channels and stand by like the onlooker in the lovely lines:

'Lo, from the channelled slope he brings the stream,
Which falls hoarse murmuring o'er the polished stones
And with its bubbling flood allays the heat
Of sun-scorched fields.' (Virgil, *Georgics* I, 108.)

Graft barren trees with buds or slips, so that you may, after a little time, pluck sweet fruit as a reward for your labours. Make hives for bees, for to them the Proverbs of Solomon[1] send you, and by watching the tiny creatures learn the ordinance of a monastery and the discipline of a kingdom. Twist lines too for catching fish, and

[1] Prov. 6, 8 in the Septuagint version.

copy out manuscripts, so that your hand may earn you food and your soul be satisfied with reading. 'Every one that is idle is a prey to vain desires.' Monasteries in Egypt make it a rule not to take any one who will not work, thinking not so much of the necessities of life as of the safety of men's souls, lest they would be led astray by dangerous imaginings, and be like Jerusalem in her whoredoms, who opened her feet to every chance comer.

When I was a young man, though I was protected by the rampart of the lonely desert, I could not endure against the promptings of sin and the ardent heat of my nature. I tried to crush them by frequent fasting, but my mind was always in a turmoil of imagination. To subdue it I put myself in the hands of one of the brethren who had been a Hebrew before his conversion, and asked him to teach me his language. Thus, after having studied the pointed style of Quintilian, the fluency of Cicero, the weightiness of Fronto, and the gentleness of Pliny, I now began to learn the alphabet again and practise harsh and guttural words. What efforts I spent on that task, what difficulties I had to face, how often I despaired, how often I gave up and then in my eagerness to learn began again, my own knowledge can witness from personal experience and those can testify who were then living with me. I thank the Lord that from a bitter seed of learning I am now plucking sweet fruits.

I will tell you of another thing that I saw in Egypt. There was a young Greek in a community there, who could not quench the fires of the flesh by any continence or any labour however severe. In his danger the father of the monastery saved him by the following device. He instructed a grave elder to pursue the young man with revilings and abuse, and after having thus insulted him to be the first to lay a complaint. When witnesses were called they always spoke in favour of the aggressor. The youth could only weep at the false charge, but no one believed the truth. The father alone would cleverly put in a plea on his behalf, lest 'our brother be swallowed up by overmuch sorrow'. To cut a long tale short, a whole year passed in this way, and at the end the youth was asked about his former imaginings, whether they still troubled him. 'Good heavens', he replied, 'how can I want to fornicate, when I am not allowed even to live?' If he had been alone, by whose help could he have overcome temptation? . . .

No art is learned without a master. Even dumb animals and herds of wild beasts follow leaders of their own. Bees have rulers, and cranes fly behind one of their number in the shape of the letter Y . . .

I want to show you that you had better not be left to your own discretion, but should rather live in a monastery under the control of one father and with many companions. From one of them you may learn humility, from another patience; this one will teach you silence, that one meekness. You will not do what you yourself wish; you will eat what you are ordered; you will take what you are given; you will wear the dress allotted to you; you will perform a set amount of work; you will be subordinate to some one you do not like; you will come to bed worn out with weariness and fall asleep as you walk about. Before you have had your fill of rest, you will be forced to get out of bed and take your turn in psalm-singing . . . You will be so busy with all these tasks that you will have no time for vain imaginings, and while you pass from one occupation to the next you will only have in mind the work that you are being forced to do . . .

If you have substance, sell it and give it to the poor. If you have none, you are free from a great burden. Naked yourself follow a naked Christ. The task is hard and great and difficult; but great also are the rewards.

57. THE VULGATE 383

In his Preface to the four Gospels addressed to his master Damasus Jerome explains how he tackled his work of revision. He compared one Latin manuscript with another, one Latin version with another (there were not only different manuscripts but different translations from the Greek in existence), and Latin manuscripts with Greek manuscripts. Clearly he did not want to shock people, and he implies that but for this he would have made more changes than he did.

This preface was written in 383 when he was perhaps half-way through his first draft of the New Testament and while he was still in Rome. He probably finished the New Testament by 386 and the whole bible in 404. For the Old Testament he worked from the Hebrew.

Earlier translations had been made from the Greek either of the Septuagint or of the revision made by the Greek Aquila, a Jewish proselyte, which was finished by about 140.

In the fourth century the Bible existed for Christians in four main living languages in addition to the Old Testament in Hebrew. Greek, the original language of the New Testament, was spoken in Greece, southern Italy, Asia Minor, and along the coasts of Syria and Egypt. Latin was the language of central and north Italy, of North Africa and the countries of the Atlantic sea-board. Syriac was the speech of what is now Syria and Iraq; Coptic, the language of the Nile Valley.

You urge me to revise the old Latin version and, as it were, to sit in judgment on the copies of the Scriptures which are now scattered throughout the whole world; and, inasmuch as they differ from one another, you would have me decide which of them agree with the Greek original. The labour is one of love, but at the same time both perilous and presumptuous; for, in judging others, I must be content to be judged by all; and how can I dare to change the language of the world in its hoary old age, and carry it back to the early days of its infancy? When a man, learned or unlearned, takes this book in his hands and sees that the text differs from the one familiar to him, will he not break out immediately into violent language, and call me a forger and a profane person for having the audacity to add anything to the ancient books, or to make any changes or corrections therein? Now there are two consoling reflections which enable me to bear the odium —in the first place, the command is given by you who are the supreme bishop; and, secondly, even on the showing of those who revile us, readings at variance with the early copies cannot be right. For if we are to pin our faith to the Latin texts, it is for our opponents to tell us which; for there are almost as many forms of texts as there are copies. If, on the other hand, we are to glean the truth from a comparison of many, why not go back to the original Greek and correct the mistakes introduced by inaccurate translators and the blundering alterations of confident but ignorant critics, and, further, all that has been inserted or changed by copyists more asleep than awake?

This short preface deals with the four Gospels only, which

are to be taken in the following order, Matthew, Mark, Luke, John, as they have been revised by the comparison of Greek manuscripts. Only early ones have been used. But to avoid any great divergences from the Latin which we are accustomed to read, I have used my pen with some restraint; and while I have corrected only such passages as seemed to convey a different meaning, I have allowed the rest to remain as they are.

58. THE BIBLE AND THE COMMON MAN   *c.* 390

Chrysostom and his school believed that the Bible was for the people. It meant what it said; and it said it in language that plain men could understand. This extract comes from two sermons that Chrysostom preached in Antioch about 390. (For Chrysostom himself, see p. 213.)

The first part of the extract makes surprising reading when one remembers that there were no printing presses and everything had to be written by hand. The process of publishing and 'printing' a book was this. A reader read slowly to a group of seven to ten trained copyists. In commercial publishing slaves did the copying and as many as seventy-five might be employed on a single book. A book might take eighteen hours to complete. Working a sixty hour week, an edition of a thousand copies could be completed in a month. Even so it is difficult to believe that Chrysostom expected his congregation to buy complete bibles. But he certainly seems to have expected them to have at least a gospel in their possession.

Source: Two sermons of Chrysostom combined: *St John* Hom. 10, vol. 8, p. 63 and *De Lazar* Concio 3, vol. 1, p. 736.

[Chrysostom is speaking of excuses for not reading the Bible]

There is another excuse employed by persons of this indolent frame of mind, which is utterly devoid of reason, namely, that they have not a bible. Now, as far as the wealthy are concerned, it would be ridiculous to spend words on such a pretext. But, as I believe many of our poorer brethren are in the habit of using it, I should be glad to ask them this question, Have they not everyone got, complete and perfect, the tools of their respective trades? Though hunger pinch them, though poverty afflict them, they will prefer to endure all hardships rather than part with any of the implements of their trade, and live by the sale of them. Many have chosen rather to borrow for the support of their families than give up the smallest of the tools of their trade. And very naturally; for they know that, if these be gone, their whole means of livelihood are lost. Now, just as the implements of their trade are the hammer or anvil or pincers, exactly so the implements of our profession are the books of the Apostles and prophets and all the Scriptures composed by Divine inspiration, and very full of profit. As with their implements they fashion whatever vessels they take in hands, so we with ours labour at our own souls, and correct what is injured, and repair what is worn out. Is it not a shame, then, if, when the tools of this world's trades are concerned, you make no excuse of poverty, but take care that no impediment shall interfere with your retaining them, here, where such unspeakable benefits are to be reaped, you whine about your want of leisure and your poverty?

But, at any rate, the very poorest of you, if he attends to the continual reading of the Scriptures that takes place here, need not be ignorant of anything that the Scriptures contain. You will say this is impossible. If it is, I will tell you why it is impossible. It is because many of you do not attend to the reading that takes place here; you come here for form's sake, and then straightway go home; and some who remain are not much the better than those who go away, being present with us only in the body, not in the spirit.

[Chrysostom goes on to deal with the objection that the Bible is too difficult to understand]

It is impossible for you to be alike ignorant of all; for it was for this reason that the grace of the Spirit appointed that publicans and fishermen, tentmakers and shepherds and goatherds, and unlearned and ignorant men, should compose these books, that none of the unlearned might be able to have recourse to this excuse; that the words then spoken might be intelligible to all; that even the mechanic, and the servant, and the widow-woman, and the most unlearned of all mankind might receive profit and improvement from what they should hear. For it was not for vainglory, like the heathen, but for the salvation of the hearers, that these authors were counted worthy of the grace of the Spirit to compose these writings. For the heathen philosophers, not seeking the common welfare, but their own glory, if ever they did say anything useful, concealed it, as it were, in a dark mist. But the Apostles and prophets did quite the reverse; for what proceeded from them they set before all men plain and clear, as being the common teachers of the world, that each individual might be able, even of himself, to learn the sense of what they said from the mere reading.

And who is there that does not understand plainly the whole of the Gospels? Who that hears 'Blessed are the meek', 'Blessed are the merciful', 'Blessed are the pure in heart',[1] and so forth, needs a teacher in order to comprehend any of these sayings? And as for the accounts of miracles and wonderful works and historical facts, are they not plain and intelligible to any common person? This is but pretext and excuse and cloak for laziness.

59. CHOOSING BOOKS FOR THE BIBLE

Jerome's Bible is our Bible as far as the books it contains is concerned. But the Church had taken a long time before finally deciding by a process or argument what ought to go in and what must be left out. These extracts show the process going on.

The first dates from about 190. It was discovered by L. A. Muratori, librarian to the Duke of Modena, and published by him in 1740. It has been suggested that it is the work of Hippolytus (see pages 60, 99). Marcion, who died about 160, was a heretic who entirely rejected the Old Testament. His followers, therefore, needed a fresh set of Psalms. *The Shepherd of Hermas* contains a series of visions, giving much moral instruction. Irenaeus and Clement of Alexandria accepted it as part of the Bible.

The second extract comes from the *Church History* (3, 3) of Eusebius and represents the state of the argument rather over a hundred years later. The statement about the Epistle to the Hebrews is interesting. It is still in the Bible and nobody would wish it out, but hardly anyone now thinks it was written by Paul.

[1] Matt. 5, 5–8.

The technical term for the list of recognized books of the Bible is 'canon'. It is a word common to both Greek and Hebrew and means a reed used as a measuring rod, or a test for straightness.

Somewhere about the year 90 the final decisions about the canon of the Old Testament had been made. During the siege of Jerusalem (see Extract 2) Rabbi Jochanan ben Zakkai left the city and secured permission from Vespasian to start a school at Jabneh on the coast. It was there that the new Judaism was formed to serve the People of God deprived of their Temple. Among the tasks that the rabbis undertook was the final review of the books of the Jewish bible. Most of its contents had long been settled but there were some disputed books. At Jabneh it was decided to include Esther, Ecclesiastes and the Song of Songs, but the books that we know as the Apochrypha were left out. The Old Testament as Christians know it is the Old Testament as the Jewish council at Jabneh settled it.

A.   FROM THE MURATORIAN FRAGMENT   c. 190

The Epistle of Jude no doubt, and the couple bearing the name of John, are accepted in the Catholic Church; and the Wisdom written by the friends of Solomon in his honour. The Apocalypse of John, and [one letter] of Peter only we receive which some of our friends will not have read in the Church. But *The Shepherd* was written quite lately in our times in the city of Rome by Hermas, while his brother Pius, the bishop, was sitting in the chair of the church of the city of Rome; and therefore it ought indeed to be read, but it cannot to the end of time be publicly read in the Church to the people, either among the prophets, who are complete in number, or among the Apostles.

But of Arsinous, called also Valentinus, or of Miltiades we receive nothing at all; those who have also composed a new book of Psalms for Marcion, together with Basilides and the Asian founder of the Cataphrygians [Montanists] are rejected.

B.   EUSEBIUS ON THE CANON   c. 320

Of Peter, then, one epistle, his former as it is called, is acknowledged; and of this also the elders of olden time have made frequent use, as a work beyond dispute, in their own treatises. But as for the second extant [epistle,] the tradition received by us is that it is not canonical; nevertheless, since it appeared profitable to many, store was set by it along with the other Scriptures. Yet as regards the book of his Acts, as it is entitled, and the Gospel named after him, and his Preaching, as it is called, and The Apocalypse (such is its name): we know that they were not handed down at all among the catholic [writings]; for no Church writer, either in ancient times or even in our day, used testimonies derived from them.

But as my history advances I shall deem it profitable to indicate, along with the successions, what Church writers in each period have made use of which of the disputed [books], and what they have said about the canonical and acknowledged writings, and anything that they have said about those that are not such.

Now the writings that bear the name of Peter, of which I recognize only one epistle as genuine and acknowledged by the elders of olden time, are so many; while the fourteen epistles of Paul are manifest and clear [as regards their genuineness]. Nevertheless it is not right to be ignorant that some have rejected the Epistle to the Hebrews, saying that it is disputed by the church of the Romans as not being Paul's. And I shall quote at the proper time what those who lived before us have said with reference to this epistle also. Moreover, I have not received his Acts, as they are called, among the undisputed writings.

CHAPTER TWELVE

THE PARTING OF THE WAYS—
East and West; New and Old;
Bishop and Emperor; Christians and Jews

The extracts in this chapter illustrate three problems which arose in the reign of Theodosius the Great (379–95; see Plate 29) and have influenced Christianity down to the present day.

What was to be done about a Christian emperor who didn't behave as a Christian? Who was to decide what a Christian emperor was to do about heretics and pagans and Jews? Was there to be one rule for the East and another for the West? Theodosius was the last man to be emperor over the whole of the Roman empire. After his death there was a definite and formal division between East and West, each with its separate line of emperors, instead of the long-standing arrangement of co-emperors with varying spheres of influence. The bishops with whom we shall be mainly concerned are Ambrose, Chrysostom and Cyril, one westerner and two easterners.

Ambrose was the son of a high civil servant. His father was Prefect of Gaul at the time of his birth, the senior civilian in France, Spain and the Rhineland to use the modern names. Ambrose himself held a responsible position in the imperial service. In 374 he was called to the great Basilica in Milan to prevent a riot over the election of a new bishop. He left the building as bishop designate himself, was baptized and eight days later enthroned. A great theologian, a compelling orator, a gifted poet, a strict, fearless and loving pastor—Ambrose deserves his reputation as one of the four traditional Doctors (teachers) of the Latin Church. A mosaic portrait of him made a few years after his death is reproduced in Plate 30. It shows a man with 'a short, delicate, elongated face; high forehead; long, straight nose; thick lips; large eyes; one eyebrow higher than the other; short hair and beard—perhaps light brown—and drooping moustache'.

For Chrysostom see pp. 192–3, 201–3, 212–20; for Cyril, 233–7.

60. AMBROSE AND SYMMACHUS: *Vicisti, Galilæe*

These were said to be the dying words of Julian the Apostate. Swinburne glossed them in his 'Hymn to Proserpine' to run 'Thou hast conquered, O pale Galilean'. The adjective was unjustified: the concession of victory a shade premature. These extracts illustrate the final struggles of official paganism to be allowed to live. They take us a generation beyond the death of Julian.

Augustus placed an Altar of Victory in the Senate House after he had defeated Mark Antony and become the first Roman emperor. It was removed by the Arian emperor Constantius in 357. Julian put it back. Gratian took it away again. But Gratian was murdered in 375. The Senate determined to try to get it put back once more.

The main duty of the seven Vestal Virgins, a proud and highly important order of unmarried priestesses, was to tend the sacred fire. They also guarded the seven sacred objects on which the power of Rome rested. The most important was the Palladium, a crude archaic statue which legend said had been brought by Aeneas from Troy.

The first extract illustrates one step in the campaign to restore the Altar of Victory and give back their endowments to the Vestal Virgins. Symmachus was Prefect of Rome, the head of the civil administration there. He made an official report to the emperors. It was delivered to Valentinian, a boy of thirteen whose sphere was Italy. Ambrose got to hear of its arrival and wrote to him saying that if he restored the Altar 'the bishops would not be able calmly to accept the fact, and to dissimulate their indignation. You may come to church if you please, but you will find no priests there, or only priests who resist your entrance and scornfully refuse your gifts, tainted with idolatry.' The second extract contains some of the arguments Ambrose supplied to Valentinian to use against Symmachus. The Altar was not restored; the Vestals lost their money.

Sources: A: The 'Relatio' (Official Report) of Symmachus; B: Ambrose, *Letters* 18.

A.   SYMMACHUS PLEADS FOR THE GODS   384

Rome herself speaks:

'Reverence my many years, to which I have attained by these holy rites; let me use these ancestral ceremonies, for I have no desire to change them. Let me live after my own manner, for I am free. It is this worship which has brought the whole world under my sway; it was these sacrifices which repelled Hannibal from my walls, the Gauls from the rock of the Capitol.[1] Have I been preserved through all these centuries only that I should now be insulted in my old age?' ......

We ask for a quiet life, for the native gods, the gods of our fatherland. It is right to believe that that which all men worship is *the One*. We look forth upon the same stars, the sky above us is common to us all, the same universe encloses us. What matters it by what exact method each one seeks for Truth? It is not by one road only that you will arrive at that so mighty Secret. ......

[Symmachus asks for the return of the confiscated endowments of the Vestal Virgins]:

The ruler should be ashamed to eke out the poverty of his treasury by such unjust gains as these. The will of the 'pious founder' should be respected. Who will have any confidence in bequeathing any property to public objects if such clear and manifest testamentary dispositions as those by which the Vestals hold their funds are set aside? It is not true that they give no return for the revenues which they receive. They dedicate their bodies to chastity; they support the eternity of the Empire by the heavenly succours which they implore; they lend the friendly aid of their virtue to the arms and eagles of your legions. You have taken the money of these holy maidens, the ministers of the gods, and bestowed it on degenerate money-changers, who have squandered on the hire of miserable porters the endowments sacred to chastity. And well have you been punished, for the crops of whole provinces have failed, and vast populations have had to live, as the first race of men lived, on the acorns of Dodona.

Finally do not be ensnared by the argument that because you are Christians, it is your duty to withold pecuniary support from every faith but your own. It is not really *you* who give these allowances to the Virgins. The dedication of the funds took place long ago, and all that you are asked to do is to respect as rulers the rights of private property. Your late brother Gratian erred through ignorance, for the evil counsellors who surrounded him would not suffer him to hear of the Senate's disapproval of

[1] Hannibal of Carthage failed to take Rome 211 B.C.; the Gauls (Senones) were driven back from the Capitol in 387 B.C.

his proceedings; but, now that you are fully informed, we call upon you with confidence to remedy that which has been unjustly ordered.

B.   AMBROSE ANSWERS SYMMACHUS

Ambrose, bishop, to the most blessed prince and most gracious emperor Valentinianus, the august. . . .

Rome complains with sad and tearful words, asking, as Symmachus says, for the restoration of the rites of her ancient ceremonies. These sacred rites, he says, repulsed Hannibal from the walls, and the Senones from the Capitol. And so at the same time that the power of the sacred rites is proclaimed, their weakness is betrayed. So, too, Hannibal long insulted the Roman rites, and while the gods were fighting against him, arrived a conqueror at the very walls of the city. Why did they suffer themselves to be besieged, for whom their gods were fighting in arms?

And why should I say anything of the Senones, whose entrance into the inmost Capitol the remnant of the Romans could not have prevented, had not a goose by its frightened cackling betrayed them? See what sort of protectors the Roman temples have. Where was Jupiter at that time? Was he speaking in the goose?

But why should I deny that their sacred rites fought for the Romans? For Hannibal also worshipped the same gods. Let them choose then which they will. If these sacred rites conquered in the Romans, then they were overcome in the Carthaginians; if they triumphed in the Carthaginians, they certainly did not benefit the Romans.

Let, then, that invidious complaint of the Roman people come to an end. Rome has given no such charge. She speaks with other words. 'Why do you daily stain me with the useless blood of the harmless herd? Trophies of victory depend not on the entrails of the flocks, but on the strength of those who fight. I subdued the world by a different discipline. Camillus was my soldier, who slew those who had taken the Tarpeian rock, and brought back the standards taken from the Capitol; valour laid those low whom religion had not driven off. What shall I say of Attilius [Regulus], who gave the service of his death? Africanus found his triumphs not amongst the altars of the Capitol, but amongst the lines of Hannibal. Why do you bring forward the rites of our ancestors? I hate the rites of a Nero.'

61. THE AFFAIR OF THE MILAN BASILICAS   386

It was Holy Week in the year 386. Justina, the empress-mother, was an Arian and wanted a church in Milan where she could keep Easter. All the churches (basilicas) were under the control of the formidable and extremely orthodox bishop Ambrose. Justina asked, begged, ordered, arrested opponents, sent in troops. Ambrose was inflexible. He told the story of what happened in a letter to his sister, Marcellina. The events up to Maundy Thursday are given in this extract. Next day, Good Friday, Ambrose preached again. He was just showing how God's pity had saved Nineveh from destruction—Jonah was the Old Testament reading at the service—when the soldiers rushed in to say that the empress had withdrawn her orders. Ambrose had won. The soldiers gave the kiss of peace to the congregation (a ceremonial gesture at Mass).

Source: Ambrose, *Letters* 21.

While I was offering (Mass), I was told that the people had carried off a certain Castulus, a presbyter by Arian reckoning. They had come upon him in the street as they went by. I burst into tears, and during the oblation I prayed for God's help to prevent any bloodshed over the church, or at least that it should be my own blood that was shed, not only for the sake of my people, but for the ungodly also. In short, I sent presbyters and deacons and rescued the man from violence.

At once very heavy penalties were decreed, first upon the whole body of merchants. So in Holy Week, when it is customary to release debtors from their bonds, we heard the grating of chains put on innocent men's necks, and two hundred pounds' weight of gold was demanded within three days. They replied that they would give as much again, and double that, if they were asked, provided they could keep their faith. The prisons were full of business men.

All the functionaries of the palace—the secretaries, the agents, the various magistrates' apparitors—were ordered to stay indoors,

on the pretext that they were being prevented from getting involved in sedition. Men of rank were threatened with severe
trouble if they did not surrender the basilica. Persecution was
flaring up, and had the door been opened, it seems likely that they
would have broken out into violence without limit.

The counts and tribunes called on me to surrender the basilica
without delay. They said that the emperor was within his rights,
since everything came under his authority. I replied that if he
asked me for anything of my own, my estates, my money, anything of mine like that, I should not refuse it, though everything
that belonged to me belonged to the poor. 'But,' I said, 'the things
of God are not subject to the authority of the emperor. If he wants
my patrimony, take it; if my body, I will go at once. Do you mean
to carry me off to prison, or to death? I shall be delighted. I shall
not shelter myself behind a crowd of people. I shall not lay hold
of the altar and beg for my life. I will gladly sacrifice myself for
the sake of the altar.'

In fact, I was horrified to learn that armed men had been sent
to occupy the basilica of the church. I was afraid that in defence
of the basilica there might be some bloodshed, which would lead
to the destruction of the whole city. I prayed that I might not
survive the ruin of so great a city, or perhaps all Italy. I shrank
with loathing from the odium of shedding blood; I offered my
own throat. Some officers of the Goths were there, and I spoke to
them, and said: 'Did Rome give you a home so that you might
show yourselves disturbers of public order? Where will you go
next if these parts are destroyed?'

I was pressed to restrain the people. I said in return that while it
lay in my power not to excite them, to pacify them was in God's
hands. To conclude, if he thought that I was instigating them, I
ought to be punished at once, or banished to whatever lonely
part of the world he chose. At these words, they went off, and I
stayed the whole day in the Old Basilica. Then I went back home
to sleep, so that if anyone wanted to arrest me, he would find me
ready.

Before daylight, when I set foot outside, the basilica was surrounded and occupied by soldiers. There was a rumour that the

soldiers had sent word to the emperor that if he wished to go there, the way was clear. If they saw him joining the catholics, they would attend him. If not, they would go over to the congregation under Ambrose.

Not one of the Arians dared go there, for there were none among the citizens, just a few in the royal household, and some Goths. Being used to a wagon for a home, they were now making their wagon a church. Everywhere that woman (Justina) goes, she transports her sect with her.

I could tell from the laments of the people that the basilica was surrounded. But during the lessons I was informed that the New Basilica was also full of people, that the crowd seemed to be larger than when they were all free, and that they were calling for a Reader. In short, when the soldiers who had occupied the basilica learned that I had given orders for their excommunication, they began to come over to our congregation. Seeing them, the women were frightened, and one of them rushed out. However the soldiers explained that they had come to pray not to fight. The people shouted a little. With restraint, but persistently and faithfully, they asked that I should go to the (new) basilica. It was said also that the people in that basilica were demanding my presence ...

[Ambrose went and preached] ... You understand the meaning of the order, 'Hand over the Basilica.' It means 'Curse God, and die.' Job was tempted by one messenger of evil after another, and he was tempted also by his wife, who said, 'Speak a word against God and die' (Job 2, 9). We know how sharp are temptations caused by women. Adam, for instance was brought down by Eve ... Need I mention how cruelly Jezebel persecuted Elijah? How Herodias had John the Baptist killed? All men suffer from some woman or other ...

62. THE CASE OF THE EMPEROR'S STATUE   387

Oratory was a great art and perhaps the main means of communication in the ancient world. The spoken word had a standing which it did not reach again until the coming of radio and television. When the empire became Christian, sermons became a principal form of oratory. The greatest Christian preacher was John of Antioch, known (though not in his lifetime) as Chrysostom—'the man with a tongue of gold'. He was born about 345. His father, who died soon after John's birth, was a senior army officer; his mother was a devout Christian. John was baptized at 18; at 21 he wanted to become a hermit. His mother persuaded him to wait until after her death—'do not plunge me into a second widowhood'—but eventually he spent six years in this way in the mountains near Antioch. When he returned to Antioch in his middle thirties crowds flocked to his sermons and enthusiastically applauded him. This was far from what John wanted, but it was the common custom and led to preachers playing to the gallery. If they get a good round of applause, John said, they are as pleased as if they had won a kingdom; but if they are heard in stony silence their gloom is almost worse than hell. We have a description of his appearance: 'a pallid little presbyter with bald pate, dome-like forehead, deep-set eyes and "spidery" frame'.[1]

Antioch was the second city of the empire, the place where men were first called Christians, and its bishop ranked with those of Alexandria, Rome and New Rome (Constantinople) as the principal figures in the Christian world. On February 26, 387 there was a serious riot in Antioch because of heavy new taxation. The bronze statues of the emperor's father and wife were knocked down from their pedestals and dragged in insult through the streets. Worse still the same thing happened to the emperor's own statue. Roman emperors no longer claimed to be gods, but their status was little less. The authorities soon put down the riot, and waited in terror for the emperor's vengeance. Old bishop Flavian set off for Constantinople to ask for mercy. John, now 42 and priested only the year before, preached twenty-one sermons 'On the Statues' between the end of February and Easter Day. They tell the story of the developing crisis with the skill of a great reporter.

In 398 John against his will was made bishop of Constantinople. He fell into disfavour, and was banished to the remotest corner of the empire on the Black Sea. He was forced to march on foot, though ill. He never reached his place of exile but died at Komana on the way there in 407, exclaiming 'Glory be to God for everything. Amen.'

'A Prayer of St Chrysostom', the last prayer of Morning and Evening Prayer in the Anglican Book of Common Prayer, is placed in the earliest MS in the Liturgy of Basil and not of Chrysostom.

Source: John Chrysostom, *Sermons on the Statues* 13, 17, 21.

---

[1] F. H. Dudden, *St. Ambrose: his life and times*, p. 361.

THE BISHOP'S EMBASSY

Although, when (bishop Flavian) set out from (Antioch), he left all of us in a state of great despondency, the sufferings he had to endure were worse than those we were enduring here at the very heart of the crisis. For, when he had made half the journey (to Constantinople), he met the commissioners who had been sent by the emperor, and learned the terms of the mission that had been entrusted to them. And when he thought of the terrible fate that awaited the city—the tumults, the confusion, the flight, the fear, the agony, the perils—it was as though his very heart had broken . . .; for it is always the case that the sufferings of parents are greatly increased when they cannot stand by their children in their time of trouble. . . .

THE DAY OF JUDGMENT

[Meanwhile the commissioners arrived in Antioch.] Think of our state on Wednesday a week ago. . . . it was on that day that the terrible tribunal was set up in our city, and caused the hearts of all of us to tremble, and made the day no better than the night. . . . Most of the people of the city had fled in terror before the impending menace, to the deserts and ravines and hidden refuges, fear driving them out in every direction. The houses were empty of women, the streets were empty of men. It was hardly possible to see two or three walking together, and those that were looked like the living dead going about the streets. I went to the place of judgment to see the end of the affair, and there I found assembled all that was left of the people of the city. The most remarkable thing of all was that, though such a crowd had come together, the silence was as deep as though not a single person had been present; all were looking one upon the other, but no one ventured to put a question or to expect an answer. Everyone suspected his neighbour, since so many had been caught up without any warning from the open street, and taken inside the judgment hall. We all, as of one mind, lifted our eyes to heaven, and raised our hands in silence waiting for the help that comes from above. We pleaded with God to stand by those who were on trial and to strengthen them, and so to soften the hearts of the judges that the sentence pronounced by them might be mild. . . .

All this was happening outside the doors. But when I went within the judgment hall, the sight that met our eyes was even more terrifying. For there we saw soldiers armed with swords and clubs, guarding the judges against any kind of disturbance. For all those related to the accused—wives and mothers and daughters and fathers—were standing close to the doors of the judgment hall. And, to make sure that, if one of the accused was led away under sentence of death, none of the watchers . . . should cause any kind of turmoil or confusion, the soldiers kept them at a considerable distance.

The most pitiable sight of all was that of the mother and sister of one of the accused, who lay close to the very door of the chamber where the judges were in session, grovelling on the floor, their faces covered, a spectacle to all those who were standing round them. No servant was with them, no neighbour or friend, and none of their relations; there they were alone, in the cheapest of garments . . . I think that their state was even more pitiable than that of those whose case was being tried. They could hear the voices of the executioners, the sound of the lash, the agonized cries of those who were being flogged. For the danger was that the evidence extorted from these might be held to prove the guilt of others. . . . So, when they heard the cries of one who was being flogged in order to make him reveal the names of the guilty, they looked up to heaven and prayed God to give him strength and endurance lest the safety of one who was dear to them might be betrayed . . .

Not only so. The very judges suffered deeply in their hearts. Perhaps their sufferings were the worst of all, since they were compelled to be the ministers of such a bitter tragedy. I myself was sitting there and saw all this. . . .

I began to think of that other dreadful judgment seat; and I said to myself, 'Here it is men who sit as judges; yet neither father nor mother nor sister nor any other can deliver those who are under trial, even though they may be innocent of the crimes that have been committed. If that is so here, who shall be able to stand by us, when we appear to be judged before the dreadful judgment seat of Christ? . . .'

THE HERMITS AND THE IMPERIAL COMMISSIONERS

When the commissioners . . . had set up that terrible tribunal . . ., the hermits who dwell on the high ridges of the mountains revealed the true quality of their manner of life. For many years they had lived apart in their seclusion; but now, though no one had called them, . . . they left their caves and their huts, and ran together from every quarter, as it were a host of angels descending from the heavens. And indeed the appearance of the city at that time was like heaven, with so many holy men . . . giving confidence to those who were in distress, and helping them to bear with equanimity the disasters that had befallen them. For who, seeing these men, would not learn to laugh at death? Who would not learn to think lightly of life?

This was only the first of the marvels. The next was these men entered the presence of the judges, and boldly appealed to them on behalf of the accused. They said that they were all ready to shed their own blood, and to lose their own heads, if only they might be allowed to deliver the captives. And they affirmed that they would not desist from their appeal, until the judges either agreed to spare the people, or consented to send them, together with the accused, as a delegation to the emperor. 'Theodosius,' they said, 'the emperor of all the world, is a believer, a man who leads a godly life. We shall certainly be able to persuade him to be merciful . . . If you do not agree to postpone sentence, we will certainly all die with them. The crimes committed were terrible; that we frankly admit; but great as was this lawlessness the human kindness of the emperor is even greater.' We hear that another of them spoke a word full of shrewd wisdom: 'The statues which were thrown down have been put back in their places . . .; in a very short time what was wrong has been put right. But, if you destroy the image of God, how will you ever be able to put right the wrong that you have done? Will you be able to bring dead men back to life? Will you be able to bring back the souls to the bodies?'

They also spoke to them at great length about the judgment of God.

Who could fail to be astonished, to be lost in admiration for the character of these men? When the mother of one of the accused . . . caught hold of the horse of one of the judges by the bridle, and ran with him through the open street, and so entered into the judgment hall, we were all amazed, we were lost in admiration of her love and courage. Ought we not to be far more amazed at the actions of these men? . . .

For, unless they had resolutely prepared themselves in advance for every kind of death, they would not have been able to use such freedom of speech to the judges and to manifest so notable a degree of courage. They remained sitting before the doors of the judgment hall all day long, ready to snatch from the very hands of the executioners those who might be led out to die. Where now are those who ostentatiously wore the philosopher's cloak, and grew their beards long, and carried a staff in their right hand, those worthless Cynics,[1] those philosophers in outward show, whose behaviour was worse than that of the dogs under the table, who were prepared to do anything for the sake of their bellies? All at that time had left the city; they had sped away, and hidden themselves in caves. And only those who by their works showed what philosophy truly is walked without fear through the open streets, as though no cloud of danger hung over the city. . . .

Those who held the first positions in the city, men of rank and power, those who had boundless wealth and ready access to the emperor, all left their houses and fled away to the wilderness, taking counsel only for their own safety. All friendship and kinship was then tested and found wanting. In this time of disaster men refused to recognize those whom previously they had known quite well, and preferred not to be recognized by them. But these hermits . . . manifested the strength of lions . . . In one single day these men came down, conferred, relieved disaster, and went back to their own dwelling place. So wonderful is the philosophy, the way of life, that has been taught by Christ to men. . . .

[1] The name of this school of philosophers derives from the Greek word for 'dog'. See page 72. There is also an allusion to Mark 7. 28.

When the commissioners . . . were appealed to by the hermits to exercise clemency and to let their judgment be tempered by mercy, they replied that their authority did not go so far as this; when the emperor had been insulted, to release without punishment those who had insulted him might be regarded as compounding the insult, and this would be fraught with grave danger for themselves. But the monks were simply unwilling to take No for an answer. . . . In the end (they) so put them to shame that they were willing to take the risk of going beyond the authority which they had received from the emperor. They were able to persuade the judges, even though the guilt of the accused had been proved, not to pronounce sentence upon them, but to refer the matter to the emperor. They undertook with absolute confidence to persuade the emperor to pardon those who had offended him, and they themselves were ready at once to set off for the capital city. In admiration for the courage of the hermits, the judges manifested the highest respect for them. But they would not agree to their undertaking this long journey. They said that the words of the monks should be recorded, and that they themselves would make the journey to the capital and prevail upon the emperor to lay aside all anger. We confidently expect that they will be successful in the attempt.

THE BISHOP AND THE EMPEROR

[By this time bishop Flavian had reached Constantinople.] When he . . . entered the royal palace, he stood at a distance from the emperor, speechless, weeping, with downcast eyes, swathed in his cloak, as though it had been he who had committed all these crimes. His purpose . . . was to work on the mind of the emperor, and even before beginning his speech in our defence to incline his heart to mercy. For, when we have done wrong, the only hope of pardon is in keeping silence, in saying not a word in defence of the wrong that has been done. . . .

You will remember that, after the people of Israel had sinned their terrible sin, Moses went up into the mountain and remained speechless before God, until God had finished his indictment of his people . . . This is just what our bishop did.

When the emperor saw him standing thus weeping and with downcast mien, he came up to him; and the effect of our bishop's tears was manifest in the words with which he addressed him. For his attitude was not one of anger or of indignation, but rather of pain ... You will understand this perfectly, when you hear the actual words of the emperor. ... He enumerated all the benefits that he had conferred on our city from the beginning of his reign until now. And after each item, he asked, 'Was it fair that I should receive such a reward as this for what I had done for them? ... Is it not the fact that I have always shown Antioch the highest honour, that I have preferred it even before the city in which I was born, that it has always been my great desire to visit that city, and that I have made public declaration of my desire?'

At this point our bishop ... could no longer keep silence. ... Groaning deeply in spirit he began:

'Your majesty, we fully admit the love which you have shown our city. It is quite impossible that we should deny it. And this it is which has made our sorrow so profound—that evil demons have bewitched this city, the object of so much love, that we have seemed ungrateful to our benefactor, and provoked to anger one who has given evidence of so much affection for us. ...

'But, your majesty, if you are willing, there can be healing for this wound and a remedy for these tremendous ills. ... For when God created man and introduced him into Paradise ... the devil could not endure this great privilege which had been given to man, but bewitched him, and expelled him from his position of eminence in the creation. But God did not desert man. Far more than that. In exchange for Paradise Lost, he opened to us Heaven Gained ... Your majesty, be an imitator of God ...

'Think of the impression that will be left on the minds of posterity, if they hear that, when so great a city was liable to punishment and vengeance, and all were in terror, and among the generals and rulers and judges there was not a single one who dared to lift up his voice on behalf of those wretched criminals, one single old man, entrusted with the authority of the priesthood, came forward, and just by his presence and by the mere fact of meeting with him, changed the mind of the emperor; and that what the emperor was unwilling to grant to any other of his subjects, he accorded to this one old man out of respect for the laws of God . . .

'Other men who go on embassies carry with them gold and silver and other gifts of the same sort. I come to your royal presence with nothing in my hand but the sacred laws of God; these I hold out to you as my sole and only gift. I urge you to imitate your Lord and Master. . . .'

Something of this kind and more to the same effect he said; and he produced so deep an effect on the emperor that . . . after (he) had finished his lengthy oration, no further discussion was necessary. . . .

When you received the news, you crowned the market-place with garlands; you lit torches; you strewed rushes before the shops; you celebrated high festival, as though the city had just been founded. . . . And let us never cease to give thanks to God for all these things . . . And, as we find it written in Scripture, proclaim these things to your children, and let them pass them on to their children, and they in turn to yet another generation so that all men who shall be born until the very end of the world, having learned of the great kindness of God . . ., may count us happy . . ., and may reverently admire our ruler . . ., and may themselves be stimulated to the pursuit of godliness by their knowledge of all the things that have happened here. . . .

63. AMBROSE AND THE SYNAGOGUE   388

Judaism was a permitted religion in the empire both before and after the reign of Constantine. To burn down a synagogue was clearly a crime which called for punishment and redress. For a bishop to encourage such a crime would seem to us an unchristian thing. It does not seem to have struck Ambrose in this way, though it did Theodosius.

Callinicum was a town on the Persian frontier of the empire. When the synagogue was burned, the authorities ordered an enquiry. The bishop was ordered to pay for the rebuilding. Ambrose objected that it would be wrong for Christians to pay for building non-Christian places of worship. Theodosius accepted this view and withdrew this part of the order. But Ambrose was not satisfied. He thought it would be just as wrong for the State to pay for the rebuilding because the

State was a Christian State. He also wanted the proceedings against the monks who had destroyed the Valentinian chapel to be dropped. It was not until he had received these further assurances that he continued the celebration of the Eucharist. The Valentinians were perhaps the largest of the Gnostic sects (see page 89).

The letter to his sister Marcellina, from which this extract is taken, contains a full report of the sermon. Gibbon said of it: 'His sermon is a strange allegory of Jeremiah's rod, of an almond-tree, of the woman who washed and anointed the feet of Christ. But the peroration is direct and personal.'

Source: Ambrose, *Letters* 41.

My dear and holy sister,

It was good of you to write and tell me that you are still anxious because you have not received my letter telling you that my composure has been restored. It had been reported that a Jewish synagogue had been set on fire by Christians, at the instigation of the bishop, and also a Valentinian chapel. While I was at Aquileia orders had been sent that the bishop should rebuild the synagogue, and the monks, who burned down the Valentinian chapel, should be punished. I took the matter up energetically but achieved nothing. So I composed a letter to the emperor and sent it off at once. When he went to church I preached this sermon. . . . When I came down (from the pulpit), he said to me: 'You have been preaching about me.' I replied: 'The sermon was meant for your own good.' Then he said: 'It is true that it was somewhat harsh of me to order the bishop to repair the synagogue, but that has been corrected. The monks do many wrong things.'

At this the general Timasius began to abuse the monks violently and I answered him: 'I am dealing with the emperor as is proper, for I know that he fears God. I shall have to deal differently with you if you are so rude.' Then, standing still for a time, I said to the emperor: 'Let me offer (the Eucharist) for you with a clear conscience; set my mind at rest.' He sat there and nodded, but did not promise openly; and as I continued to stand he said he would alter the rescript.

At once I asked him to stop the whole investigation . . . He promised he would do so. I said to him: 'I act (celebrate the

Eucharist) relying on your honour.' 'Act on my honour,' he said.
Only then did I go to the altar, and I would not have gone unless
he had distinctly promised. And truly the offering was so full of
grace that I felt myself that the favour he had granted was acceptable to God. . . .

64. AMBROSE EXCOMMUNICATES THE EMPEROR   390

Theodosius we have already met. Ecclesiastical diplomacy and flattery saved Antioch; it did not save Thessalonica (the modern Salonika),
the city where Theodosius had been baptized. The commander-in-
chief in Illyricum had arrested the favourite charioteer of that city and
proposed to punish him for a sexual offence. The people were furious.
They rioted, caught the general and killed him and some other Roman
officers.

The news reached Theodosius when he was at Milan of which city
Ambrose was bishop. The emperor, naturally and rightly, was furious.
The punishment should be what is optimistically called exemplary.
But Ambrose interceded as Flavian had done. The emperor agreed to
be moderate in his action. But then he thought again. He ordered what
amounted to a general massacre. About 7,000 people were collected in
the Circus, where the chariot races were held, and massacred. Theodosius had apparently regretted his order and tried in vain to counter-
mand it; he ordered a general delay of thirty days between sentence
and execution in future.

Ambrose left Milan before the emperor returned from a visit elsewhere and wrote him the letter which is given here. It was two months
before Theodosius was allowed to attend the Eucharist, and Christmas
before he was admitted to receive communion after doing public
penance. Ambrose had asserted, and Theodosius had accepted the right
of the bishop to exercise Christian discipline over the head of the state.
It happened in Milan; it could not have happened in Constantinople.
The West begins to part company from the East.

Note the use by Ambrose of the word 'Sacrifice' in relation to the
Eucharist.

Source: Ambrose, *Letters* 51.

Listen August Emperor. You have zeal for the faith, I own it; you
have fear of God, I confess it. But you have a vehemence of
temper, which, if soothed, may speedily be changed into com-

passion, but which, if inflamed, becomes so violent that you can scarcely restrain it . . .

A deed has been perpetrated at Thessalonica which has no parallel in history, a deed which I in vain attempted to prevent, a deed which, in the frequent expostulations which I addressed to you beforehand, I declared would be most atrocious, a deed which you yourself, by your later attempt to cancel it, have confessed to be heinous. This deed I could not extenuate. When the news of it first came, a council was in session on account of the arrival of bishops from Gaul. All the assembled bishops deplored it; not a single one viewed it indulgently. Your act could not be forgiven even if you remained in the communion of Ambrose; on the contrary the odium of the crime would fall even more heavily on me, if I were not to declare to you the necessity of becoming reconciled to our God . . .

I advise, I entreat, I exhort, I admonish. It grieves me that you, who were an example of singular piety, who exercised consummate clemency, who would not suffer individual offenders to be placed in jeopardy, should not mourn over the destruction of so many innocent people. Successful as you have been in war, and worthy of praise in other respects, yet piety has ever been the crown of your achievements. The devil has grudged you your chief excellence—overcome him while you have the means. Add not sin to sin by following a course which has proved the ruin of many.

For my part, debtor as I am to your goodness in all other things, grateful as I must ever be for it (for your goodness has surpassed that of many emperors, and indeed has been equalled only by one), I am not free from apprehension, though I have no ground for supposing that you will show yourself contumacious. I dare not offer the Sacrifice[1] if you determine to attend. For can it possibly be right, after the slaughter of so many, to do that which may not be done after the blood of only one innocent person has been shed? I trust not!

I write with my own hand what I wish to be read by yourself

[1] Ambrose seems to have been one of the first to speak of the Eucharist as a Sacrifice, the commemoration and repleading of Christ's sacrifice on the Cross.

alone. Doubtless you desire to be approved by God. You shall make your oblation when you have been given liberty to sacrifice, when your offering will be acceptable to God . .

65. DESTRUCTION OF THE SERAPEUM   391

Rome was the main centre of conservative paganism, but it would be quite wrong to think that the rest of the empire had given up entirely the worship of the old gods. In Alexandria, for instance, which was always a riotous city, the Christians still found that street attacks were mounted on them from the great temple called the Serapeum. In 391 Theodosius issued a general order against pagan sacrifices. He also ordered the destruction of the Serapeum. Theophilus, bishop of Alexandria (385–412) led the attack. He was under orders not to let this become a police action, in retaliation for the anti-Christian disturbances. Theodosius wrote: 'The Christians who have fallen in these disturbances are martyrs. Their blessed state exempts us from the necessity of seeking to avenge their blood: and accordingly free pardon is given to the idolaters who have been concerned in the late disturbances. But we condemn the vain superstition of the Gentiles, and we order the destruction of their temple.'

Osiris outlived and absorbed all the gods of ancient Egypt. Under the name of Serapis (Osiris-Apis) he was identified with the Greek Hades or Pluto, and worshipped by Egyptians and Greeks alike. For this purpose the Ptolemies, the Greek rulers of Egypt, built the Serapeum. The emperor Hadrian, writing to the consul Servian, said, rather too inclusively, that the Alexandrians had 'one god, Serapis, who was worshipped by Christians, Jews and Gentiles.' A second century papyrus discovered at Oxyrhynchus runs: 'Chaeremon requests your company at dinner at the table of the lord Serapis in the Serapeum to-morrow, the 15th, at 9 o'clock.'

Source: Rufinus, *Church History* (continuation of Eusebius) 11, 23.

Everyone, I suppose, has heard of the temple of Serapis at Alexandria, and many people actually know it. It is a place elevated not by nature but by artificial construction on a hundred or more steps and extending on all sides into large rectangular areas. Every part providing a way out to the topmost pavement is constructed of vaulted work. There are enormous windows above and secret passages separated off internally from one another, which used to enable various operations and secret activities to be practised. Coming to the upper parts, the outermost area of the whole circuit was occupied by halls and chapels and lofty chambers in which the temple officials or those they called 'hagneuontes' (i.e. those purifying themselves) used to live together. Cloisters also ran round the whole circuit behind these buildings, separated into rectangular compartments. In the middle of the whole area was the temple, raised on pillars of precious stone and constructed outside with a rich and magnificent display of marble. Within was an image of Serapis so enormous that it touched one wall with its right hand, the other with its left. This portentous statue was said to be built out of every species of metal and timber.

The walls of the inner shrine were kept sheathed with thin layers first of gold, then of silver, and finally of bronze to protect the more precious metals. There were also some features constructed with an art and cunning that roused wonder and amazement in the beholder. A very small window facing the sunrise had been adapted in such a way that on the day when it was customary for the statue of the Sun to be carried in to salute Serapis, by a careful attention to time, just as the statue came in, a sunbeam entered through this window and lit up the mouth and lips of Serapis. Thus before the eyes of the people Serapis appeared to be greeted by the Sun with a kiss.

There was also another kind of trick. The magnetic stone is said to have the power of seizing iron and drawing it towards itself. With this in mind the statue of the Sun had been made by the sculptor's hand of the finest iron. Thus, when the stone whose nature, as we have mentioned, was to draw iron to itself was fixed in the ceiling above, and the statue, exactly balanced, was meticulously placed beneath the exact spot from which its influence was exerted, the stone by its natural force attracted the iron and the statue was seen by the people to rise and hang in the air. In order that it might not be given away by its sudden fall the managers of the trick used to say, 'The Sun has risen that he may bid farewell to Serapis before departing to his own realm.' Many other devices for purposes of deception had been constructed by the ancients in this place, which it would be tedious to describe individually.

But, as we began by remarking, when the proclamation had been read aloud, the crowds on our side were prepared to overthrow the author of error. However, a certain belief had been spread around by the heathen themselves that if this statue were touched by human hand the earth would immediately gape asunder and be dissolved into chaos and the sky would suddenly crash down. This caused a kind of immobility to descend on the crowds for a little, but suddenly one of the soldiers, fortified more by faith than by his weapons, seized a battle-axe and, rising up, smashed it with all his force into the jaw of the old deceiver. A shout arose from the crowds on either side. However, the sky did not fall, nor did the earth sink away. Then, renewing the attack again and again, he cut at the smoke-stained knee of rotten wood. When this had been thrown down fire was applied and it blazed up as easily as touchwood. After this the head was wrenched from the neck and dragged from its socket; then the feet and other limbs were cut off with axes, attached to ropes and dragged down, and, under the gaze of the Alexandria that worshipped him, the aged, dormant deity was burnt limb by limb in separate places. Last of all, the trunk, which had survived, was consumed by fire in the amphitheatre. Such was the end of the vain superstition and ancient error of Serapis.

66. SACRIFICE FORBIDDEN

The year after the destruction of the Serapeum, Theodosius issued a general law (Extract A) against all pagan worship, public or private. Yet the same year there was a pagan restoration in Rome under the usurping emperor, Eugenius, a nominal Christian, and the Frankish general Arbogast who had never become one. Ambrose left Milan when Eugenius approached. He wrote to the new emperor: 'Though the imperial power is great, Sire, consider how great is God. He sees the hearts of all. He questions their innermost consciences. He knows all deeds before they are done. He knows the secrets of your breast. A king will not allow one of his subjects to deceive him. Do you think you can hide anything from God?'

Two years passed before the issue was decided in favour of the Christians. Theodosius gathered his armies and marched through what is now Yugoslavia until he reached the summit of a pass that leads down into Italy. He looked down on the army of Eugenius encamped below under the banner of Hercules. Theodosius rode to the head of his troops and, shouting 'Where is the Lord God of Theodosius?', led them down to battle. The first day's battle went badly; but on the second Theodosius decisively beat the pagans. Eugenius was executed; Arbogast killed himself. Theodosius knocked down the statues of Jupiter which Eugenius had put up to guard the pass. In the hands of each Jupiter was a golden thunderbolt ready poised for discharge. Theodosius gave the thunderbolts to his men—'by such lightnings,' they said, 'may we often be struck.' The emperor, who was usually austere and aloof, relaxed and, as Augustine put it, 'permitted the merriment of the soldiers'.

Among the officers of Theodosius was a young Visigoth called Alaric (see page 289).

Theodosius and his young son Honorius went on to Rome. There the tireless Senate, in spite of the edict of Theodosius, in spite of the defeat of Eugenius, asked for money to continue the sacrifices. They were, of course, refused.

It would be wrong to suggest that there was not also a minority Christian party in the Senate. The letter from Jerome (Extract B) describes what one of its members did.

Sources: A: *The Theodosian Code* 16, x, 12; Jerome, *Letters* 107.

A.   THE EDICT OF EMPEROR THEODOSIUS

8 November 392

Hereafter no one of whatever race or dignity, whether placed in office or discharged therefrom with honour, powerful by birth or humble in condition and fortune, shall in any place or in any city sacrifice an innocent victim to a senseless image, venerate with fire the household deity (as it were the genius of the house or the Penates) by a more private offering, and burn lights, place incense, or hang up garlands.

If anyone undertakes by way of sacrifice to slay a victim, or to consult the smoking entrails, let him, as guilty of lese-majesty, receive the appropriate sentence, having been accused by a lawful indictment . . .

If anyone, by placing incense, venerates either images made by mortal labour, or those which are enduring, or if anyone in ridiculous fashion forthwith venerates what he has represented, either by a tree encircled with garlands, or an altar of cut turfs . . . let him, as guilty of sacrilege, by punished by the loss of that house or possession in which he worshipped according to the heathen superstition. For all places which shall smoke with incense, if they shall be proved to belong to those who burn incense, shall be confiscated.

But if anyone should venture this sort of sacrifice, in temples or public sanctuaries or buildings and fields belonging to another, and if it shall appear that the acts were performed without the knowledge of the owner, let him be compelled to pay a fine of 25 pounds of gold, and let the same penalty apply to those who connive at this crime as well as those who sacrifice.

B.   JEROME SURVEYS THE FIELD OF VICTORY   403

Jerome to Laeta

Did not your own kinsman Gracchus, whose name shows his patrician origin, when he was prefect of the city a few years ago, overthrow, wreck and pulverize the grotto of Mithras and all its dreadful images? I mean those by which the worshippers were initiated as Raven, Bridegroom, Soldier, Lion, the Persian, Sun, Crab, and Father . . . Even in Rome itself paganism is deserted. Those who were once the gods of the nations linger under their lonely roofs with horned owls and night-birds. The standards of the army are emblazoned with the sign of the Cross. The emperor's purple robes and his crown glittering with jewels are ornamented with symbols of that shameful but saving gibbet. Already the Egyptian Serapis has been made a Christian.

67. THE LAST GLADIATORS   404

The triumph of Christianity had one humane consequence. It stopped the shows. The games in the Colosseum at Rome and in every sizeable town in the empire were cruel and degrading beyond imagining. Christian sentiment was against them not only because Christians had so often been the victims. Thus Prudentius begged in verse for their abolition (Extract A). He was a Spaniard who worked as a lawyer in

Rome until he retired about the age of fifty to write Christian poetry
and theology. This extract comes from verses *Against Symmachus*. For
Symmachus see p. 207; for Prudentius as hymn-writer see pages 251–4.

The circus games took as much suppression as pagan worship. Constantine had issued an edict against them nearly a hundred years before
they were finally ended. The occasion seems to have been the visit of
the twenty-one-year-old emperor Honorius to Rome. The story is associated with the name of Telemachus, a monk from Syria. The only
source for the story is Theodoret, bishop of Antioch—a fellow Syrian—
who was about eleven years old at the time. The name of Telemachus
is found in one of the martyrologies, the official lists of those who
suffered. This is the Hieronymian Martyrology compiled in Italy about
450. What Theodoret had to say is given in Extract B. Gibbon's comment is characteristic: 'I wish to believe the story of St. Telemachus. Yet
no church has been dedicated, no altar has been erected to the only
monk who died a martyr in the cause of humanity.'

Sources: A: Prudentius, *Against Symmachus* 2, 1121–31; B: Theodoret,
Church History 5, 26.

A.   PRUDENTIUS PLEADS

Theodosius prohibited bull's blood from tainting the city:
May you, sire, forbid wretched men being sent to the slaughter.
Let none die in Rome to accord by his agony pleasure,
Nor boast in her bounds that a maid is amused by such carnage.
Let only wild beasts quench the thirst of the baleful arena,
And stage us no more of these murders in blood-spattered armour.

B.   TELEMACHUS ACTS

Honorius, who inherited the empire of Europe, put a stop to the
gladiatorial combats which had long been held at Rome. The
occasion of his doing so arose from the following circumstance.
A certain man of the name of Telemachus had embraced the
ascetic life. He had set out from the East and for this reason had
repaired to Rome: there, when the abominable spectacle was being
exhibited, he went into the stadium and, stepping down into the
arena, endeavoured to stop the men who were wielding their
weapons against one another. The spectators of the slaughter were

indignant, and, inspired by the mad fury of the demon who delights in those bloody deeds, stoned the peacemaker to death.

When the admirable emperor was informed of this, he numbered Telemachus in the army of victorious martyrs, and put an end to that impious spectacle.

68. THE AUTHORITY OF THE BISHOP OF ROME

For nearly three hundred years there was no doubt that Rome was the effective as well the ancient capital of the Roman empire. It was beyond doubt the chief city. Its bishop was clearly the key man once the Church began to form a parallel organization to that of the empire. These six extracts illustrate the growth from that position of eminence towards that of supremacy.

The first extract is from a letter of Cyprian, bishop of Carthage, to another bishop in the course of his controversy with Stephen, bishop of Rome over the validity of heretical baptism which Stephen accepted as part of the apostolic tradition of his see and Cyprian denied.

A hundred years later Athanasius was banished by the Arian emperor from his see of Alexandria and took refuge in Rome. Julius, bishop of Rome, wrote in 339 on his behalf and that of another banished bishop to the Council of Antioch making claims of disciplinary jurisdiction (Extract B). A similar claim is made in Extract C about the same time. Thirty years later Jerome writes in terms which foreshadow the fully developed teaching about the position of Peter and his successors as bishop of Rome (Extract D).

Extract E is important in a different way. It takes for granted the precedence, the primacy of honour, of Rome. There was, and perhaps had never been, any dispute about that. The point of the canon is that the bishop of New Rome—a nobody yesterday—is recognized as second in order of precedence in the whole church, ranking above Alexandria and Antioch which had occupied that place. Precedence in the church follows precedence in the empire. This precedence was confirmed by the Council of Chalcedon in 451, but on that occasion Rome objected.

Between Extracts E and F there had been great events. Rome itself was becoming of less and less importance in the actual running of the empire. It had been visited only four times by an emperor in a hundred years. The working capital of the eastern half of the empire was Constantinople; in the west the imperial headquarters might be at Milan,

Ravenna or Trier. On the death of Theodosius in 395 the empire was permanently divided into two. In the eastern empire the bishop of Constantinope was manifestly first in precedence; but he was essentially the emperor's bishop, living in the capital under the emperor's eye. In the west the bishop of Rome was, as he had always been, first and, as he rapidly became, supreme. He was under no emperor's eye. As civilization crumbled and civil rulers rose and fell in bewildering succession the permanence of the bishop of Rome and his curia, his staff, provided a refuge to which men turned. Rome, the Eternal City, still stood first in the allegiance of men's hearts. But Rome now meant its bishop, its pope (for this was the customary style of fifth-century bishops)— the Pope. Leo deserved his title of 'the Great' on both religious and secular grounds as chapter 15 shows.

Just as there were now two empires, so there were beginning to be two churches: a western Catholic Church and an eastern Orthodox Church, but formal separation was still some way off.

Sources: A: Cyprian, *Letters* 74; B: Athanasius, *Against Arians*; C: Canon 3 of the Council of Sardica; D: Jerome, *Letters* 15; E: Canon 3 of the Council of Constantinople; F: Leo the Great, *Letters* 11 (quoting the Order of Valentinian).

A.   *Cyprian to Bishop Pompey*   c. 255

I have sent you a copy of the answer which our brother Stephen (bishop of Rome) has sent to our letter, on reading which you will mark the error of him who endeavours to maintain the cause of heretics against the Church of God; for among other things, either insolent or irrelevant, or self-contradictory, which he has rashly and thoughtlessly written, he has added this: 'If anyone comes to us from any heresy whatever, let no innovation be made on the tradition (of the Roman church) that hands be laid on him unto repentance (but not baptism). Whence comes that tradition? Does it descend from the authority of our Lord and the Gospels? Does it come from the commands and Epistles of the Apostles? ... What do you do when the water in a conduit fails? You go back to the source.'

B.   *Bishop Julius of Rome to the Council of Antioch*   339

Suppose, as you allege, these men were guilty of some offence, the trial should have been conducted not in this way, but according to the Canons of the Church. We should all have been informed of it in writing, so that a just verdict might have been reached by us all. For the accused were bishops, and the churches concerned were no ordinary ones, but those which the Apostles had governed in person.

And why, with regard to the church of Alexandria, was nothing written to us? Don't you know that it is customary for word to be sent first to us, that a just verdict may be secured from this place? If, therefore, any suspicion fell upon the bishop there, word should have been sent to the bishop here; but they neglected to inform us, and proceeded on their own authority at their own pleasure, and now wish us to approve their decisions, though we never condemned him (Athanasius). This is not in accord with the constitutions of Paul or the tradition of the Fathers. What we have received from the blessed Apostle Peter, that I make known to you.

C.   CANON 3 OF THE COUNCIL OF SARDICA[1]   343

If any bishop has had judgment passed against him in a case, and considers that he has good grounds for a re-trial, let us honour the memory of the Apostle Peter and agree that letters should be sent to the bishop of Rome, either from those who tried the case or from the neighbouring bishops. He may decide that judgment should be given afresh and appoint arbitrators, or he may be unable to agree that the case needs re-trial, and the first decision shall hold good.

D.   *Jerome to Pope Damasus*   376

Though your eminence alarms me, your kindness draws me to you. From the priest I claim the saving of a victim, from the shepherd the protection due to the sheep ... It is to the successor of the fisherman that I appeal, to the disciple of the cross. As I follow no leader but Christ, so I address none but your Beatitude, that is, the chair of Peter. For this, I know, is the rock on which the

[1] This was put forward by Hosius, bishop of Cordova (see pages 175, 177, 178).

Church is built. This is Noah's ark and he who is not found in it shall perish when the flood prevails.

E. CANON 3 OF THE COUNCIL OF CONSTANTINOPLE 381

The Bishop of Constantinople is to have primacy of honour next after the Bishop of Rome, because Constantinople is New Rome.

F. AN ORDER OF VALENTINIAN III 445

It is certain that the only defence for us and our empire is the favour of the God of heaven; and to deserve it our first care is to support the Christian faith and its venerable religion. So, because the pre-eminence of the Apostolic See is assured by the merit of the prince of bishops St Peter, by the leading position of the city of Rome, and also by the authority of a sacred Synod, let none presume to attempt anything contrary to the authority of that See. For then at last the peace of the churches will be preserved everywhere, if the whole body recognizes its ruler . . .

So that no disturbance, however slight, may arise among the churches, and that religious discipline may never appear to be weakened, we decree by this perpetual edict that it shall not be lawful for the bishops of Gaul or any other province to do anything without the authority of the venerable pope of the Eternal City. Whatever the authority of the Apostolic See has enacted or may enact hereafter shall be the law for all.

69. CYRIL NO SAINT AT ALEXANDRIA 414-15

Like uncle, like nephew. Theophilus, bishop of Alexandria, had personally supervised the destruction of the Serapeum. His nephew, Cyril, was his adviser. He succeeded him as bishop and personally led a mob attack on the Jews of Alexandria. This extract from the historian Socrates tells the story of this and surrounding incidents. To understand it properly it is important to remember that:

a. the incidents happened in Alexandria; Socrates was a lawyer who lived in Constantinople;
b. Alexandria was a much older city and Christian centre than Constantinople, which as a major town was under a hundred years old, as its name suggests;

   c. Constantinople was the capital, and its bishop—the bishop of
New Rome—now ranked second in precedence in the empire
and the church, having been promoted over the bishop of
Alexandria's head (pp. 230, 233). There was as little love lost
between the two towns and the two churches as was consistent
with their both being Christian.

   d. the conflict between the civil and the religious power which in the
West was waged between Ambrose and Theodosius was paralleled
here in the East between Cyril and Orestes, the emperor's representative, with this difference: Orestes is the humane Christian,
Cyril (one would suspect) the sinner in need of repentance.

   e. the Jews of Alexandria had been a large and thriving community
for some 600 years; Cyril's pogrom, whatever the provocation,
is an ugly beginning to Christian anti-semitism.

   f. Cyril, like so many men of his generation, had spent a long
apprenticeship in the desert—six years. He had allies there.

Cyril of Alexandria is reckoned a saint. Three comments may be
quoted. Gibbon said that this was a mark that his opinions and his
party had finally prevailed. Salmon remarked that in the fourth century
the title, applied to an orthodox bishop, meant, perhaps, little more
than the title 'reverend' applied to a clergyman of the present day. And
Cardinal Newman admitted: 'Cyril, I know is a saint; but it does not
follow that he was a saint in the year 412'—or he might have added in
414 and 415.

Source: Socrates, *Church History* 7, 13-15.

Alexandrians love riots more than any other people . . . and a disturbance arose out of an evil that has become very popular in
almost all cities: a love of dance shows. Because Jews are free from
work on the Sabbath, and spend their time not in hearing their
Law, but in theatrical entertainments, dancers usually attract great
crowds on that day, and rioting almost always follows . . . And
although Jews are always hostile to Christians, they were roused
to still greater opposition because of the dancers.

   Orestes the prefect was proclaiming an order in the theatre for
the regulation of the shows, and some of bishop Cyril's party were
present to learn what sort of rules were to be imposed. One of
them was Hierax, a teacher of elementary literature and an
enthusiastic listener to the bishop's sermons, one who made him-

self conspicuous by leading the applause. When the Jews saw this man in the theatre, they immediately cried out that he had come to excite the people to sedition.

Now Orestes had long been jealous of the growing power of the bishops, because they encroached upon the jurisdiction of the emperor's officers. Cyril, in particular, wished to set spies on his proceedings; Orestes therefore had Hierax seized and put publicly to the torture in the theatre. When Cyril heard of it, he sent for the chief Jews and threatened to take the severest measures unless they ceased to molest Christians.

Hearing these menaces the Jewish people, instead of restraining their violence, only became more furious and were driven to form conspiracies for the destruction of the Christians. One of these was so savage that it led to their complete expulsion from Alexandria, and this I shall now describe.

They determined to make a night attack upon the Christians and agreed that each man should wear a palm-fibre ring on his finger for mutual recognition. Then they sent people into the street to cry that the church called Alexander was on fire. Hearing this, many Christians came running out from all sides, very anxious to save their church. The Jews fell upon them and slew them, readily recognizing each other by their rings. At daybreak the perpetrators of this atrocity could not be concealed, and Cyril, with a huge crowd of people, went to the synagogues, seized them, and drove the Jews out of the city, allowing the mob to plunder their goods. Thus the Jews, who had lived in the city from the time of Alexander the Macedonian, were expelled from it, stripped of all their possessions, and dispersed in all directions.

But Orestes, the governor of Alexandria, was highly indignant at what was done and exceedingly sorry that a city of such magnitude should be suddenly bereft of so large a part of its population. He therefore reported the whole affair to the emperor. Cyril also wrote to him, describing the outrageous behaviour of the Jews; and he sent emissaries to Orestes to negotiate a reconciliation, as the people had urged him to do so. And when Orestes refused to listen to such friendly overtures, Cyril offered him the book of the gospels, thinking that he would put aside his resentment out of respect for religion. But this failed to pacify the prefect, who remained in unrelenting hostility to the bishop. Then this next event occurred.

Some monks living in the mountains of Nitria, of a very fierce temper . . . decided to fight for Cyril. About five hundred of them therefore left their monasteries, entered the city, met the prefect in his chariot and called him a pagan idolater, with many other terms of abuse. Thinking this to be some trap laid for him by Cyril, Orestes shouted that he was a Christian and had been baptized by Atticus, the bishop of Constantinople. They paid very little attention to his protests and one of them, Ammonius, threw a stone at him, which struck him on the head and covered him with blood from the wound. With but few exceptions all the guards plunged through the crowd and fled in all directions, fearing to be stoned to death.

The people of Alexandria, however, ran to the governor's rescue, and after arresting Ammonius and handing him over to the prefect, they put the rest of the monks to flight. Orestes immediately put Ammonius publicly to the torture, which was inflicted with such severity that he died under it; whereupon the governor sent an account of what had happened to the emperor.

So did Cyril, and he had the body of Ammonius buried in one of the churches . . . and ordered his name to be put on the roll of martyrs, praising him in church as one who had died in defence of religion. But the more sober-minded, although they were Christians, did not accept Cyril's prejudiced estimate of him, for they knew very well that he had suffered as a result of his own rashness and had not died under torture for refusing to deny Christ. And Cyril himself, conscious of this, allowed the memory of this business to fade gradually away. The hostility between Cyril and Orestes, however, did certainly not subside then, but was roused again by another event like the last.

There was a woman of Alexandria called Hypatia who . . . far surpassed all the other philosophers of her time . . . Having succeeded to the school of Plato and Plotinus, she would explain the principles of philosophy to her hearers, many of whom came from afar to learn from her.

It was slanderously reported among the Christians that she was responsible for preventing the reconciliation of Orestes to the bishop. Some of them, therefore, carried away by a fierce fanaticism under a ringleader, a reader called Peter, waylaid her as she was returning home and dragged her from her carriage. They took her to the church called Caesareum, where they stripped her and murdered her with potsherds. After tearing her body in pieces, they took the mangled remains to a place called Cinaron and burnt them ... This happened in March during Lent (415).

This affair brought great reproach, not only upon Cyril, but also the whole Church in Alexandria; and surely nothing can be farther from the spirit of Christianity than to tolerate massacres and murders of this sort.

CHAPTER THIRTEEN

THE LIFE OF CHRISTIANS IN THE WEST
Fourth and Fifth Centuries

The extracts in this chapter illustrate a few aspects of the ordinary daily life of orthodox Christians in the West—the normal run of things, not the fortunately exceptional happenings when barbarians sack a city or bishop and emperor clash. They show us men writing poems, singing hymns, holding family prayers, electing a bishop or hoodwinking an heiress, and women firmly leading a truly Christian life in the permissive world of upper-class Rome.

70. TWO POETS CORRESPOND

A.   AUSONIUS: ON FAMILY PRAYERS

Ausonius (310-95), was the son of a doctor. He became a professor of rhetoric and had two famous pupils: Paulinus of Nola was a more fervent Christian and a better poet than his old teacher and friend, Gratian became emperor and made his old tutor one of his two chief ministers. He, too, was a more fervent Christian than Ausonius—it was he who removed the Altar of Victory from the Senate House (see p. 207). The best-known poem of Ausonius is one in which he praises the wine-growing Moselle, which flows through Trier where he lived, because it reminds him of the vineyards of Bordeaux where he was born.

This extract comes from a poem, only the beginning of which survives, in which he describes a day in his life. His Christianity seems a natural, accepted part of his life, but one that did not go very deep into his inner life—family prayers seem to be rather less trouble than the worship of the household gods which they had replaced.

Source: Ausonius, *Poems*; 'Ephemeris' (Translated by Thomas Hodgkin).

> Now the bright-eyed Morn re-illumes the window;
> Now the wakeful swift in her nest is chirping;
> You, my slave! as though it were scarcely midnight,
>   Parmeno! sleep still.

Dormice sleep, 'tis true for a livelong winter;
Sleep, but feed not. You, like a lazy glutton,
Drink deep draughts before you lie down to slumber;
    Therefore you snore still.

Therefore voice of mine cannot pierce those ear-flaps,
Therefore slumber reigns in your vacant mind-place,
Therefore Light's bright beams with a vain endeavour
    Play on your eye-lids.

Bards have told the tale of a youth whose slumbers
Lasted on, unbroken, a mortal twelvemonth,
Nights and days alike, while the Moon above him
    Smiled on his sleeping.

Rise! you dawdler; rise! or this rod corrects you.
Rise! lest deeper sleep, when you least expect it,
Wrap your soul:[1] your limbs from that couch of softness,
    Parmeno! lift now.

Ah! perhaps my gentle harmonious Sapphics
Soothe his brain and make but his sleep the sweeter.
Drop we then the Lesbian tune, and try the
    Sharper Iambus.

    Here: boy! Arise! My sandals bring
    And fetch me water from the spring,
    That I may wash hands, eyes and face;
    And bring my muslin robe apace;
    And any dress that's fit to wear
    Bring quick, for I abroad would fare.
    Then deck the chapel, where anon
    I'll pay my morning orison.
    No need of great equipments there,
    But harmless thoughts and pious prayer;

[1] (Taken over from Horace, Carm. 3. 11.)

No frankincense I need to burn;
The honeyed pastry-cake I spurn.
The altar of the living sod
I leave to others, while to God
The Father with coëqual Son
And Spirit, linked in unison,
I pray in this my morning hour.
I think upon the present Power:
My spirit trembles. He is here,
Yet what have Hope and Faith to fear?'

B. PAULINUS OF NOLA: ON GETTING AWAY FROM THINGS

Helen Waddell in *Desert Fathers* describes Paulinus thus: 'A member of a great French house, an accomplished scholar, ex-Senator, ex-Consul, and finally parish priest of Nola [near Naples], who lived in poverty after spending the last of a royal fortune in ransoming the prisoners taken in the sack of Rome'.

Paulinus had a genius for friendship. He was on intimate terms with Martin of Tours, Ambrose, Pope Anastasius I, Augustine, and Ausonius; he sympathized with Pelagius, and wrote a poem on the marriage of Julian of Eclanum (see pages 283–5). But he liked his friends to become pen-friends. Augustine, the warmer-hearted African, 'yearned' to see him; the physical presence of his friend was what he 'greatly craved' (*Letters* 27, 28). His old tutor Ausonius was almost heartbroken when Paulinus went off to Spain before retiring to Nola, and this poem is a kind of defence of his retreat and an exaltation of the ascetic life.

Source: Paulinus of Nola, *Carmen* 10, lines 162–80, translated by Helen Waddell, *Mediaeval Latin Lyrics*.

Not that they beggared be in mind, or brutes,
That they have chosen their dwelling place afar
In lonely places: but their eyes are turned
To the high stars, the very deep of Truth.
Freedom they seek, an emptiness apart
From worthless hopes, din of the market-place,
And all the noisy crowding up of things,
And whatsoever wars on the divine,
At Christ's command and for his love, they hate;
By faith and hope they follow after God,

And know their quest shall not be desperate,
If but the Present conquer not their souls
With hollow things: that which they see they spurn
That they may come at what they do not see,
Their senses kindled like a torch, that may
Blaze through the secrets of eternity.
The transient's open, everlastingness
Denied our sight; yet still by hope we follow
The vision that our minds have seen, despising
The shows and forms of things, the loveliness
Soliciting for ill our mortal eyes.
The present's nothing: but eternity
Abides for those on whom all truth, all good,
Hath shone, in one entire and perfect light.

71. AMBROSE, WRITER OF HYMNS   *c.* 380

Juvencus, a Spanish noble and a priest, was the first notable Latin-
Christian poet; he turned the story of the gospels into an epic poem in
skilful imitation of the style of Virgil. Damasus, another Spaniard, who
became bishop of Rome in 366, composed epigrams for the tombs of
martyrs in the catacombs on the Appian Way, which he had restored,
and composed his own epitaph. His hexameters are poor poetry, but
good history.

Jerome states that Hilary, bishop of Poitiers (*c.* 310–66), wrote a
Book of Hymns. This has been lost, but three of his hymns have been
recovered. One consists of seventy verses in honour of the Trinity, each
verse starting with a different letter of the alphabet, a trick as old as
Psalm 119. The third hymn, celebrating the victory of the second
Adam over Satan, is notable because it is written in trochaic tetra-
meters, a rhythm as old as Julius Caesar's legions, which, Suetonius
reported, sang as they marched:

See our Caesar now triumphant from his Gallic victory!

Prudentius was to use it (see pages 251–3); it became popular in Ireland,
and many of our familiar hymns are in this metre. *Praise the Lord! ye
heavens adore him*, to Haydn's great tune *Austria*, is one of the finest.

Ambrose is the acknowledged inventor of the mediaeval Latin hymn
of uniform stanzas, suited to congregational singing. Augustine, whom
he baptized, described how these hymns came to be written in his

Confessions (Book 9), which, it must be remembered, were addressed to God.

'Not long had the church of Milan begun to use this kind of conso-lation and exhortation, the brethren zealously joining with harmony of voice and hearts. For it was a year, or not much more, that Justina, mother to the emperor Valentinian, a child, persecuted thy servant Ambrose, in favour of her heresy, to which she was seduced by the Arians. The devout people kept watch in the church, ready to die with their bishop thy servant. There my mother thy handmaid, bearing a chief part of those anxieties and watchings, lived for prayer. Then it was first instituted that, after the manner of the Eastern churches, hymns and psalms should be sung, lest the people should wax faint through the tediousness of sorrow. And from that day to this the custom is retained, almost all thy congregations throughout other parts of the world following herein . . . How I did weep in thy hymns and can-ticles, touched to the quick by the voices of thy sweet-attuned Church!'

Perhaps to make the lines more easily memorable Ambrose used a number of rhymes, no doubt a vulgar innovation in the opinion of classical poets. Conservative churchmen seem to have criticized Ambrose for starting a craze for hymns, and he defends the practice in one of his sermons:

'They assert that the people are charmed by the strains of my hymns. I don't deny it. It's a lofty strain and most powerful. For what can be more powerful than the confession of the Trinity, daily affirmed by the mouth of the whole people? All are zealous to profess their faith, and now they can do it—in verse. Thus all become teachers who were scarcely able to be disciples.'

So popular were Ambrose's hymns that all such hymns came to be described as Ambrosian. Scholars allow some 18 to be genuine. We give the morning hymn here, *Splendor Paternae gloriae*. The first verse is from the translation for the *Yattendon Hymnal* by Robert Bridges (1899), but we have made a new translation of the other verses to show, by a more literal version, the homely vigour of Ambrose's hymns. The oxymoron in verse 5 might shock a modern congregation; verse 4 could not express more exactly the needs of our own times.

> O splendour of God's glory bright,
> O thou that bringest light from light,
> O Light of light, light's living spring,
> O Day, all days illumining!

True Sun, pour down on us who sing
Thy brightness ever-shimmering,
Thy Holy Spirit radiate,
And all our senses saturate.

Our daily toil direct aright,
And blunt the tooth of envy's spite,
Make the rough going smooth and clear,
Our burdens give us grace to bear.

Under thy rule let mind be placed,
The body true to thee and chaste;
Let faith boil up with fervent heat,
But keep from us the drugs that cheat.

And Christ shall be to us our food,
And faith shall be the wine he brewed;
So let us drink of happiness,
The Spirit's sober drunkenness.

In gladness let the day go by,
Shy as the dawn our modesty,
Our faith the midday's burning glow,
And darkness may we never know.

72. MARTIN MADE BISHOP OF TOURS 371

Martin was a Christian catechumen (a convert undergoing instruction) in the Roman army when he met a beggar and gave him half his cloak. He then saw a vision of Christ which led him to be baptized. In 360 he founded the first monastery in Gaul, at Ligugé.

Like many early bishops, notably Ambrose, Cyprian, and Eusebius of Caesarea, Martin was consecrated by demand of the people, as this witness by his friend Sulpicius Severus shows. It is interesting that the Ordinal drawn up by the Anglo-Methodist Unity Commission, 1968, restores this element in the ordination services, the people answering with a loud voice, 'We trust he is worthy, to God be the glory.'

Source: Sulpicius Severus, *Life of St. Martin.*

About this time Martin was asked to accept the bishopric of Tours. As, however, it was no easy matter to get him to leave his monastery, a citizen of Tours named Rusticus resorted to this ruse. He threw himself at Martin's feet, pretending his wife was ill, and so lured him away. Groups of citizens lining the road at intervals made it look as if he were conducted to the city under guard.

There was an incredibly large crowd assembled to cast their vote in his favour, not only from the city of Tours but also from nearby towns, all of one mind, one wish, one and the same purpose: Martin was the most worthy candidate, happy the church that had him as its bishop.

A few, however, and some of them among the prelates summoned to appoint a new bishop, set up an unworthy opposition. They objected that he was a person of low quality, dress filthy, hair untidy, quite unfit to fill the office of a bishop. Most of the people, however, with better judgment, laughed down this foolish view. In fact, the abuse levelled at this excellent man only seemed to recommend him more highly. There was no course left to the bishops but to consent to the wishes of the people, which indeed were inspired by the will of God.

A leader among the opposing bishops was a certain Defensor, whose very name brought condemnation on his head through a prophetic reading which was heard by all. It happened that the lector (reader), whose turn it was to read that day, was unable to make his way through the crowd. While the clergy were put out by his failure to arrive, a bystander seized the Psalter and sang the first verse that leapt to his eye, which happened to be this, from the Psalms (8, 2):

'Out of the mouths of babes and sucklings thou hast perfected praise, because of thine enemies, that thou mayest destroy the enemy and the *defender*.' (Defensor in Latin.)

When they heard this the people lifted their voices in triumph at the confusion of the opposite party. The reading of that Psalm was taken for a divine intervention, so that this Defensor might hear judgment pronounced on his cause. Out of the mouth of a babe and suckling—in Martin, as it were—divine praise was perfected, and as clearly was the enemy denounced and destroyed.

Martin's wonderful manner of life as a bishop is beyond our skill to relate. He strove to become all the more what he had been before, showing the same humility of heart, the same poverty of dress, while lacking nothing of dignity and grace as he fulfilled the bishop's office. Yet he achieved this without giving up his vocation as a monk. For some time he made use of a cell adjacent to the cathedral church, but when he found the flow of visitors more disturbing than he could bear, he founded a monastery for himself some two miles beyond the city.

This was as remote and secluded a place as the desert solitude. It is a level piece of ground enclosed on one side by a lofty cliff and on the other by a sweep of the river Loire. There was only one approach and that a narrow one. Martin himself, and some of the brethren, lived in huts built of timber, but the majority excavated for themselves rock dwellings out of the overhanging cliff.

There were about eighty disciples, whose way of life followed the example set by the blessed master. No one had anything as his own but all was held in common. To buy or sell anything, as many monks do, was forbidden them. They practised no crafts, except that of the copyist,[1] and this was reserved to the younger brethren; the seniors had all their time for prayer. It was rare for anyone to leave his cell, except to go to the oratory. They fasted except for one meal a day and never touched wine, except in the case of sickness. Many wore camel-hair garments, and it was considered a sin to wear softer material, which is all the more surprising since so many among them were of noble birth and, after an upbringing of quite a different sort, had been trained to such austerity by penance and humility. Many of these men we now know as bishops. What church or city would not be glad to have a bishop from Martin's monastery?

73. TWO PATRICIAN WOMEN OF ROME

Jerome had a gift for friendship with women, and many of his most

---

[1] Copying manuscripts: an important task until the discovery of printing.

interesting letters were written to them and about them. The fourth-century Libanius, one of the last of the great pagan philosophers, once exclaimed, 'Heavens! What women you Christians have!' Blesilla and Fabiola are two fine examples, and see Jerome's description of Marcella, pages 291–6.

Source: Jerome, *Letters* 38 and 77.

A.   BLESILLA   384

In the past our dear widow used to deck herself with jewels, and spent whole days before her glass looking for anything wrong in her appearance. Now she boldly says: 'We all with unveiled face, beholding as in a glass the glory of the Lord, are changed into the same image, from glory to glory, even as by the spirit of the Lord.'[1] In those days lady's maids used to arrange her hair, and her poor head, which had done no harm, was imprisoned in a head-dress crammed with curls. Now it is left alone, and knows that it is sufficiently cared for when it is covered by a veil. At that time the softest down seemed hard to her limbs, and she could scarcely rest upon a pile of cushions. Now she rises in haste from her bed to pray, and with tuneful voice forestalls her comrades' 'Alleluia,' herself ever the first to praise her Lord. She kneels on the bare ground, and with frequent tears cleanses the face that was once defiled with white lead [i.e. a cosmetic]. After prayer comes the singing of psalms; her neck grows weary, her knees totter, her eyes drop off to sleep; but her ardent spirit will hardly give them leave to rest. Her dress is of dark stuff; therefore it is scarcely soiled by lying on the ground. Her slippers are of a cheap sort; the price of gilded boots will be given as alms to the needy. Her girdle is not adorned with jewels or gold; it is made of wool, perfectly simple and clean, and it is intended to keep her dress close rather than to cut her figure into two halves.

B.   FABIOLA   399

On this occasion you give me as my subject Fabiola, the glory of the Christians, the wonder of the Gentiles, the sorrow of the poor, and the consolation of the monks. Whatever point I take first

[1] 2 Cor. 3, 18.

pales in comparison with what is to come. Shall I tell of her fastings? Her alms are greater still. Shall I praise her humility? It is outstripped by the ardour of her faith. Shall I mention her studied squalor, her plebeian dress, and the slave's garb she chose in condemnation of silken robes? It is a greater thing to change one's disposition than to change one's dress. We part with arrogance less easily than with gold and jewels. Even when these are thrown away, we sometimes pride ourselves on our ostentatious shabbiness and make a bid for popular favour by offering poverty as its price. A virtue that is concealed and cherished in the inner consciousness looks to God alone as judge. So the eulogy I bestow upon her must be altogether new; I must neglect all the rules of rhetoric and begin my story at the cradle of her conversion and penitence . . .

As at the very outset there is a rock in the path, and I am faced by the storm of censure that was directed against her for having taken a second husband and abandoned her first, I shall not praise her for her conversion until I have cleared her from this charge. We are told that her first husband was a man of such heinous vices that even a prostitute or a common slave could not have put up with them. If I describe them, I shall mar the heroism of the woman, who preferred to bear the blame of separation rather than to expose to shame the man who was one body with her, and thus reveal the stains upon his character. This only I will say, and it is a plea sufficient to excuse a chaste matron and Christian wife. The Lord ordained that a wife must not be put away except for fornication, and that, if she was put away, she must remain unmarried . . . With us what is unlawful for women is equally unlawful for men, and as both sexes serve God they are bound by the same conditions.

Fabiola, as men say, put away a vicious husband; she put away a man who was guilty of this and that crime; she put him away because—I almost mentioned the scandal which the whole neighbourhood proclaimed but which his wife alone refused to reveal. If she is blamed because after repudiating her husband she did not remain unmarried, I will readily admit her fault, provided that I may put in the plea of necessity. 'It is better,' says the apostle, 'to

marry than to burn'. She was a very young woman and she could
not remain a widow. She saw 'another law in her members war-
ring against the law of her mind',[1] and she felt herself dragged like
a chained captive into carnal intercourse. She thought it better to
confess her weakness openly and to accept the dark stain that such
a lamentable marriage would bring, rather than to claim to be the
wife of one husband and under that disguise to ply the harlot's
trade. The same apostle expresses his wish that 'young widows
should marry, bear children, and give no handle to calumny'[2]
And then at once he gives his reason: 'For some are already
turned aside after Satan.' Fabiola therefore had convinced herself, and thought that she was justified in putting away her
husband. She did not know the Gospel's strict ordinance, which
precludes Christian women from marrying again in their first
husband's lifetime, whatever their case may be. Thus she evaded
the other assaults of the devil, but this one wound from him she
unwittingly received.

But why do I linger over the forgotten past, seeking to excuse
a fault for which she herself confessed her penitence? Who would
believe that after the death of her second husband, at a time when
widows, having shaken off the yoke of slavery, are wont to grow
careless and indulge in licence, frequenting the public baths, flit-
ting to and fro in the squares, showing their harlot faces everywhere—who, I say, would believe that it was then that she came
to herself, put on sackcloth and made public confession of error?
On the eve of passover, in the presence of all Rome, she took her
stand among the other penitents in the church of that Lateranus
who perished formerly by Caesar's sword. There before bishop,
presbyters, and weeping populace she exposed to view her dishevelled hair, wan face, soiled hands, and dust-stained neck. What
sins would not such lamentation purge away? What stains so deep
that these tears would not wash them out?

When she was restored to communion before the eyes of the
whole Church, what did she do? Did she forget her sorrows in the
midst of happiness, and determine after being shipwrecked to face

[1] References are to 1 Cor. 7, 9 and Romans 7, 23.
[2] 1 Tim. 5, 14.

once more the dangers of the main? Nay, she preferred to break up and sell all that she could lay hands on of her property—it was a large one and suitable to her rank—and when she had turned it into money she disposed of everything for the benefit of the poor. First of all she founded an infirmary and gathered into it sufferers from the streets, giving their poor bodies worn with sickness and hunger all a nurse's care. Need I describe here the diverse troubles from which human beings suffer, the maimed noses, the lost eyes, the scorched feet, the leprous arms, the swollen bellies, the shrunken thighs, the dropsical legs, and the diseased flesh alive with hungry worms? How often did she carry on her own shoulders poor filthy wretches tortured by epilepsy! How often did she wash away the purulent matter from wounds which others could not even endure to look upon! She gave food with her own hand, and even when a man was but a breathing corpse, she would moisten his lips with drops of water . . .

She showed the same generosity to the clergy, monks, and virgins. What monastery was there which her purse did not aid? What naked or bed-ridden sufferer did she not supply with clothes? On what indigent person did she not pour out her swift and lavish donations? Rome was not large enough for her compassionate kindness. She went from island to island, and travelled round the Etruscan Sea, and through the Volscian province,[1] with its lonely curving bays, where bands of monks have taken up their home, bestowing her bounty either in person or by the agency of holy men of the faith.

Then suddenly, and to everyone's surprise, she sailed to Jerusalem, where she was welcomed by a great concourse of people, and for a short time was my guest. When I remember that meeting, I seem to see her still as I saw her then. Blessed Jesus, with what fervour and zeal did she study the sacred volumes! In her eagerness to satisfy her hunger, she ran through the prophets, the gospels and the psalms; she suggested questions and stored up my answers in her heart's repository.

But let me continue the task I have begun. While I was seeking a dwelling suitable for so great a lady, whose desire for solitude

[1] i.e. up and down the west coast of Italy.

included an unwillingness not to visit the place where Mary once lodged, suddenly messengers flew this way and that and the whole Eastern world trembled. We were told that swarms of Huns had poured forth from the distant Sea of Azov, midway between the icy river Tanais and the savage tribes of the Massagetae, where the Gates of Alexander keep back the barbarians behind the rocky Caucasus. Flying hither and thither on their swift steeds, said our informants, these invaders were filling the whole world with bloodshed and panic. At that time the Roman army was absent, being kept in Italy by reason of civil war ... The general report was that they were making for Jerusalem, and that it was their excessive greed for gold that urged them to flock to that city. The walls of Antioch, neglected in the careless days of peace, were hastily repaired. Tyre, desirous of cutting herself off from the land, sought again her ancient island. We too were compelled to prepare ships, and to wait on the sea-shore as a precaution against the enemy's arrival; to fear the barbarians more than shipwreck, however fierce the winds might be; for we had to think not so much of our own lives as of the chastity of our virgins. At that time also there was a certain dissension amongst us, and our domestic quarrels seemed more important than any fighting with barbarians. I myself clung to my fixed abode in the East, and could not give up my inveterate longing for the Holy Land. Fabiola, however, who only had her travelling baggage and was a stranger in every land, returned to her native city to live in poverty where she had been rich, to lodge in the house of another, she who had once entertained many guests, and—not to prolong my story unduly—to pay over to the poor before the eyes of Rome all that she had sold with Rome for witness ...

How great had been the wonder of Fabiola's life Rome showed when she was dead. She had scarcely drawn her last breath and paid the debt of her soul to Christ, when

'Flying rumour heralding such woe'

brought the peoples of the whole city to attend her funeral ...

I hear it still: the crowds that went before the bier, the swaying multitude that attended her obsequies in throngs; no streets, no colonnades could contain, no overhanging roofs could hold the eager onlookers. On that day Rome saw all her peoples gathered together. Every one flattered himself that he had a share in the glory of her penitence. No wonder that men exulted in her salvation, seeing that the angels in heaven rejoiced over her conversion.

This, the best gift of my aged powers, I present to you, Fabiola, as a funeral offering of respect.

74. THREE HYMNS OF PRUDENTIUS   *c.* 410

From a brief autobiography in verse we know that Prudentius (see pages 228–9) was a Spanish gentleman, bred to the law and attaining high judicial office under the emperor Theodosius, another Spanish gentleman. In 404 at the age of fifty-six he dedicated the rest of his life to the service of God. Two books of poetry are fruits of this service. *Peristephanon*, 'the garland', is a collection of hymns in praise of martyrs, many of them Spaniards; it is valuable history as well as good poetry. He has a special love for Saragossa, where 'Christ dwells in every street', and whose many martyrs shall win a special grace at the last day. He describes how he had halted at Imola on the way to Rome, and visited the tomb of the martyr Cassian to say his prayers. Looking up he saw, in vivid mosaic, the story of how Cassian, the schoolmaster, was stabbed to death by the *stili*[1] of his pupils. 'I hug the tomb, the altar and stone are wet with my weeping . . .'

His other book of poems, *Cathemerinon*, is a collection of hymns 'for the hours of the day'. The poems are too long—and too good—for congregational singing, but parts of them may be found in our church hymnals. We give three extracts, the first to show his use of the trochaic tetrameter (see page 241), the others, beautifully translated by Helen Waddell, to show the quality of his poetry at its best.

I

A Hymn for every hour

Of the Father sole begotten,
    Ere the worlds began to be,
He the Alpha and Omega,
    He the source, the ending he,

---

[1] Sharp writing instruments for writing on wax tablets.

Of the things that are, that have been,
  And that future years shall see,
    Evermore and evermore.

O that ever-blessèd birthday,
  When the Virgin, full of grace,
By the Holy Ghost conceiving,
  Bore the Saviour of our race,
And the boy, the world's redeemer,
  First revealed his sacred face,
    Evermore and evermore.

Laud and honour to the Father,
  Laud and honour to the Son,
Laud and honour to the Spirit,
  Ever Three and ever One,
Con-substantial, co-eternal,
  While unending ages run,
    Evermore and evermore.

II

Before Sleep

The toil of day is ebbing,
The quiet comes again,
In slumber deep relaxing
The limbs of tired men.

And minds with anguish shaken,
And spirits racked with grief,
The cup of all forgetting,
Have drunk and found relief.

The still Lethean waters
Now steal through every vein,
And men no more remember
The meaning of their pain . . .

Let, let the weary body
Lie sunk in slumber deep.
The heart shall still remember
Christ in its very sleep.

III

The Burial of the Dead

Take him, earth, for cherishing,
To thy tender breast receive him.
Body of a man I bring thee,
Noble even in its ruin.

Once was this a spirit's dwelling,
By the breath of God created.
High the heart that here was beating,
Christ the prince of all its living.

Guard him well, the dead I give thee,
Not unmindful of his creature
Shall he ask it: he who made it
Symbol of his mystery.

Comes the hour God hath appointed
To fulfil the hope of men,
Then must thou, in very fashion,
What I give, return again.

Not though ancient time decaying
Wear away these bones to sand,
Ashes that a man might measure
In the hollow of his hand:

Not though wandering winds and idle,
Drifting through the empty sky,
Scatter dust was nerve and sinew,
Is it given man to die.

Once again the shining road
Leads to ample Paradise;
Open are the woods again
That the Serpent lost for men.

Take, O take him, mighty Leader,
Take again thy servant's soul,
To the house from which he wandered
Exiled, erring, long ago.

But for us, heap earth about him,
Earth with leaves and violets strewn,
Grave his name, and pour the fragrant
Balm upon the icy stone.

75. THE FEAST OF ST JUST AT LYONS   *c.* 464

Sidonius Apollinaris is regarded as the last representative of classical culture. Son-in-law to Avitus, the future emperor, Sidonius was elected bishop of Clermont-Ferrand in 469, apparently while still a layman, and partly to defend Clermont against the Goths. Reluctantly and humbly he accepted the responsibility, giving up his country pursuits and practice of poetry. After repeated sieges, Clermont fell, but Sidonius was restored to his see after a short captivity.

Lyons was his birth-place. The Vigil and Mass of St Just was held on September 1st and 2nd; we cannot be sure which year's celebration is here described by Sidonius. It is interesting to see how the Roman way of life lingered in certain pockets of the empire. In an earlier letter, he discusses, in a single paragraph, works of Plato and Origen and Cicero's translation of the *Ctesiphon* of Demosthenes.

Source: Sidonius, *Letters* 5, 17.

We had assembled at the tomb of St Just. The annual procession before daylight was over, attended by a vast crowd of both sexes which even that great church could not hold with all its cincture of galleries. After Vigils were ended, chanted alternately by the monks and clerics, the congregation separated. We could not go far off, as we had to be at hand for the next service at Terce,[1] when the priests were to celebrate the Mass.

We felt oppressed by the crowding in a confined space, and by the great number of lights which had been brought in. It was still almost summer, and the night was so sultry that it suffocated us, imprisoned as we were in that steaming atmosphere. Only the first freshness of the autumn dawn brought some welcome relief. Groups of the different classes dispersed in various directions, the principal citizens assembling at the monument of Syagrius, which is hardly a bowshot from the church. Some of us sat down under an old vine, the stems of which were trained trellis-wise and covered with leaves and drooping fronds; others sat on the grass, odorous with the scent of flowers.

The talk was enlivened with amusing jests and pleasantries. Above all (and what a blessed thing it was!), there was not a word about officials or taxes, not an informer among us to betray, not a syllable worth betrayal. Every one was free to tell any story worth relating and of a proper tenor. It was a most appreciative audience; the vein of gaiety was not allowed to spoil the distinct relation of each tale. After a time, we felt a certain slackness through keeping still so long, and we voted for some more active amusement.

We soon split into two groups according to our ages; one shouted for the ball, the other for the board-game, both of which were to be had. I was the leader of the ball-players: you know that book and ball are my twin companions. In the other group, the chief figure was our brother Domnicius, that most engaging and attractive of men. There he was, rattling some dice which he had got hold of, as if he sounded a trumpet-call to play. The rest of us had a great game with a party of students, doing our best at the healthful exercise with limbs which sedentary occupations made much too stiff for running . . .

They came to tell us that our time was up, and that the bishop was leaving his retreat. We therefore rose to go to Mass.

[1] Terce was one of the seven times of prayer observed by strict Jews (Psalm 119, 164), and adopted by Christians for monastic life. Terce was at the third hour of the day.

76. THE BISHOPS AND THE FORTUNE HUNTER *c.* 475

Sidonius Apollinaris, Bishop of Clermont-Ferrand, had introduced Amantius, one of his lay readers ('lectors'), to the bishop of Marseilles, commending him as a rising business man with an import business. He soon discovered that the honest young man was not so honest, and wrote a second letter to explain what had happened.

Source: Sidonius, *Letters* 3, 3.

His native country is Auvergne; his parents are persons in a some-what humble position in life, but free and unencumbered with debt; their duties have been in connection with the service of the Church rather than of the State. The father is a man of extreme frugality, more intent on saving up money for his children than of pleasing them. This lad accordingly left his home and came to your city with a very slender equipment in all respects. Notwith-standing this hindrance to his ambitious projects he made a fairly successful start among you. Saint Eustachius, your predecessor, welcomed him with deeds and words of kindness, and put him in the way of quickly obtaining comfortable quarters. He at once began to cultivate assiduously the acquaintance of his neighbours, and his civilities were well received. He adapted himself with great tact to their different ages, showing deference to the old, making himself useful to his coëvals, and always exhibiting a modesty and sobriety in his moral conduct which are as praiseworthy as they are in young men. At length, by well-timed and frequent calls, he became known to and familiar with the leading personages of your city, and finally even with the Count himself. Thus the assiduous court which he paid to greatness was rewarded with ever-increasing success; worthy men vied in helping him with their advice and good wishes; he received presents from the weal-thy, favours of one kind or another from all, and thus his fortune and his hopes advanced 'by leaps and bounds'.

It happened by chance that near the inn where he was lodging there dwelt a lady of some fortune and high character, whose daughter had passed the years of childhood, yet had scarcely reached the marriageable age. He showed himself very kind to this girl, and made, as her youth allowed him to do, trifling presents to her of toys and trash that would divert a girl, and thus, at a very trifling expense, obtained a firm hold on her affections. Years passed on; she became old enough to be a bride. To make a long story short, you have on the one side a young man, alone, poorly off, a stranger, a son who had skulked away from home not only without the consent, but even without the knowledge of his father; on the other, a girl not inferior to him in birth, and superior to him in fortune; and this fellow, through the introduction of the bishop because he was a reader, by favour of the Count because he had danced attendance in his hall, without any investigation as to his circumstances by the mother-in-law because his person was not displeasing to her daughter, woos and wins and marries that young lady. The marriage articles are signed and in them some beggarly little plot of ground which he happened to possess near our borough is set forth with truly comic pomposity. When the solemn swindle was accomplished, the poor beloved one carried off his wealthy spouse, after diligently hunting up all the possessions of his late father-in-law, and converting them into money, besides adding to them a handsome gratuity drawn from the easy generosity of his credulous mother-in-law, and then, unrivalled humbug that he was, he beat a retreat to his own native place.

Some time after he had gone, the girl's mother discovered the fraud, and had to mourn over the dwindling proportions of the estates comprised in her daughter's settlement, at the very time when she should have been rejoicing over the augmented number of her grandchildren. She wanted to institute a suit for recovery of her money, on the ground that he had fraudulently overstated his property; and it was in fact in order to soothe her wrath that he set forth for Marseilles, when he first brought you my letter of introduction.

Now, then, you have the whole story of this excellent young man, a story, I think, worthy of the Milesian Fables[1] or an Attic comedy. It remains for you to show yourself a worthy successor of bishop Eustachius by discharging the duties of patronage to the

---

[1] A collection of Greek vulgar tales, now lost.

dear youth whom he took under his protection. You asked me for a long letter, and therefore if it is rather wordy than eloquent you must not take it amiss. Condescend to keep me in your remembrance, my lord Pope.[1]

---

[1] 'Papa' was the common form of address to all bishops at this time.

CHAPTER FOURTEEN

BEYOND THE BOUNDS

In a characteristic purple patch which, also characteristically, has significance, Jerome showed how the Christian faith was being carried outside the now Christian empire: 'From India, from Persia, from Ethiopia we daily welcome monks in crowds. The Armenian bowman has laid aside his quiver, the Huns learn the Psalter, the chilly Scythians are warmed with the glow of the Faith. The Goths, ruddy and yellow-haired, carry tent-churches about with their armies: and perhaps their success in fighting against us may be due to the fact that they believe in the same religion.' (*Letter* 107.)

The extracts illustrate the growth of Christianity beyond the empire northwards across the Danube to the Goths, south into Ethiopia, east into Persia and west to Ireland. Two of these outward thrusts were ultimately sterile because Islam cut them off from the main body. But the northward thrust probably saved Christianity from disappearing with the empire in which it grew up, while the westward movement doubled back to convert the still pagan Saxons and Norsemen and ensure that all Europe should be Christian.

The extracts also serve to introduce two new heresies—Nestorianism and Monophysitism—and to carry forward the story of Arianism. They are concerned more with the followers of these heresies than with the heresies themselves for heretics play a vital part in what those who live this side of Hadrian's Wall may like to think of as extra-mural Christianity. It may be noted that, while Arianism may be thought of as a heresy for metaphysicians, Nestorianism and Monophysitism concern psychologists as well.

77. ULFILAS CONVERTS THE GOTHS

Bishop Ulfilas (*c.* 311–83) was one of the great men of the fourth century. He was himself in every respect but ancestry a Goth—his family had been captured in the great Gothic invasion of the eastern part of the empire which had taken place in 259. It was on that occasion that, as the writer of Extract B put it, Troy was sacked a second time when it had scarcely recovered from its destruction by Agamemnon!

The rich civilization of the empire, the Romania of Extract A, had a strong attraction for the poor barbarians outside. As a young man Ulfilas went to Constantinople, accepted Christianity and was consecrated bishop. He returned to his people.

Ulfilas was perhaps the first of the many missionaries who have reduced a native language to writing and given it a grammar in order that people might read the Bible which he translated for them. Ulfilas thought his people took more than sufficient delight in war so he left out the books of Samuel and Kings. Most of his Old Testament is lost but the greater part of the New Testament survives in a wonderful manuscript written in silver and gold on a purple parchment, the Codex Argentius in Uppsala.[1] It is the first in the noble family of translations into Germanic languages which came into full flower with Martin Luther in Germany and Tyndale in England. Here are the first four petitions of the Lord's prayer with a literal translation made by Thomas Hodgkin:

ATTAR UNSAR THU IN HIMINAM   VEIHNAI NAMO THEIN.
Father our   thou in the heavens hallowed be name thine.

QIMAI THIUDINASSUS THEINS: VAIRTHAI VILJA THEINS, SVE IN
Let come kingdom   thine: be done   will   thine, as in

HIMINA JAH ANA AIRTHAI. HLAIF UNSARANA THANA SINTEINAN
heaven and on earth.   Loaf   our   the   enduring

GIF UNS HIMMA DAGA.
give us   today.

Extract A comes from Auxentius, bishop of Dorostorum on the Danube, a friend of Ulfilas. It tells how, when persecution came from a hostile Gothic ruler, Ulfilas led his Christian Goths across the Danube into what is now Bulgaria and settled there inside the empire. Extract B is from Jordanes, the historian of the Goths, who wrote two centuries later. He himself came from the same part of the world. It appears that Ulfilas had done his pacifying work well among his immediate converts.

But Christianity was not confined to those Goths who settled in Bulgaria. It spread back across the Danube and in time virtually all the Goths became Christian. This too did not happen without persecution. After a heavy defeat by the Roman emperor, the Gothic ruler Athanaric took revenge on those of his fellow tribesmen who followed

[1] See Plate 27.

the religion of Rome. Extract c tells the story of the martyrdom of Sabas. It comes from the letter sent to the Cappadocian churches with the body of Sabas in response to a request from Basil.

Thanks to Ulfilas western Europe did not cease to be Christian when the Goths finally invaded Italy and conquered Rome. It was a legacy of inestimable worth. But it might have been even more valuable but for the divisions that plagued fourth-century Christianity. When Ulfilas lived in Constantinople all the official world was Arian. It was the peak of the time when Athanasius was 'contra mundum'. Ulfilas naturally accepted the Arian form of doctrine, lived and died in it. Extract D is his dying confession of faith. It should be compared with the Nicene formula. The last short extract, from his friend Auxentius, explains some of the differences. The unfortunate moment of Ulfilas' conversion meant that western Europe was plagued by the Arian controversy throughout the whole period of the barbarian invasions.

Sources: A: Auxentius, *Life of Ulfilas*; B: Jordanes, *Of the Affairs o the Goths* 51; C: *Letter to the Cappadocian Churches*; D: Socrates, *Church History* 2, 41; E: Auxentius, *Life of Ulfilas*.

A.   THE MIGRATION OF THE CHRISTIAN GOTHS   348

When through the envy and mighty working of the enemy, there was kindled a persecution of the Christians by an irreligious and sacrilegious Judge of the Goths, who spread tyrannous affright through the barbarian land, it came to pass that Satan, who desired to do evil, unwillingly did good; that those whom he sought to make deserters became confessors of the faith; that the persecutor was conquered, and his victims wore the wreath of victory. Then after the glorious martyrdom of many servants and handmaids of Christ, as the persecution still raged vehemently, after seven years of his episcopate were expired, the blessed Ulfilas being driven from Barbaricum[1] with a great multitude of confessors, was honourably received on the soil of Romania by the emperor Constantius of blessed memory. Thus as God by the hand of Moses delivered his people from the violence of Pharaoh and the Egyptians, and made them pass through the Red Sea, and ordained that they should serve him (on Mount Sinai), even so did God

[1] The country of the Barbarians as opposed to Romania.

deliver the confessors of his only begotten Son afrom the Barbarian land, and cause them to cross over the Danube, and serve him upon the mountains (of Haemus) like his saints of old.

B.   THE PEACEFUL GOTHS   *c.* 550

There were also certain other Goths, who are called Minores, an immense people, with their bishop and primate Ulfilas, who is said, moreover, to have taught them letters. They are at this day (*c.* 550) dwelling in Moesia, in the district called Nicopolitana, at the foot of Mount Haemus, a numerous race, but poor and unwarlike, abounding only in cattle of divers kinds, and rich in pastures and forest timber, having little wheat, though the earth is fertile in producing other crops. They do not appear to have any vineyards: those who want wine buy it of their neighbours; but most of them drink only milk.

C.   THE MARTYRDOM OF SABAS   372

After a little lull the persecution broke forth again: and again the friendly Pagans interposed with their proffered oath,
'There is no Christian in our village.'
'Let no one swear on my behalf,' Sabas burst in with a loud voice. 'I am a Christian.'
Then the Pagan mediators were forced to modify their oath: 'No Christian in our village save one, this Sabas.'
He was brought before the prince, who asked the bystanders what property he possessed.
'Nothing save the robe he wears.'
'Such a man,' said he, 'can do neither good nor harm,' and he drove Sabas scornfully from his presence.
A third time the persecution was set on foot, and now Sabas was keeping his Easter feast with a presbyter named Sansala, just returned to Gothland, to whom he had been directed by a heavenly vision. While he was thus engaged, Atharid, son of King Rhotesteus, broke in upon the village with a band of wicked robbers, dragged Sansala and Sabas from their beds, bound them and carried them off to punishment. Sansala was allowed to ride in a chariot, but Sabas, all naked as he was, was dragged over the

lately burned heather, his captors urging him onwards with cruel blows. When day dawned the saint said to his persecutors,

'Have you not been dragging me all night through thorns and briars, yet where are the wounds upon my feet? Have you not been striking me with whips and cudgels, yet where are the weals upon my back?'

No trace could be found of either.

When the next night came he was laid prostrate on the ground with his outstretched hands tied to one shaft of the wagon and his feet to the other. Next morning a woman, touched with pity, came and unbound him, but he refused to escape and assisted her in preparing breakfast for his captors.

In the morning Atharid ordered him to be hung by his bound hands from a rafter in the room of a cottage. The servants brought some meat which had been offered to idols saying,

'See what the lord Atharid has sent you that you may eat and not die.'

'There is only one Lord, the Lord of heaven and earth,' replied Sabas. 'These meats are tainted and unholy, like Atharid who has sent them.'

At this, one of the servants, enraged at the insult offered to his master, struck him on the breast with the point of a dart. The by-standers thought he must be killed, but he said,

'You think you have dealt me a grievous blow, but I felt it no more than a snowflake.'

Nor was there in fact any mark found on his body.

When Atharid heard of these things he ordered that Sabas should be put to death by drowning. The saint gave himself up to prayer and to praising God, until they reached the banks of the river Musaeus [Buzeo in Wallachia?]. And now some relentings began to stir in the hearts of his persecutors.

'Why should we not let this man go?' they said, one to another. 'He is innocent, and Atharid will never know.'

'Why are you loitering,' said the saint, 'instead of doing that which is commanded you? I see that which you cannot see, those waiting on the other side who shall receive me to glory.'

Still praising God he was thrown into the river, with his neck tightly bound to a beam, so that he seems to have been strangled rather than drowned. His body, untouched by beast or bird, was brought to Julius Soranus, the Roman Duke of Scythia, and by him sent as a precious gift to his native country of Cappadocia.

D.   THE CREED OF ULFILAS   383

This was the confession of faith which, according to custom, bishop Ulfilas made on his death bed:

I, Ulfilas, bishop and confessor, have ever thus believed, and in this, the alone true faith, do I make my testament to my Lord. I believe that there is one God the Father, alone unbegotten and invisible: and in his only-begotten Son our Lord and our God, artificer and maker of every creature, having none like unto himself...; and in one Holy Spirit, an illuminating and sanctifying power, neither God nor Lord, but the minister of Christ, subject and obedient in all things to the Son, as the Son is subject and obedient in all things to the Father.

E.   COMMENT OF HIS FRIEND AUXENTIUS

By his sermons and his tracts he showed that there is a difference between the divinity of the Father and the Son, of the God unbegotten and of the God only-begotten: and that the Father is the Creator of the Creator, but the Son the Creator of the whole creation; the Father, God of our Lord, but the Son the God of every creature.

78. NESTORIUS AND THE OPENING TO THE EAST

Rome's neighbours to the north were barbarians, anxious both to rob and to imitate. To the east was the great kingdom of Persia, a very different matter. It was as hostile as the barbarians but without their desire to copy. Christianity had become the religion of the Roman empire; then it could not be the religion of Persians. To be a Christian was to be suspect as a fifth columnist.

Nestorius (d. *c.* 451) was the unwitting finder of a way out. Nestorians could be tolerated in Persia because they were outcasts in the empire. The totally unchristian intolerance of Cyril proved in this way an asset to the Christian faith. Extracts A–C illustrate the process by which Nestorianism was rejected. This is their setting. Nestorius him-

self came originally from a town on the Persian frontier. He went to
Antioch and was a monk there. The emperor chose him to be bishop
of Constantinople in 428. There he distinguished himself by a bitter
persecution of the remaining Arians. So far Cyril and he would have
agreed. But it was almost unnatural for Alexandria and Antioch, or
Alexandria and Constantinople to agree. Cyril and Nestorius soon fell
out. The key word in their quarrel was 'theotokos', mother of God,
just as 'homoousion' had been in the Arian controversy. What was the
relation of the divine and the human in Christ? Nestorius distinguished
and denounced the new-fangled epithet being applied to Mary. Cyril
approved it.

The bishops from Asia cautiously inclined towards Nestorius. Celes-
tine in Rome took the opposite side and wanted Cyril to depose
Nestorius. The emperor called a council to Ephesus. Cyril hurried
there with a boatload of Egyptian bishops and his own armed followers.
The bishop of Ephesus (which was to claim the Virgin's tomb)
took his side. Cyril refused to wait for the opposition. Why should
they lose the advantage of quick travel by sea? They held a session and
excommunicated Nestorius in his absence. It is to this proceeding of
theirs that Extract A, the protest of the emperor's representative, refers.
When bishop John of Antioch and his party arrived they too called a
council, and they excommunicated Cyril.

It was now up to the emperor. The longest purse won. How expensive the process was is shown by extract B, a plaintive letter from
Dioscorus the archdeacon of Alexandria (i.e. the bishop's right hand
man) to the new bishop of Constantinople. Nestorius was sent to a
lonely part of Upper Egypt and there he died probably about 451. It
was in these years of exile that he wrote the reasoned defence of his
position from which Extract C is taken. This work has the misleading
title of *The Bazaar of Heracleides*. It has survived in a Syriac translation
which was discovered in 1895 and published in 1910. It is incomplete:
at one of the chief gaps there is a manuscript note: 'From here twelve
pages have been torn out and lost from the original by the troops of
Bedr Khan Bey when they captured the district of Das in the year 2154
of the Greeks' (1854). Bazaar seems to have been a mistaken translation
for a Greek word which can mean either 'treatise' or 'business'—and
where else would a Syrian transact business but in a bazaar?

The last extract illustrates the active functioning of a Nestorian church
in Persia fifty years after the break. The writer is Barsumas, bishop of
Nisibis in that country. He is writing to Acacius, the new bishop of

Ctesiphon, the headquarters of the Persian church. They had been fellow-pupils of bishop Ibas at his famous Academy at Edessa, a town within the Roman empire. Now that Nestorianism was repressed in the empire its place had been taken by a similar Academy at Nisibis. The council referred to in the letter was finally held in 486. It sanctioned the right of bishops and priests to marry and take a second wife if the first died. In the West celibacy had by now become the rule if not always the practice. In the East priests but not bishops were allowed to marry. It must have done its work well, for from this time on the Nestorian church was active and successful in spreading Christianity further eastwards.

Sources: A and C: Nestorius, *The Bazaar of Heracleides*; B: Synodicon: *Concilia* 5, 988; D: Ditto 2, 56–8; E: Barsumas, *Letter to Acacius*.

A.   THE PROTEST OF COUNT CANDIDIANUS   431

To the holy Cyril, bishop of Alexandria and Metropolitan, and to the bishops who have assembled together with him, Flavius Candidianus, the great and illustrious Count of the most religious household. Since I reached the city of Ephesus, nothing else have I demanded of the congregation of the holy Council except that the questions of the orthodox faith should be settled in peace and unity, as the faithful, the victorious emperor also has commanded . . . But when I learned that you were ready to assemble together in the holy Church without the will of the other bishops . . . I rested not from persuading and invoking each one of you not to think of holding a Council incomplete . . . that you should introduce no innovations before all the holy bishops were gathered together unto the Council, but that you should wait four days only for the holy John, bishop of Antioch, Metropolitan, and those who were with him, and those again who were with the holy and pious Nestorius, bishop of Constantinople . . . Then, by the consent of you all, it would be known who was found to believe improperly and outside the canons. . . . But you have not accepted aught of what has been said, while I also have surely been driven out by you.

B.   THE COST OF ORTHODOXY   *c.* 432

[This letter was written by archdeacon Dioscoros of Alexandria,

on behalf of his bishop, Cyril, to the bishop of Constantinople
while the rival decrees of the factions at the Council of Ephesus
were still under consideration by the emperor.]

My master, your brother bishop, has written to the Lady Pul-
cheria, the most reverend servant of God;[1] the prefect Paul;
Romanus, the chamberlain; the Lady Marcella, lady of the bed-
chamber; and the Lady Droseria. Suitable presents (lit. 'blessings') have been sent to them. And his magnificence Aristolaus is
ready to write to the prefect Chrysoretus, who is opposing the
Church, about some things which your messenger ought to obtain.
Suitable gifts (lit. 'eulogies') have also been sent to him. My
master, your most holy brother, has written also to the Lord the
professor of Rhetoric and to his magnificence Arthebas asking
them to meet and persuade Chrysoretus to stop his opposition to
the Church. And indeed suitable presents have been sent to them
. . . . A schedule shows to whom gifts have been sent from here
so that you yourself may be aware how much the church of
Alexandria exerts itself for your holiness . . . Indeed the clergy
here are upset because the church of Alexandria is stripped of its
goods on account of this conflict. In addition to the gifts sent from
here it owes count Ammonius 15,000 pounds of gold. Now a
second letter has been sent to him asking him to carry out his
undertaking. But, as for your church, be careful lest the greed of
some whom you know should reduce the church of Alexandria
to sorrow.

C.   THE COMMENT OF BISHOP NESTORIUS   *c.* 450

Cyril was the whole tribunal, for everything which he said they
all said together, for without doubt it is certain that he in person
took the place of a tribunal for them. For if all the judges had been
assembled and the accusers had risen in their place and the accused
also likewise, all of them equally would have had freedom of
speech, instead of his being in everything both accuser and emperor and judge. He did all things with authority after excluding

---

[1] Sister of the emperor and, as her title shows, a woman following a strict
religious rule.

from authority him who had been charged by the emperor, and he exalted himself. And he assembled all those whom he wanted, both those who were far off and those who were near, and he constituted himself the tribunal.

And I was summoned by Cyril who had assembled the Council, even by Cyril who was the chief thereof. Who was judge? Cyril. And who was the accuser? Cyril. Who was the bishop of Rome? Cyril. Cyril was everything. Cyril was the bishop of Alexandria and took the place of the holy and saintly bishop of Rome, Celestinus.

D.   UPROAR IN THE COUNCIL OF CHALCEDON   451

The most illustrious judges and the right honourable senators[1] said: 'Let the most reverend bishop Theodoretus come in and take his seat as a member of the Council because the most holy archbishop Leo has restored him to his see, and the most sacred and pious emperor has ordered that he should be present at the sacred Council.' When the most reverend bishop Theodoretus[2] came in, the most reverend the bishops of Egypt, Illyria and Palestine shouted out: 'Lord, have mercy upon us. The Faith is in danger. He is expelled under the Church's canons. Out with this man. Out with the man who taught Nestorius.' The most reverend the bishops of the Orient, Pontus, Asia and Thrace shouted: 'We signed a blank piece of paper. We were beaten up. That was why we signed. Out with the Manichees.[3] Out with Flavian's[4] enemies. Out with the enemies of the Faith.' The most reverend Dioscoros, bishop of Alexandria, said: 'Why was Cyril deprived, who was excommunicated by that man?' The most reverend the bishops of the Orient, Pontus, Asia and Thrace shouted: 'Out with Dioscoros the murderer. Everybody knows what Dioscoros did.'

[1] The imperial commissioners who, with the legates from Rome, presided over the Council, which defined the doctrine of the Person of Christ.

[2] Theodoret, the church historian.   [3] See pages 280–2.

[4] Flavian, bishop of Constantinople who died as a result of injuries received at the Council of Ephesus in 449. The 'blank piece of paper' refers to the fact that the minority party were kept by force in the church where the Council met until they had signed a blank cheque.

. . . And after the most reverend bishop Theodoretus had taken his seat the bishops of the Orient and their allies shouted: 'He is worthy, worthy.' The bishops of Egypt and their party shouted: 'Don't call him bishop. He's no bishop. Out with God's enemy. Out with the Jew.' The bishops of the Orient and their friends shouted: 'The orthodox for the council; out with the rebels.' The Egyptians: 'Out with God's enemy; out with the man who slandered Christ. Long live the empress. Long live the emperor. Long live the Catholic emperor.' . . . The Eastern bishops: 'Out with the murderer Dioscoros. Long live the Senate . . . He stands condemned in the face of the whole council.' Basil, the most reverend bishop of Trajanopolis, rose and said: 'And Theodoretus is condemned by us.' The Egyptians: 'And Theodoretus accused Cyril. If we accept Theodoretus, we banish Cyril. . . .'

The most illustrious judges and the right honourable senators said: 'These vulgar interjections are not seemly for bishops. . . .'

E.   AVOIDING A COUNCIL IN PERSIA   485

People who don't know, think that the Bishop of Nisibis has a fine time of it; but for two years we have been having plague and famine, and now the Tu'an Arabs have been on the raid, plundering round Nisibis and across the Roman border; and the Romans with their Arabs, the Tai'ans, are threatening reprisals. The marquis is trying to make terms on condition of mutual return of plunder; and that necessitates a meeting between him and the Roman general, with a big official from Seleucia, and all the chiefs of both Arab tribes, and goodness knows how long that will take to arrange!

Last August (when I came to a council to oblige you) we got the general to come to Nisibis for a talk; and those Tu'ans must needs choose that time to go a-raiding, and of course the Romans thought it was our treachery, and there was no end of a fuss! I cannot come to any council now, in spite of your request and the King's order. The marquis will not hear of it, and will not even summon my suffragans and let them go. Besides, you are just starting on this embassy of yours to Constantinople, and you really had better put off the council till your return. By the way,

T

among the Romans there is a devil of a row ecclesiastically, and you will be delighted at the contrast with our splendid union. If you will have the council, I will agree beforehand to all of its decisions that are in accordance with the faith. We have already dropped the Beit Lapat canons.

Your humble disciple and subject. Take care of yourself and pray for us.

79. THE ETHIOPIAN CUL-DE-SAC   c. 340

There was nothing in the least heretical about the spread of Christianity down the Nile valley and into Ethiopia as this extract shows. It took place with the help of Athanasius himself. But it became involved in heresy about a century later through the fact that bishop Dioscorus, Cyril's successor at Alexandria, had gone too far in the opposite direction to Nestorius. He had adopted the view that there was in Christ only one nature, the divine. In 449 he forced this view through the 'robber council' of Ephesus, to use the nickname given it by Leo the Great. Leo's indignation was understandable since the Council excommunicated him. Monophysitism ('one nature') became the official Christian teaching. Two years later the Council of Chalcedon reversed the decision—in the interval there had been a change of emperor. Dioscorus was excommunicated and banished; Monophysitism became a heresy—but remained the belief of the Coptic (Egyptian) and Ethiopian Churches, which were in this way cut off from the main body. This may be one reason why there was no outgoing activity from Ethiopia. It has remained a Christian country to this day. Its emperor is styled 'the Lion of Judah'. It is the only African state with a continuous Christian history—something to be proud of but yet to regret.

This account comes from Rufinus' *Church History* 1, 9. Rufinus states that he got the facts from Edesius, 'who was afterwards ordained to the priesthood at Tyre'. Frumentius appears in the official records of Ethiopia as Fremonatos.

A Tyrian philosopher, Meropius, decided to explore the country of the Ethiopians, inspired by the example of the philosopher Metrodorus, who had previously travelled through it. He took with him two lads, who were relations of his and knew the Greek language well. They reached the country by boat, and when

Meropius had observed what he had wished to see, he put in at a place with a safe harbour to procure some necessary supplies.

It so happened that the treaty between the Romans and the Ethiopians had been lately violated. Consequently the Ethiopians seized the philosopher and those who sailed with him and killed them all except his two young kinsmen; these they spared out of pity for their tender age and sent them as a gift to the king. He was pleased with the boys' good looks, and appointed one of them, whose name was Edesius, to be cup-bearer at his table. The other, named Frumentius, was entrusted with the care of the royal records.

The king died soon afterwards and left them free, the government devolving on his wife and infant son. The queen then, seeing her son thus left in his minority, begged the youths to take charge of him until he should come of age. They accepted the commission and began to administer the kingdom. The chief authority was in the hands of Frumentius, and he made a point of enquiring of the Roman merchants trading with that country, whether there were any Christians to be found. And when some were found, he told them who he was and urged them to select suitable sites for the celebration of Christian worship.

In a short time he built a house of prayer, instructed some of the Ethiopians in Christian principles and trained them to take part in the services.

When the young king came of age, Frumentius resigned to him the administration of public affairs, in which he had so honourably acquitted himself, and begged leave to return to his own country. Though both the king and his mother implored him to remain he, yearning to visit his home again, would not be persuaded. So both of them departed.

Edesius hurried to Tyre to see his parents and kin, but Frumentius stopped at Alexandria and told the whole story to Athanasius the bishop, who had just been invested with that dignity. He said how he hoped that steps could be taken to bring Christianity to the Ethiopians and begged Athanasius to send a bishop and clergy there and not to neglect those who might thus be brought to salvation.

Athanasius considered how this could best be done, and asked Frumentius himself to accept the bishopric, as there was no one more suitable than he. So this was done. Frumentius, invested with episcopal authority,[1] returned to Ethiopia, became there a preacher of the gospel, and built several churches. Helped by God's grace, he performed various miracles, healing the diseases of many souls and bodies.

80. PATRICK OF IRELAND   *c.* 405–12

Ireland was always outside the Roman empire. Patrick was born on the west coast of its westernmost province (Britain) in the last days of Roman rule there. His birth-place cannot be identified nor do we know where he served as a slave in Ireland, nor where he landed in Gaul from a ship that apparently carried a cargo of Irish wolf-hounds. But we do know that he was consecrated bishop by Germanus of Auxerre, a town some hundred miles south-east of Paris. Germanus had close associations with the British Isles. He twice visited what is now England. The first time was in 429 to deal with Pelagian heretics[2] at St Albans; the second, eighteen years later to encourage British troops to victory over Picts and Saxons with shouts of Alleluia. Patrick was sent to Ireland to help bishop Palladius and to take over when he left. His success paved the way for the remarkable flowering of Christianity in Ireland at a time when it was everywhere else in retreat, and prepared for the rescue later by Celtic missions of much moribund European Christianity and the conversion of northern Europe.

His work in Ireland lasted from about 431 to his death in 461. He worked largely through the sons of petty kings and chiefs whom he took to 'walk with him' and learn what he had to teach.

Source: Patrick, *The Confession.*

I am Patrick, a sinner, most unlearned, the least of all the faithful, and utterly despised by many. My father was Calpurnius, a deacon, son of Potitus, a priest, of the village Bannavem Taburniae; he had a country seat nearby, and there I was taken captive.

I was then about sixteen years of age. I did not know the true God. I was taken into captivity to Ireland with many thousands of people—and deservedly so, because we turned away from God,

---

[1] As bishop of Axum.   [2] See pages 281, 283–6.

and did not keep his commandments, and did not obey our priests, who used to remind us of our salvation. And the Lord brought over us the wrath of his anger, and scattered us among many nations, even unto the utmost part of the earth, where now my littleness is placed among strangers.

And there the Lord opened the sense of my unbelief that I might at last remember my sins and be converted with all my heart to the Lord my God, who had regard for my abjection, and mercy on my youth and ignorance, and watched over me before I knew him, and before I was able to distinguish between good and evil, and guarded me, and comforted me as would a father his son. . . .

For this reason I long had in mind to write, but hesitated until now; I was afraid of exposing myself to the talk of men, because I have not studied like the others, who thoroughly imbibed law and sacred Scripture, and never had to change from the language of their childhood days, but were able to make it still more perfect. . . .

As a youth, nay, almost as a boy not able to speak, I was taken captive, before I knew what to pursue and what to avoid. Hence today I blush and fear exceedingly to reveal my lack of education; for I am unable to tell my story to those versed in the art of concise writing—in such a way, I mean, as my spirit and mind long to do, and so that the sense of my words expresses what I feel. . . .

But after I came to Ireland—every day I had to tend sheep, and many times a day I prayed—the love of God and his fear came to me more and more, and my faith was strengthened. And my spirit was moved so that in a single day I would say as many as a hundred prayers, and almost as many in the night, and this even when I was staying in the woods and on the mountain; and I used to get up for prayer before daylight, through snow, through frost, through rain, and I felt no harm, and there was no sloth in me—as I now see, because the spirit within me was then fervent.

And there one night I heard in my sleep a voice saying to me: 'It is well that you fast, soon you will go to your own country.' And again, after a short while, I heard a voice saying to me: 'See, your ship is ready.' And it was not near, but at a distance of perhaps two hundred miles, and I had never been there, nor did I know a living soul there; and then I took to flight, and I left the man with whom I had stayed for six years. And I went in the strength of God who directed my way to my good, and I feared nothing until I came to that ship.

And the day that I arrived the ship was set afloat, and I said that I was able to pay for my passage with them. But the captain was not pleased, and with indignation he answered harshly:

'It is of no use for you to ask us to go along with us.' And when I heard this, I left them in order to return to the hut where I was staying. And as I went, I began to pray; and before I had ended my prayer, I heard one of them shouting behind me;

'Come, hurry, we shall take you on in good faith; make friends with us in whatever way you like.' And so on that day I refused to suck their breasts for fear of God, but rather hoped they would come to the faith of Jesus Christ, because they were pagans. And thus I had my way with them, and we set sail at once.

And after three days we reached land, and for twenty-eight days we travelled through deserted country. And they lacked food, and hunger overcame them; and the next day the captain said to me:

'Tell me, Christian: you say that your God is great and all-powerful; why, then, do you not pray for us? As you can see, we are suffering from hunger; it is unlikely indeed that we shall ever see a human being again.'

I said to them full of confidence: 'Be truly converted with all your heart to the Lord my God, because nothing is impossible for him, that this day he may send you food on your way until you be satisfied; for he has abundance everywhere.' And, with the help of God, so it came to pass: suddenly a herd of pigs appeared on the road before our eyes, and they killed many of them; and there they stopped for two nights and fully recovered their strength, and their hounds received their fill, for many of them had grown weak and were half-dead along the way. And from that day they had plenty of food. They also found wild honey, and offered some of it to me, and one of them said:

'This we offer in sacrifice.' Thanks be to God, I tasted none of it.

Also on our way God gave us food and fire and dry weather

every day, until, on the tenth day, we met people. As I said above, we travelled twenty-eight days through deserted country, and the night that we met people we had no food left.

And again after a few years I was in Britain with my people, who received me as their son, and sincerely besought me that now at last, having suffered so many hardships, I should not leave them and go elsewhere.

And there I saw in the night the vision of a man, whose name was Victoricus, coming as it were from Ireland, with countless letters. And he gave me one of them, and I read the opening words of the letter, which were, 'The voice of the Irish'; and as I read the beginning of the letter I thought that at the same moment I heard their voice—they were those beside the Wood of Voclut, which is near the Western Sea—and thus did they cry out as with one mouth:

'We ask thee, boy, come and walk among us once more.'

And I was quite broken in heart, and could read no further, and so I woke up. Thanks be to God, after many years the Lord gave to them according to their cry.

And another night—whether within me, or beside me, I know not, God knoweth—they called me most unmistakably with words which I heard but could not understand, except that at the end of the prayer he spoke thus:

'He that has laid down his life for thee, he it is that speaketh in thee': and so I awoke full of joy.

CHAPTER FIFTEEN

DARKNESS AND DAWN
Augustine and the Fall of Rome

The events illustrated in this chapter can be regarded either as the break-down of civilization or the clearing away of worn-out forms to make way for a new growth. In almost every material way, things were getting worse in Western Europe; they were to get worse still before the long winter ended. The catalogue of the great names in secular history tells its own tale—Alaric the Goth, Attila the Hun, Gaiseric the Vandal. But to set against them are Leo the Great, who gave the West a church strong enough to survive the fall of the empire and to take over much of its work, and Augustine whose thinking is inescapable in all later Christian theology.

81. THE CONVERSION OF AUGUSTINE 385

Augustine was born in 354 at Tagaste in North Africa, of a dissolute father and a Christian mother, Monica. At the age of thirty he went to Rome to teach Rhetoric, but became disgusted by the behaviour of his pupils and took a professorship at Milan. The two great influences leading to his conversion were the prayers of his mother who, now a widow, followed him to Rome and Milan, and the sermons and ex-ample of Ambrose. Two incidents also helped and these are described here. Extracts A and B come from his book, *Confessions* (8: 14–15, 28–9), the greatest of early autobiographies (which, readers must always remember, was addressed to God). Extract C is from Augustine's *The Advantage of Believing*, written in 391. For notes on the Manichees see pages 280–1.

A. ATTRACTION OF THE ASCETIC LIFE

One day there called to see Alypius and me a countryman of mine from Africa. His name was Ponticianus and he held an important post at court. I forget on what business he called, but when we sat down to discuss it he happened to notice a book lying on the gaming table before us. He picked it up, opened it, and to his astonishment found it was the Epistles of St Paul. He had expected it to be one of the text-books I exhausted myself teaching. He smiled, however, and in his glance showed his pleasure and surprise at suddenly finding this book before my eyes, and no other. For he was a Christian, one of the faithful, and he often went to church to kneel before you, our God, in long and frequent prayer.

When I had explained to him that I was engaged in a close study of those Scriptures, he began to tell us about the Egyptian monk Antony, whose name enjoyed a great reputation among your servants, though we had never heard of him till that moment. When, to his surprise, he discovered this, he pursued the theme even more warmly, enlightening our ignorance on so worthy a subject. For our part we were amazed to hear of such wonderful things, well proven, happening within recent memory, almost of our own day, in the true faith and in the Catholic Church. So we were all surprised, he because we had not heard, and we to hear of news so great.

Then his conversation turned to monastic communities leading a life devoted to you, O God, and to the fertile solitudes of the desert of which we knew nothing. Even here in Milan there was such a monastery of holy brethren outside the walls, under the direction of Ambrose. We had not heard of it. He carried on, and we listened in captivated silence.

Then he began to relate how, one afternoon at Trier when the emperor was at the Circus, he had taken a walk with three companions in some pleasant meadows just outside the city walls. They walked in pairs; one accompanied him, the others fell behind. In the course of their wanderings this latter pair came to a simple dwelling where some of your servants—the poor in spirit of whom is the kingdom of heaven[1]—were living together. There they found a book of the Life of St Antony. One of the two began to read it; he marvelled at what he read till it set him afire, and the idea came to him to adopt that way of life, abandoning a worldly career for your service—he was at the time in the civil service. Suddenly, overcome by holy love, and with a sober shame vexed at his own life, he turned to look at his friend, and said: 'I ask you;

[1] Matt. 5, 3.

tell me what is the object of all our labours? What are we aiming at? What is the true end of our service? Does our position at court offer any higher hope than becoming intimates of the emperor, and that a fragile, perilous ambition? How many dangers have we to step over to reach the danger greater than them all, and how long will that take? Yet to be God's friend, if I choose that, can be mine even now!'

Then, in toil with this new life bursting within him, he followed the page again, and as he read he was changed inwardly where you alone can see, and the world fell away from his mind, as soon became clear. Yes, even as he read his heart was tossed in a storm; he disputed with himself, but finally he chose the better way. Then, already belonging to you, he said to his friend: 'Right now I give up our ambitions and decide to prefer God's service, and here is where my new life begins. If you cannot follow, at least do not dissuade me.' The other replied that he too would engage in such a good service to aspire to so great a reward . . .

Then along came Ponticianus and his companion who had taken their stroll by other paths. They had been looking for them, and now they reminded them that it was getting late; they should be on their road back. But they explained to them their new resolution, what had befallen and how they had reached such a resolve, and asked them, if they would not join them, at least not to take it ill. Ponticianus and his companion, however, were not changed inwardly, as were the other two, but they wept for themselves (as he told us), and warmly congratulated the others, recommending themselves to their prayers. So, trailing their hearts in the dust, they returned to the palace, while their companions, setting their hearts in heaven, remained in that dwelling.

B.   TAKE UP! READ!

I flung myself down under a certain fig-tree and completely gave way to my tears . . . 'How long, O Lord, how long wilt thou be angry? For ever? Remember not our former sins'[1]—for I felt I was held by them . . . 'Tomorrow and tomorrow? Why not now? Why is there not an end to my uncleanness here and now?'

[1] Cf. Psalm 85, 5.

I was speaking like this and weeping in the most bitter contrition of my heart, when lo! I heard a voice from a nearby house, as of a boy or girl—I could not tell—chanting and repeating 'Tolle! Lege! Take up! Read!' Immediately, my countenance changed and I began seriously to consider whether children used to sing such words in any of their games, but I could not remember ever hearing the like. So, stemming the torrent of my tears, I arose, judging it to be no other than a command from God, to open the book and read the first chapter I should find. For I had heard that Antony, coming in during the reading of the Gospel, received what was being read as an admonition to himself: 'Go, sell all that thou hast, and give to the poor, and thou shalt have treasure in heaven; and come, follow me.'[1] And by such an oracle he was immediately converted unto thee.

Eagerly then I returned to the place where Alypius was sitting, for there I had laid the Apostle's book, when I arose thence. I seized, opened, and in silence read that passage my eyes first fell on: 'Not in rioting and drunkenness, not in chambering and wantonness, not in strife and envying; but put ye on the Lord Jesus Christ, and make not provision for the flesh'[2]—in lust. I read no further, nor needed to. For instantly, at the end of this sentence, it was as though a calm light flooded my heart, and all the darkness of doubt vanished away.

C.   FOR AND AGAINST THE MANICHEES   *c.* 374–83

You know, my dear Honoratus, that what made me fall into the snares of the Manichees was their assertion that without using the imperious path of authority, they would lead to God, and free from error, those who should follow their teaching. In truth, what decided me to follow them, and to listen to them assiduously for nearly nine years, rejecting the holy religion which had been taught me in my childhood, was that they guaranteed that this same religion imposed the yoke of a superstitious belief on us, and obliged us to believe things, without understanding them; whilst they asked no one to believe anything, without having first penetrated the truth, in such a way as to make it evident. How

---

[1] Matt. 19, 21.   [2] Romans 13, 13–14.

should I not have been attracted by such promises, in the state of mind in which I found myself, when I fell into their hands, being full of the presumption of youth; loving the truth, no doubt, but inflated with the pride which one usually contracts in the schools, where one hears men who are accounted able discoursing on all subjects? I, myself, cared only to argue and to discuss, treating as songs and fables all that was not according to my ideas, at the same time having an ardent desire to possess this truth, which they promised to make me see clearly. . . .

That which hindered me from giving myself up entirely to them, and that which made me confine myself to those whom they called 'hearers' without abandoning the interests and hopes that I might have in the world, was that I perceived they were far richer in specious arguments for attacking the doctrine of the Church, than in proofs for establishing their own. I had taken them for able men, because they showed a great abundance of developments on this subject, and because they had the art of saying ever the same things in a great variety of ways. I had then a bias for this form of talent, and I only understood, later, that there is nothing in it which is not within the range of every man who is a little learned. As to their principles, they had the skill only to show a few of them, and without approving them altogether, I thought that I could hold them, and content myself with them, not knowing any others which appeared to be more satisfying. But you must not think that the least ray of light enlightened me at this time, when I breathed only the love of the world, and when I was possessed with the criminal hope of feasting my eyes on the frail beauty of a woman, passionately fond of luxury, of the ex-hibition of riches, and the false renown of honours, and, in short given up to all the most culpable delights. For you must surely have remarked that it was after these things, alone, I aspired, during the time that I listened to the Manichees with more assiduity than pleasure.

82. BORN BAD OR BORN GOOD? A MANICHEE OR PELAGIAN?

Manes (called Manichaeus in the West) was a Persian, born at Ctesiphon about 215. The Zoroastrians got him exiled to India, where he preached far and wide; then he returned home and was flayed alive by the emperor Sapor I in 275. His followers were banished and Islam eventually destroyed them in the East, but documents discovered in Turfan in Sinkiang show that his teaching survived until the thirteenth century there. Manichaeism was popular in North Africa in Augustine's time and he confesses that he was a Manichee from the age of nineteen to twenty-eight. It seems permanently to have affected his attitude to sex.

Manes taught that it was Satan who created this dark world of ours, and all matter was evil. But he stole particles of God's light and shut them in man's brain, and Jesus, the prophets, Buddha, and Manes had been sent to help release these particles of light, the main purpose of religion. Extreme asceticism, involving celibacy and vegetarianism, was necessary. This asceticism appealed to Augustine, reacting from his youthful venery. It is worth remembering that Augustine had a common law wife and a son of whom he was intensely fond, Adeodatus. Father and son were baptized on the same day.

That we are all born in sin—the doctrine of Original Sin—was stressed by Didymus the Blind at the Alexandrian School for Catechumens. It was based on Paul's words in Romans 5, 12: 'As by one man sin entered into the world, and death by sin, so death passed upon all men, for that all have sinned.' The sin of Adam was transmitted through the act of human procreation. This doctrine, held by Augustine and Tertullian and Cyprian and Ambrose, became the doctrine of the Catholic Church, and was held, even more strongly, by Puritan reformers. Only today is it strongly challenged.

But it was resisted in Augustine's day by Pelagius, a lay monk from Britain, who came to Rome about 400. Celestius became his chief supporter. They were opposed by Augustine and Jerome, and excommunicated in 417. Pelagius went to Palestine and seems to have died there.

Sources: A: *Acts of Thomas* (Apocryphal New Testament); B: Augustine, *Retractationes* I, 16; C: Augustine, *Confessions* 10, 29–30; D: Augustine, *On Original Sin* 14, quoting Pelagius, *On Free Will*; E: Augustine, *On Original Sin* 5–6.

A. GNOSTIC ADVICE TO A BRIDE AND BRIDEGROOM *c.* 250

If ye abstain from this foul intercourse, ye become holy temples, pure, being quit of impulses and pains, seen and unseen, and ye will acquire no cares of life or of children, whose end is destruction. And if indeed ye get many children, for their sakes ye become grasping and covetous, stripping orphans and over-reaching widows, and by so doing subject yourselves to grievous punishments. For most children become useless, oppressed by devils, some openly and some invisibly, for they become either lunatic or half withered or blind or deaf or dumb or paralytic or foolish; or if they be sound, again they will be vain, doing useless or abominable acts; for they will be caught either in adultery or murder or theft or fornication, and by all these will ye be afflicted.

Be persuaded and keep your souls chaste before God . . .

B.   AUGUSTINE REJECTS MANICHAEAN TEACHINGS ON THE ORIGIN OF EVIL

About that period in my presbyterate, I held a disputation with one Fortunatus, a presbyter of the Manichaeans, who had lived for some time at Hippo and had perverted so many that, for their sakes, it pleased him to make his home there. This disputation was taken down by notaries, just as minutes are made: with a date (Aug. 28–29, 392) and the name of the consul. We have taken care to have it placed on record and brought together in the form of a book. The question there propounded is, Whence is evil? And whereas I maintain that evil in man arises out of his voluntary free will, my opponent endeavours to show that the nature of evil is co-eternal with God. Next day, however, he at length confessed that he found nothing to say against my contention. He did not, indeed, become a Catholic; but he left Hippo.

C.   AUGUSTINE'S SEXUAL CODE

Thou commandest chastity: give me what thou commandest, and command what thou wilt . . . Thou commandest me to refrain from the lust of the flesh, the lust of the eyes, and the ambitions of the world. Thou commandest me to refrain from having a mistress, and, for marriage itself, thou hast advised something better than what thou hast permitted . . .

Increase thy gifts in me, Lord, more and more, that my soul may be brought to thee, disentangled from the bird-lime of lustfulness. May it not rebel against itself, not even in dreams through sensual images, committing those degrading defilements, even to the pollution of the flesh.

D.   PELAGIUS DENIES ORIGINAL SIN

Nothing good and nothing evil, for which we are judged to be worthy either of praise or blame, is born with us, but is done by us. For we are born not fully developed, but with a capacity for either conduct. We are made naturally without either virtue or vice, and before the action of our own proper will, the only thing in man is what God has formed in him.

[Augustine added this comment]: 'Now you see in these words of Pelagius the dogma of both him and Celestius, that infants are born without the contagion of any sin from Adam'.

E.   CELESTIUS UPHOLDS INFANT BAPTISM BUT NOT ORIGINAL SIN

We quite agree that infants ought to be baptized for the remission of sins, according to the rule of the universal Church and to the meaning of the gospel. For the Lord has ruled that the kingdom of heaven is only to be given to baptized persons; and since this cannot belong to the resources of nature, it must be conferred by the grace of God.

But that infants must be baptized for the remission of sins was not admitted by us to imply that we agree with the doctrine of original sin, a doctrine very foreign to Catholic sentiment. Because sin is not born with a man; it is subsequently committed by the man. For it is shown to be a fault of the human will, not of nature.

F.   JULIAN AGAINST AUGUSTINE

Pelagianism won its most formidable advocate when the cause was already lost. This was Julian of Eclanum, whose father was a bishop, and who, when a priest, married the daughter of a bishop. Paulinus of Nola (see page 240), wrote one of his songs about this wedding, praising the simplicity of the ceremony as reminiscent of the innocence of Adam and Eve before the fall (Song 25).

Julian became bishop of Eclanum in South Italy, and sold his estates to relieve a famine that followed the ravages of a Gothic army (Symmachus, Letter 1). In 419, however, he was exiled from his see and never recovered it. Julian fastened on Augustine's doctrine of the necessity to baptize infants for the remission of sins as the supreme error, even a blasphemy, and attacked the old African in open letters, manifestos, and twelve great volumes of criticism. As they were the works of a heretic, they have perished, and we can only recover Julian's words from the lengthy quotations in Augustine's last works. In fact Augustine was engaged in writing a second treatise 'against Julian' when he died, a treatise known as the *Unfinished Work* from which this extract is taken (3, 67 and 1, 48).

You ask me why I would not consent to the idea that there is a sin that is part of human nature? I answer, it is improbable, it is untrue; it is unjust and impious; it makes it seem as if the Devil were the maker of men. It violates and destroys the freedom of the will ... by saying that men are so incapable of virtue that in the very wombs of their mothers they are filled with bygone sins. You imagine so great a power in such a sin, that not only can it blot out the new-born innocence of nature, but, forever afterwards, will force a man throughout his life into every form of viciousness ... What is as disgusting as it is blasphemous, this view of yours fastens, as its most conclusive proof, on the common decency by which we cover our genitals.

Tiny babies, you say, are not weighed down by their own sin, but they are being burdened with the sin of another. Tell me then, who is this person who inflicts punishment on innocent creatures ... You answer, God. God! He who commended his love to us, who has loved us, who has not spared his own son for us ... He it is, you say, who judges in this way; he is the persecutor of newborn children; he it is who sends tiny [unbaptized] babies to eternal flames ... It would be right and proper to treat you as beneath argument. You have come so far from religious feeling, from civilized thinking, so far, indeed, from mere common sense, in that you think that your Lord God is capable of committing a crime against justice such as is hardly conceivable even among the barbarians.

G. AUGUSTINE AGAINST JULIAN

Augustine's views on sex are chiefly set forth in his book, *Of Marriage and Sexual Desire* and in Sermon 151. In the latter he instances again the fall of Adam and Eve. When they had disobeyed God by eating the forbidden fruit, they were ashamed and covered their genitals with fig-leaves. 'That's the place! That's the place from which the first sin is passed on.' And Augustine goes on to explain to his congregation that this shame at the uncontrollable stirring of the genitals was the punishment for the sin of disobedience and so is the shame of his hearers at night pollutions.

This extract comes from his first treatise *Against Julian* 3, 14.

Really, really: is that your experience? So you would not have married couples restrain that evil—I refer, of course, to your favourite good? So you would have them jump into bed whenever they like, whenever they feel tickled by desire? Far be it from them to postpone this itch till bedtime: let's have your 'legitimate union of bodies' whenever your 'natural good' is excited. If this is the sort of married life you led, don't drag up your experience in debate.

83. A LETTER FROM PELAGIUS   414

As a result of his condemnation, many of the writings of Pelagius have perished. We have his *Commentary on St Paul's Epistles*, and perhaps there are other works of his transmitted under other names. The one letter which is certainly his was addressed to Demetrias, a woman of noble rank who became a nun, part of which we give here. As the first man from Britain to make an impact upon Christian theology, he deserves a special notice. It is a pity we know so very little about him. He seems to have been the most attractive of the heretics. It is a tragedy that the Church should have become like Procrustes and chopped down or stretched out on a rack those who could not exactly fit her bed! The disciples boasted that they had met one who cast out devils in Jesus' name 'and we forbade him for he was not following us', but their action was repudiated by Christ (Mark 9. 38–40). We cannot help thinking that the lives of many Christians would have been happier if some of the views of Pelagius had been accepted.

As this letter shows, he put a special emphasis on the value of man's own moral efforts.

Source: Pelagius, *Letter to Demetrias.*

U

Like proud and worthless servants, we shout in God's face and say, 'It's hard! It's difficult! We can't! We are but men, encompassed by the frailty of the flesh!'

What blind folly, what rash profanity! We make the God of knowledge guilty of twofold ignorance: of not knowing what he has made, and of not knowing what he has commanded. As if, in forgetfulness of human frailty—which he has made—he had laid upon men commandments which they could not bear. At the same time (oh, the shame of it!) we ascribe unrighteousness to the just one and cruelty to the holy one, first by complaining that he has commanded something impossible, and next by thinking that a man will be condemned by him for things that he could not help; so that—it is sacrilegious even to hint it—God seems to have been seeking not so much our salvation as our punishment . . .

No one knows better the measure of our strength than he who gave us our strength; and no one has a better understanding of what is within our power than he who endowed us with the very resources of our power. He has not willed to command anything impossible, for he is righteous; and he will not condemn a man for what he could not help, for he is holy.

84. AUGUSTINE, THEOLOGIAN: FREE WILL AND GRACE

No one since St Paul has shaped the beliefs of Christians more than Augustine. He was no innovator; in fact he found his theology largely in St Paul's Epistles, but he developed and stressed certain themes. His teaching on grace and free will, faith, predestination, the need for confession, discipline and the last judgment, have become the accepted tenets of both Catholic and Protestant churches. The most important of these tenets are perhaps the first two, grace and free will, and we illustrate Augustine's views on them, not from his formal treatises, but from a letter to Archbishop Hilary of Arles, a 'semi-Pelagian'. Pelagius, as we have seen, was one who 'boasted of personal ability' to follow the Christian life; Augustine was far too conscious of his own weakness and need of supernatural grace. The literal meaning of 'grace' is 'free gift'.

Source: Augustine, *Letters* 157.

Freedom of choice avails for the performance of good works if it receives divine assistance; and this comes about by praying and acting with humility. But if a man is deprived of divine assistance, then, be he never so excellent in knowledge of the Law, he will in no wise be firm and solid in righteousness, but blown up with the deadly swelling of an irreverent pride . . .

Now free will will be the more free the more it is healthy; and it will be the more healthy the more it is subject to the divine mercy and grace. For of itself the will prays and says, 'Direct my steps, according to thy word, and no unrighteousness shall have domination over me' (Psa. 119, 133). How can a will be free if it is under the domination of unrighteousness? And observe who it is that is invoked, in order to escape that domination. It does not say, 'Direct my steps according to free choice', but 'according to thy word'. It is a prayer, not a promise, a confession, not a profession; a desire for the fullness of liberty, not a boast of personal ability . . .

This freedom of will is not therefore removed because it is assisted; it is assisted just because it is not removed. For he that says to God 'be thou my helper' confesses that he wills to fulfil what he has commanded, but that he asks the aid of him who commanded that he may have power to fulfil it . . .

Grace will assist us if we are not presumptuous about our own virtues, and 'mind not high things but are of one mind with the humble' (Romans 12, 16: Vulgate); if we give thanks for what we already have power to do, while for those things for which we have not yet power we entreat God in supplication with yearning desire; if we support our prayer with fruitful works of kindness, by giving, that it may be given to us, by forgiving, that we may be forgiven.

85. AUGUSTINE, THE BISHOP OF HIPPO 396–430

Hippo was the second port of North Africa, 150 miles west of Carthage. At Milan, Augustine was one of a brilliant society of Christian Platonists, and when he became bishop of Hippo he tried to gather a similar circle of cultured men about him in his monastery-palace. But his friends were soon taken off to be bishops, though there was always a great traffic of visitors and suppliants. Augustine moved further and further away from Plato and Plotinus in his efforts to influence the

Africans in his diocese, most of whom were Donatists when he first came to Hippo (see pages 297–9).

These brief extracts show the more attractive qualities of Augustine, easily overlooked if we concentrate on his theological treatises and controversies. We see this ascetic's love of music, his nostalgia for the ordinary monk's hours of labour in the garden, the warmth of his friendships, his concern for the most wayward of his flock, his joy in expounding the Scriptures, the book open on his lap as he sits in his 'cathedra' at Hippo.

Most of these extracts are from such *Expositions of the Psalms*: A, Psalm 32; D, Psalm 54 and 30, No 2; E, Psalm 18 and 30, No 2. B is from the *Commentary on Genesis* 8, 8, 16; C is from *Letters* 84.

A. So men who sing like this—in the harvest, at the grape-picking, in any task that totally absorbs them—may begin by showing their contentment in songs with words; but they soon become filled with such a happiness that they can no longer express it in words, and, leaving syllables aside, strike up a wordless chant of jubilation.

B. When all is said and done, is there any more marvellous sight, any occasion when human reason is nearer to some sort of converse with the nature of things, than the sowing of seeds, the planting of cuttings, the transplanting of shrubs, the grafting of slips? It is as though you could question the vital force in each root and bud on what it can do, and what it cannot, and why.

C. But when you yourself begin to have to surrender some of the very dearest and sweetest of those you have reared to the needs of churches situated far from you, then you will understand the pangs of longing that stab me on losing the physical presence of friends united to me in the most close and sweet intimacy.

D. The man you cannot put right is still yours. He is part of you; either as a fellow human being, or very often as a member of your church, he is inside with you . . .

Therefore, brother, among these shocking conditions, there is only one remedy: do not think ill of your brother. Strive humbly to be what you would have him be, and you will not think that he is what you are not.

E.   We should understand what this Psalm (18) means. Sing it
with human reason, not like birds. Thrushes, parrots, ravens, mag-
pies and the like are often taught to say what they do not understand. To know what we are saying—that was granted by God's
will to human nature. We know only too well the way bad loose-
living men sing, as suits their ears and hearts. They are all the
worse for knowing too well what they are singing about. They
know they are singing dirty songs—but the dirtier they are, the
more they enjoy it ... And we, who have learnt in the Church
to sing God's words, should be just as eager ... Now, my friends,
what we have all sung together with one voice—we should know
and see it with a clear mind.

Let me try to winkle out the hidden secrets of this Psalm (30)
we have just sung, and chip a sermon out of them, to satisfy your
ears and minds.

86. ALARIC TAKES ROME; AUGUSTINE SEES THE CITY OF GOD
410–26

We know virtually nothing of the actual taking of Rome by the
Goths under Alaric. Orosius writing only seven years after the fall
tells the story in only seven words. It was probably stormed, possibly
betrayed by treachery. But we do know a good deal of what happened
after the Goths had broken in. Alaric was a Christian, though an
Arian one. So, probably, were most of his soldiers. Of course, a city
that had been stormed had to expect to be sacked. Rome was. But
Alaric set bounds to what his men could do. The first extract from a
passage written by Augustine probably within three years of the siege
describes what these were. The second extract is what we should call
Jerome's obituary notice of Marcella, one of those aristocratic Christian
women of Rome who lived a life rather like that of a Sister of Charity.
He had been asked to write it by her young friend, Principia, who had
been with her during the siege and at her death. There is, therefore, no
room to doubt the source of his information. It illustrates by a particular instance what Augustine described in general terms.

Orosius was a young Spanish priest who had been befriended by
Augustine. In 415 Augustine sent him to Palestine with a message to
Jerome about the Pelagians. Extract C recounts what he heard in
Bethlehem. Ataulfus (or Atawulf) was Alaric's brother-in-law and suc-
ceeded him as king of the Goths when Alaric died soon after the taking

of Rome. He was at Narbonne in 414 and there in January he married the Roman princess Placidia who was in Rome at the time of the two first sieges by Alaric and had been taken as a hostage. The Goths wanted to take over Rome, not to destroy it as the Romans had destroyed Hannibal's Carthage. Ataulfus was murdered in 415; Placidia remarried and ruled the Western Empire as regent for 25 years from Ravenna where she is buried (Plate 32).

The effects of the fall of Rome were world-wide—far greater than might seem to be justified by the news of one city sacked, one among many, or even of one city spared. Rome had long ceased to be the strategic or the administrative centre of the empire. It had become an embarrassment with its huge population having to be fed each year from the cornfields of Africa. But Rome was—Rome. In his cell in Bethlehem Jerome was writing the third book of his commentary on Ezekiel when he heard the news. With it came refugees: 'I was long silent, knowing that it was the time for tears. Since it was impossible for us to relieve them all we could only join our lamentations with theirs. In this state of mind I had no heart for explaining Ezekiel, but seemed likely to lose all the fruit of my labour.' He filled his letters with quotations from the Psalms about the fall of Jerusalem and from Virgil on the fall of Troy. Best of all perhaps, since it catches the mood of the civilized world, he amends Lucan's 'What is enough, if Rome be deemed too small?' to 'What can be safe, if Rome in ruins fall?'

Augustine in his strenuous way prepared to give the answer. He had to meet the argument that Rome fell because the gods were neglected, that Christianity was the destroyer. He spent thirteen years writing his immensely long, immensely influential book *On the City of God*. When he finished the task in 426 he turned to review and revise his earlier works. Extract D comes from this book, his *Retractationes*.

The *City of God* is perhaps the first philosophy of history ever written. Its theme is the tension between the two interwoven societies—'confused together in this world but distinct in the other'—the City of God and the city of men. The former had its origin with the creation of the angels, the other with the fall of Satan. On earth, the one was founded by the pious Abel, the other by the impious Cain. Augustine asks the question 'If it is the fate of earthly dominion to pass away, is there a city which endures?' His answer is that the city which shall have no end is the city of God, which has its latest and most perfect terrestial manifestation in the Christian Church. But what did Augustine mean by the Church—the visible Catholic Church or the invisible society of the elect, known only to God? And what did he mean by the city of men—the State, the Roman empire, or the residuum of all who did not acknowledge the predominance of the spiritual motive in their lives? There is no certain answer because Augustine himself moves from one thought to another. But at least it is clear that Augustine was certain that he was on the winning side: the City of God remaineth.

Sources: A: Augustine, *City of God* 1, 7; B: Jerome, *Letter to Principia*; C: Orosius, *Against the Pagans* 7, 43; D: Augustine, *Retractationes*.

A.   CLEMENCY OF THE GOTHS

The dreaded atrocity of the barbarians has shown itself so mild in the event that churches providing ample room for asylum were designated by the conqueror and orders were given that in these sanctuaries nobody should be smitten with the sword and nobody carried away captive. Indeed, many prisoners were brought to these churches by soft-hearted enemies to receive their liberty, while none were dragged out of them by merciless enemies in order to be enslaved.

B.   MARCELLA

Jerome to Principia, 412

You have often and earnestly begged me, Principia, virgin of Christ, to honour in writing the memory of that saintly woman Marcella, and to set forth the goodness we so long enjoyed for others to know and imitate. It is, however, something of a grief to me that you should spur a willing horse, or that you should think I need your entreaties, seeing that I do not yield even to you in love for her. In recording her signal virtues I shall indeed receive more benefit myself than I confer upon others. That I have kept silence up till now, and have allowed two years to pass without speaking, has not been due to any wish to repress my feelings, as you wrongly think, but rather to my incredible grief; which has so overwhelmed my mind that I judged it better to remain silent for the moment than to produce something unworthy of her fame. And even now I shall not follow the rules of rhetoric in praising your, mine, or to speak more truly, *our* Marcella, the glory of all the saints and peculiarly of the city of Rome. I shall not describe her illustrious household, the splendour of her ancient lineage, and the long series of consuls and praetorian prefects who have been her ancestors. I shall praise nothing in her save that which is her own, the more noble in that, despising wealth and rank, by poverty and lowliness she has won higher nobility.

On her father's death she was left an orphan, and she also lost her husband seven months after marriage. Thereupon Cerealis, a man of high consular rank, paid her assiduous court, attracted by her youth, her ancient family, her modest character, and those personal charms which always find such favour with men. Being an old man he promised her all his money, and offered to make over his fortune as though she were his daughter, not his wife. Her mother Albina was excessively anxious to secure so illustrious a protector for the widowed household, but Marcella's answer was this: 'If I wished to marry and did not rather desire to dedicate myself to perpetual chastity, I should in any case look for a husband, not an inheritance.'

Gentile widows are wont to paint their faces with rouge and white lead, to flaunt in silk dresses, to deck themselves in gleaming jewels, to wear gold necklaces, to hang from their pierced ears the costliest Red Sea pearls, and to reek of musk. Rejoicing that they have at length escaped from a husband's dominion, they look about for a new mate, intending not to yield him obedience, as God ordained, but to be his lord and master. With this object they choose poor men, husbands only in name, who must patiently put up with rivals, and if they murmur can be kicked out on the spot. Our widow, on the other hand, wore clothes that were meant to keep out the cold, not to reveal her bare limbs. Even a gold signet ring she rejected, preferring to store her money in the stomachs of the needy rather than hide it in a purse. Nowhere would she go without her mother, never would she interview, without witnesses, one of the monks, or clergy, which was often necessary for the needs of her large household. Always her retinue consisted of virgins and widows, and they were all staid women; for she knew that a saucy maid is a reflection on her mistress' character, and that women usually prefer the company of people like themselves. Her ardent love for God's Scriptures surpasses all belief. She was for ever singing: 'Thy words have I hid in my heart that I might not sin against thee'; and also the passage about the perfect man: 'His delight is in the law of the Lord; and in his law he doth meditate day and night.'[1] Meditation in the law meant for her not a mere reperusal of the Scriptures, as the Jewish Pharisees think, but a carrying it out in action . . . However fine a man's teaching may be, it is put to the blush when his own conscience reproves him; and it is in vain that his tongue preaches poverty and teaches almsgiving, if he himself is swollen with the wealth of a Croesus, and though he wears a coarse cloak fights to keep the moths from the silken robes in his cupboard.

Marcella practised fasting, but in moderation; and she abstained from eating meat. The scent of wine was more familiar to her than the taste, for she drank it only for her stomach's sake and her frequent infirmities. She seldom appeared in public and carefully avoided the house of ladies of rank, that she might not be forced to see there what she herself had rejected; but she frequently visited the churches of the apostles and martyrs for quiet prayer, avoiding the people's throng. To her mother she was so obedient that occasionally she did for her sake things that went against her own inclination. For example, Albina was devoted to her own kinsfolk, and wished to leave all her property to her brother's children, being without sons and grandsons; Marcella would have preferred to give it to the poor, but still she could not go against her mother, and handed over her necklaces and other effects to people already rich for them to squander. She chose rather to see money lost than to vex her mother's feelings.

At that time no great lady in Rome knew anything of the monastic life, nor ventured to call herself a nun. The thing itself was strange and the name was commonly accounted ignominious and degrading. It was from some priests of Alexandria and from pope Athanasius and from Peter afterwards, who to escape the persecution of the Arian heretics had all fled to Rome as being the safest refuge for their communion, that Marcella was told of the life of the blessed Antony, then still in this world, and of the monasteries founded by Pachomius in the Thebaid, and of the

1 Psalms 119, 11 and 1, 2.

discipline laid down there for virgins and widows. She was not ashamed to profess a life which she knew was pleasing to Christ; and many years later her example was followed by Sophronia and by some other ladies. Her friendship was also enjoyed by the revered Paula, and in her cell that paragon of virgins Eustochium was trained. Such pupils as these make it easy for us to judge the character of their teacher.[1]

Lastly, when the needs of the Church brought me also to Rome in company with the holy pontiffs Paulinus and Epiphanius, directors respectively of the churches of Syrian Antioch and of Salamis in Cyprus, I in my modesty was inclined to avoid the gaze of ladies of rank. But Marcella was so urgent 'both in season and out of season', as the Apostle says, that her persistence overcame my timidity. At that time I had some repute as a student of the Scriptures, and so she never met me without asking me some question about them, nor would she rest content at once, but would bring forward points on the other side; this, however, was not for the sake of argument, but that by questioning she might learn an answer to such objections as she saw might be raised. What virtue and intellect, what holiness and purity I found in her I am afraid to say, both lest I should exceed the limits of men's belief, and also that I may not increase the pain of your grief by reminding you of the blessings you have lost. This only will I say; all that I had gathered together by long study, and by constant meditation made part of my nature, she first sipped, then learned, and finally took for her own. Consequently, after my departure from Rome, if any argument arose concerning the testimony of the Scriptures, it was to her verdict that appeal was made.

I have heard that you at once took my place as her close companion, and that you never left her side even for a finger's breadth, as the saying goes. You lived in the same house, and had the same cell and bed, so that you had found a mother and she a daughter. A farm near Rome was your monastery, the country being chosen because of its loneliness. You lived thus together for a long time,

---

[1] A letter from Jerome to Julia Eustochium on virginity caused such a stir in Rome that she and her mother Paula left Rome and founded four monasteries at Bethlehem.

and as many other ladies followed your example and joined your company, I had the joy of seeing Rome become another Jerusalem. Monastic establishments for virgins were founded in many places, and the number of monks in the city surpassed all counting. Indeed, so great was the crowd of God's servants that the name, which previously had been a term of reproach, was now one of honour. Meanwhile we consoled ourselves for our separation by an interchange of conversation, discharging in the spirit the debt that we could not pay in the flesh. Our letters always crossed, outvied in courtesies, anticipated in greetings. Separation brought no great loss, since it was bridged by a continual correspondence.

A dreadful rumour reached us from the West. We heard that Rome was besieged, that the citizens were buying their safety with gold, and that when they had been thus despoiled they were again beleaguered, so as to lose not only their substance but their lives. The speaker's voice failed and sobs interrupted his utterance. The city which had taken the whole world was itself taken; nay, it fell by famine before it fell by the sword, and there were but a few found to be made prisoners. The rage of hunger had recourse to impious food; men tore one another's limbs, and the mother did not spare the baby at her breast, taking again within her body that which her body had just brought forth . . .

Meanwhile, as you might expect in such a turmoil, the blood-stained conquerors burst their way into Marcella's house. 'Be it mine to say what I have heard,' nay, rather to relate what was seen by those holy men who were present at that hour, and found you, Principia, at her side in the time of danger. They tell me that she confronted the intruders with fearless face, and when they asked her for gold and hidden treasures pointed to her coarse gown. However, they would not give credence to her self-chosen poverty, but beat her with sticks and whipped her. She felt no pain, but throwing herself in tears at their feet begged them not to take you from her or force your youth to endure the fate which her old age had no occasion to fear. Christ softened their hard hearts, and even among blood-stained swords a sense of duty found place. The barbarians escorted both her

and you to the church of the apostle Paul,[1] for you to find there
either safety or a tomb. There she burst into cries of joy, thank-
ing God for having kept you unharmed for her. 'By heaven's
grace,' she said, 'captivity has found me a poor woman, not made
me one. Now I shall go in want of daily bread, but I shall not feel
hunger since I am full of Christ and can say in word and deed:
"Naked came I out of my mother's womb, and naked shall I
return thither: the Lord gave and the Lord hath taken away;
blessed be the name of the Lord".'[2]

Some months after this she fell asleep in the Lord, sound in
mind and not suffering from any malady, with her poor body
still active. She made you the heir of her poverty, or rather she
made the poor her heirs through you. In your arms she closed her
eyes, your lips received her last breath; you were weeping, but she
smiled, conscious of having lived a good life and hoping for a
reward hereafter. This letter to you, revered Marcella, and to you,
my daughter Principia, I have dictated in the wakeful hours of one
short night. I have used no charms of eloquence; my one wish
has been to show my gratitude to you both, my one desire to
please both God and my readers.

C.   ROMANIA OR GOTHIA?

When I[3] was at Bethlehem I heard a citizen of Narbonne, who had
served with distinction under Theodosius, and who was besides a
wise and religious person, tell the most blessed Jerome that he had
been on terms of the greatest intimacy with Ataulfus at Narbonne,
and that he had frequently heard him say that, in the first exuber-
ance of his strength and spirits, he had made this his most earnest
desire—utterly to obliterate the Roman name, and bring under
the sway of the Goths all that had once belonged to them—in fact,
to turn Romania into Gothia, and to make himself all that Caesar
Augustus had once been. But he had learnt by long experience
that the Goths would obey no laws on account of the unrestrained
barbarism of their character. He had learnt too that it would be
wrong to deprive the State of the rule of law since a state without
law ceases to be a state. He at least for his part had chosen to have

---

[1] See Plate 21.   [2] Job I, 21.   [3] Orosius.

the glory of restoring the Roman name to its old standing and increasing its potency by Gothic vigour.

D.   AUGUSTINE SEES THE CITY OF GOD

Rome, by the invasion of the Goths under king Alaric, was devasted through the ruin of a mighty slaughter. The worshippers of many and false gods, whom we describe as pagans, tried to connect this destruction with the Christian religion, and therefore began to blaspheme against the name of the true God with more than their usual malevolence.

I, therefore, burning with zeal for the house of the Lord, resolved to write a treatise on The City of God, in order to correct the mistakes of some and refute the blasphemies of others. This work occupied me for several years as I was interrupted by many other engagements which demanded immediate attention. But this great work, *De Civitate Dei*, is at last completed in twenty-two books.

87. NORTH AFRICA ON THE EVE: THE DONATISTS

For a hundred years before the barbarians came, North Africa had been in a state of religious, and often of military civil war. It started in 311 when a new bishop of Carthage was consecrated by one who had been a 'traditor', a traitor who handed over Christian books for burning under Diocletian's orders.[1] Other North African bishops refused to accept a man, however orthodox—and Caecilian was strictly orthodox —who had been consecrated in this way. They set up a rival bishop of Carthage called Donatus. Thus there started a schism which lasted till the Moslems swept away both Catholics and Donatists four hundred years later. The only point of heresy was that the Donatists believed that the validity of sacraments depended on the personal fitness of the minister.

Donatist persistence was largely the result of local nationalist feeling which objected to domination by Rome and Roman Carthage. It was inflamed by poverty and economic injustice: the highlands produced corn and olives in plenty—for export, but brought prosperity only to the owners of the great slave-run estates. It was inspired by the fanatical rigorist faith of the Donatists, the Covenanters of the early church.

The emperors backed the Catholics. They took the strongest possible

[1] See pages 132–5.

steps to put Donatism down in 316–21, 347–61 and again in the first twenty years of the fifth century. Bishops were banished, their followers heavily fined. All this proved ineffective. Many African towns had both Catholic and Donatist bishops. The coastal strip was largely Catholic, the hinterland Donatist. Augustine, the writer of this extract, and Optatus, another bishop from North Africa, wrote strongly against the Donatists, and their writings are almost our sole source of information about these strange, fierce people—not a very satisfactory position to be in. Augustine argued against the Donatists that the church was 'holy' not because her members were holy but because her purposes were good. She contained within her fold both good and bad men—only at the final judgment would the latter be weeded out.

The extreme wing of the Donatists were called Cicumcellions—the people who lived 'around the tombs' of the martyrs. Excavations have shown that these Numidian shrines contained around them silos, troughs and storage jars for food. The Circumcellions, as the Catholics called them, or the Agonistici (Soldiers of Christ) as they called themselves, went about armed with clubs which they called Israels. They fought a guerilla war with the Catholics and the troops who supported them, matching their war cry, 'Praise God' against the 'Thank God' of the Catholics. They gladly encountered martyrdom; sometimes they seem to have been driven to mass suicide. Augustine said: 'They lived as robbers, they died as Circumcellions, and were honoured as martyrs.' (*Letter* 88.)

With this long history of trouble North Africa was clearly going to be an easy prey to the first northern barbarians who crossed the sea. One might have expected one persecuted sect of heretics to throw in their lot with another conquering body of heretics. It was not so. The Donatists seem to have stood aside when the Vandals came.

Source: Augustine, *Letters* 185.

Among the Donatists mobs of lawless men were disturbing the peace of the innocent for one reason or another in the spirit of the most reckless madness. What master was there who was not compelled to live in dread of his own servant, if that servant had put himself under the protection of the Donatists? Who dared even threaten one who sought his ruin with punishment? Who dared to exact payment of a debt from one who consumed his stores, or from any debtor whatever that sought their assistance or protection?

Under the threat of beating, and burning, and instant death, all documents compromising the worst of slaves were destroyed, so that they might depart in freedom. Notes of hand that had been extracted from debtors were returned to them. Any one who showed contempt for their hard words were compelled by harder blows to do what they desired. The houses of innocent persons who had offended them were either razed to the ground or burnt. Certain heads of families, of honourable parentage and brought up with a good education, were carried away half dead after their deeds of violence, or were bound to the mill and compelled by blows to turn it round, in the manner of the meanest beasts of burden.

For what legal aid could the civil powers render that was ever of any avail against them? What official ever dared so much as to breathe in their presence? What agents ever exacted payment of a debt if they were unwilling to discharge it? Except, indeed, that their own madness took revenge upon themselves, when some provoked against themselves the swords of men whom they forced to choose either to kill or be killed; others by throwing themselves over various precipices, others by water, others by fire, gave themselves over on several occasions to a voluntary death, giving their lives as offerings to the dead, by punishments inflicted on themselves by their own hands.

88. VANDALISM; DEATH OF AUGUSTINE

The Goths were not the only barbarians seeking inside the Roman empire a place in the sun. The Vandals were their near relations. Like them, wrote Procopius, who fought against the Vandals, they 'have fair skins and yellow hair; they are tall and handsome. They possess the same laws, the same faith, Arian Christianity; and the same language, the Gothic.' They were generally reckoned less brave than the Goths, more greedy and crueller. Loot was their heart's delight. They moved from Spain across into North Africa which under their king, Gaiseric, they conquered between 428 and 439. This account of their behaviour there is from the book, *On the Persecution of the Vandals* by Victor, bishop of Vita, in North Africa, written when he had been driven into exile in 485. He is describing the events of a generation before, but there is no reason to doubt the general accuracy of his picture, though obviously his interpretation of the reasons behind specific Vandal actions, as in the last sentence of Extract A, is nonsense.

One of the early towns to be besieged was Hippo. Other bishops from the neighbourhood asked Augustine whether they might take refuge there, leaving their dioceses. At first he demurred. They pleaded the words of Christ 'When they persecute you in one city, flee into another.' Augustine thought again, and the outlying bishops came in to be shut up in Hippo for the fourteen months of the siege. Among them came Possidius, bishop of Calama, who had been a monk at Hippo. In command was Boniface, the count or military governor of Africa. Augustine in happier days had written a letter to him explaining his interpretation of a Christian soldier's duty (Extract B). Before the fall of Carthage Augustine was dead. The account of his last days is by Possidius (Extract C). Note the use of the Eucharist as a requiem.

Sources: A: Victor, bishop of Vita, *On the Persecution of the Vandals* I, I; B: Augustine, *Letter to Count Boniface*; C: Possidius, *Life of Augustine* 31.

A.   VANDALISM

The wicked rage of the Vandals was especially directed against the churches and basilicas, the cemeteries and the monasteries, and they made bigger bonfires of the houses of prayer than of whole cities and towns. If by chance they found the door of the holy house fast closed, it was who should soonest force an entrance by thumping it down with his right hand; so that one might truly say, 'They break down the carved work thereof at once with axes and hammers. They have cast fire into thy sanctuary; they have defiled by casting down the dwelling-place of thy name to the ground.'[1]

Ah, how many illustrious bishops and noble priests were put to death by them with divers kinds of torments in the endeavour to compel them to reveal what treasures they had of gold or silver, belonging to themselves or to their churches! If, under the pressure of the torture, they easily revealed their possessions, the persecutors plied them with yet more cruel torments, declaring that part only had been surrendered, not the whole; and the more they gave up the more they were supposed to be keeping back. Some

[1] Psalm 74, 6-7.

had their mouths forced open with stakes and crammed with noisome filth ... Some had bladders filled with sea-water, with vinegar, with the dregs of the olive-presses, with the garbage of fishes, and other foul and cruel things laid upon their lips. The weakness of womanhood, the dignity of noble birth, the reverence due to the priesthood—none of these considerations softened those cruel hearts; nay, rather, where they saw that any were held in high honour, there was their mad rage more grievously felt. I cannot describe how many priests and illustrious functionaries had heavy loads piled upon them, as if they were camels or other beasts of burden, nor how with iron goads they urged them on their way, till some fell down under their burdens and miserably gave up the ghost. Hoary hairs enwrapping the venerable head like whitest wool won for the bearer no pity from those savage guests. Innocent little children were snatched by the barbarian from the maternal embrace and dashed to the ground. Well might our captive Zion sing 'The enemy said that he would burn my borders and slay my infants and dash my little ones to the earth.' (See Psalm 137, 9).

In some large and stately buildings [probably churches], where the ministry of fire had proved insufficient to destroy them, the barbarians showed their contempt of the edifice by levelling its fair walls with the ground; so that now those beautiful old cities have quite lost their former appearance, and many whole towns are now occupied by a scanty remnant of their former inhabitants, or even left altogether desolate.

Yes, and even today, if any buildings remain, they are continu-ally laying them waste, as, for instance, the Temple of Memory, that worthy appendage to the Theatre of Carthage, and the street called the Street of Heaven, both of which they have destroyed from top to bottom. Then too, the large basilica, where the bones of the blessed martyrs Perpetua and Felicity are laid, the church of Celerina, and others which they have not destroyed, they have, with the licence of tyrants, enslaved to their own religious rights. Did they see any strongholds which they were unable to carry by the rush of their barbarian fury, they collected vast multitudes around the walls and slew them with the bloody sword, leaving

v

their carcases to putrefy under the ramparts, that they might slay with the stench those whom their arms were powerless to assail.

B. THE CHRISTIAN SOLDIER

Think then of this, first of all, when you are arming for a battle, that even your bodily strength is a gift from God; for considering this, you will not employ the gift of God against God. When faith is pledged, it is to be kept with the enemy against whom the war is waged, but much more with the friend, for whom the battle is fought. Peace should be the object of your desire, and war should be waged only as a necessity, and waged only in such a way that God may deliver men from the necessity, and preserve them in peace. For peace is not sought in order that war may be kindled, but war is waged, in order that peace may be obtained.

Therefore, even in waging war, cherish the spirit of a peacemaker, that by conquering those whom you attack, you may lead them back to the advantages of peace, for our Lord says: '*Blessed are the peacemakers for they shall be called the children of God*'.[1] If, however, peace among men is sweet, as procuring temporal safety, how much sweeter is that peace with God which procures for men the eternal felicity of the angels? Let necessity, therefore, and not your will, slay the enemy who fights against you. As violence is used towards him who rebels and resists, so mercy is due to the vanquished and the captive, especially in the case where future troubling of the peace is not to be feared. Let the manner of your life be adorned with chastity, sobriety and moderation, for it is exceedingly disgraceful that lust should subdue him, whom man finds invincible, and that wine should overpower him, whom the sword assails in vain.

C. THE DEATH OF AUGUSTINE

Truly the saint had length of years divine allotted to him for the benefit and joy of the holy Catholic Church. He lived for seventy-six years and was in the clerical state and the episcopacy for nearly forty years.

In friendly converse he was often wont to say to us that after

---

[1] Matt. 5, 9.

receiving baptism, the Christian, however laudable his work, and priests especially, should not pass out of this mortal state without doing ample and worthy penance for sin. This he did himself, and during the illness in which he died he had the penitential Psalms written down, and these were hung in order upon the wall where he could see them whilst lying in bed. During that illness he recited them continuously and whilst he did this he shed bitter and abundant tears. And lest his reflections might be disturbed by anyone, during the ten days before he departed this life, he asked that he might be left alone, and that no one would enter his room except at the hours when the doctor came to see him, or when his food was being brought him; and we observed his wishes and did not disturb him. He spent all the time in prayer.

Up to the days of his last illness, he continued with great perseverance, ardour, and strength, and with clearness of mind and judgment, to preach the Word of God. He was sound in all the members of his body, and enjoyed good sight and hearing.

Whilst we stood around him, watching him, and at the same time joining with him in prayer, he sank into sleep with his fathers, having reached a good old age. And for his eternal repose, on the day of his burial the holy sacrifice was offered up, at which we were all present.

He made no will, for, as a poor man of God, he had no possessions. He desired that his library and manuscripts might be carefully preserved for posterity by those succeeding him in the Church, whilst those things that he owned in the church, whether offerings or sacred vessels, be left to the priests of his household who had charge of the church. With regard to his relations, whether in the religious state or not, he treated them in the ordinary manner. Where he had something to spare, and when necessity arose, he gave to them just as he gave to others, not to enrich them, but to help them in need.

He left the Church supplied with sufficient clergy, with monasteries filled with holy men and nuns living according to their religious profession, and in continency. He also left the Church his library containing books and treatises written by himself, or by other holy men. In these works it can be seen how, with God's help, Augustine became so great in the Church, and in these works the faithful shall find that Augustine lives for ever.[1]

89. WHY ROME FELL: ANOTHER ANGLE

Augustine had begun his argument about the fall of Rome and the barbarian irruptions by denying that the Christians were to blame. His starting point was a defence against the pagans who were still powerful enough to be bothering with their belief that it was the neglect of the old gods which had proved fatal. A generation later Salvian finds more to blame in his fellow Christians than in the old Christians. He contrasts the temperance and the strict sexual morality of most of the barbarians—heathen and Arian Christian alike—with the depravity and decadence of his fellow Catholic Christians. He is, of course, a man with a grouse and a case to prove. He probably paints the barbarians in too fair, the Romans in too dark colours; but there is truth in his picture.

Salvian was born in the Rhineland about 400 and lived to be eighty. As a young man he lived at Trier, the capital of all Gaul, the favourite city of Constantine the Great (until he built Constantinople), where Ambrose was born, Ausonius wrote his poems, and Jerome first turned his mind to the monastic life. In the first half of the fifth century Trier was four times sacked by the heathen Franks, finally passing into their hands and out of the empire between 450 and 455. Salvian left it in 424, finally settling near Marseilles. He wrote the book *About God's Rule* from which these three extracts are taken some time between 440 and 450.

A.   BARBARIAN VIRTUE: ROMAN VICE

You, Romans and Christians and Catholics, cheat your brethren, grind the faces of the poor, and fritter away your lives in the obscene and heathenish shows of the amphitheatre, wallowing in wantonness and drunkenness. The barbarians, however, though heathens or heretics and though fierce with us, are just and fair in their dealings with one another. Members of a clan, followers of one king, they love one another with true affection. The indecencies of the theatre are unknown among them; many tribes are free from

---

[1] According to Victor, bishop of Vita, Augustine wrote '232 books, besides innumerable letters, an exposition of the Psalter and the Gospels, and popular "tractates" called "homilies" by the Greeks, the number of which it is impossible to ascertain'.

drunkenness; and, for all except the Alans and the Huns, chastity is the rule. . . . If they have their vices they have also virtues, clear, sharp, and well defined. Whereas you, my dear fellow Romans, I regret to say, with the exception of a few holy men among you, are altogether bad . . . notwithstanding that you have the sacred Scriptures in your hands . . . [he objects to the bad language used by Christians and especially to their habit of swearing 'by Christ' and tells how he tried to persuade a rich man not to rob a poor man of his last possessions]: but he was furious at my daring to interfere, and said that it was now his religious duty, and one which he dared not neglect, to do what I had asked him not to do. I asked him 'Why?' and he gave me the astonishing answer, 'Because I have sworn "by Christ" that I would take that man's property away from him.'

B.   THE INCURABLE FRIVOLITY OF TRIER

Are you asking for games in the circus, people of Trier, when your countryside has been devastated and your city captured? After all the bloodshed, after your citizens have been tortured and made prisoner, and after all the disasters that have overtaken your city which lies in ruins? Can you imagine anything more pitiable than such folly? I admit that I thought you were the most miserable of all men when I heard of how your city had been destroyed. But now that you are begging for games I think you are still more miserable. . . . Where, pray, shall they be held? Over the tombs, the ashes, the bones and the blood of the slain? What part of the city is free from these dreadful sights? . . . The city is black from her burning, and do you want to put on the sleek face of a merrymaker? All around you is mourning; will you rejoice? Worse still, will you with your wicked pleasures provoke the Most High, and draw down upon you the wrath of God by the vilest kind of idolatry? I am not now surprised that all these evils have come upon you. If three catastrophes failed to correct you, you deserve to perish by the fourth.

C.   EMPTY CHURCHES: FULL THEATRES

If it happens, as it often does, that a Church Festival and public plays are held on the same day, I ask you all to search your conscience and say which of the two has the greater crowd of Christians there, the seats of the theatre or of the house of God? Do they all rather flock to the temple or the theatre? Do they love the words of the Gospel more, or those of the players, the words of life or of death, the words of Christ or the words of a mimic?

There is no doubt that we prefer what we put first. For on every day of these deadly sports, if there happen to be any feasts of the Church, they who call themselves Christians not only fail to come to church, but if they chance to have come, not having heard of any such thing, as soon as they hear there are plays they quickly leave the church. The Church of God is despised as they hurry to the theatre: the church emptied, the circus filled. We leave Christ on the altar to feast our eyes which go a whoring after lascivious sights . . .

90. THE INTERVENTIONS OF LEO

Leo the Great was bishop of Rome from 440 to 461. We have already met him twice. It was he who obtained from the emperor Valentinian III an official recognition of Rome's supremacy over all other bishoprics in the West (pp. 231–3). It was his formula which was accepted by the Council of Chalcedon to settle the bitter disputes about the human and divine in the person of Christ (pp. 265, 270). We have now to meet him when on two occasions he was able to make favourable bargains with the barbarians on behalf of the people of Rome. The secular prestige which this brought the Roman Church and the religious prestige which Chalcedon brought him were two pillars on which the medieval papacy was shortly afterwards to be raised by Gregory the Great.

The first extract concerns the great invasion by Attila and the Huns, a tribe of small, dark, intrepid horsemen from the steppes. Rome was in danger. Leo went north to meet Attila. Extract A tells the story of their meeting in the country of Virgil and Catullus at a crossing of the Mincio. It is from Jordanes, the historian of the Goths, who wrote a hundred years later. But, as he tells us, he draws on Priscus, a contemporary who had actually met Attila when sent on an embassy to him by the emperor at Constantinople. The part of his history which deals with Leo's mission is lost, but we still have his description of his own meeting with Attila in his log-hut palace in the Hungarian plain. Extract B is taken from this.

The importance which later ages attached to Leo's successful mission is shown by the legends which gathered round it. They tell how 'the hammer of God', a title given generations later to Attila, was over-awed by an appearance of the apostles Peter and Paul in the sky forbidding him to move on Rome. This is the subject of a famous painting by Raphael in the Vatican.

Three years after Attila had turned back from Rome the Vandals, who had become great sea raiders, crossed from Carthage and marched on the defenceless city. The sober prose of Extract c is from Prosper of Aquitaine, who was Leo's secretary. Leo was successful in saving Rome from the horrors of a sack. Instead the city suffered a fortnight's orderly treasure hunt. Among the loot were the sacred vessels from the temple at Jerusalem which Titus had brought to Rome after the Jewish war.

Sources: A: Jordanes, *The Gothic History*; B: Priscus, *Of Byzantium*; c: Prosper, *Chronicles to the year 445.*

A.   LEO AND ATTILA   452

The siege of Aquileia (the metropolis of Venetia) was long and fierce, but of no avail, since the bravest of the Romans withstood him from within. At last his army was discontented and eager to withdraw. Attila chanced to be walking around the walls, considering whether to break camp or delay longer, and noticed that the white birds, the storks, who build their nests in the gables of houses, were bearing their young from the city and, contrary to their custom, were carrying them out into the country. Being a shrewd observer of events, he understood this and said to his soldiers.

'You see the birds foresee the future. They are leaving the city as it is sure to perish.'

Why say more? He inflamed the hearts of his soldiers to attack Aquileia again. Constructing battering rams and bringing to bear all manner of engines of war, they quickly forced their way into the city, laid it waste, divided the spoil and so cruelly devastated it as scarcely to leave a trace to be seen. Then growing bolder and still thirsting for Roman blood, the Huns raged madly through the remaining cities of the Veneti. They also laid waste Mediolanum

(Milan) ... Then they destroyed the neighbouring country in their frenzy and demolished almost the whole of Italy.

Attila's mind had been bent on going to Rome. But his followers, as the historian Priscus relates, took him away, not out of regard for the city to which they were hostile, but because they remembered the case of Alaric, the former king of the Visigoths. They distrusted the good fortune of their own king, inasmuch as Alaric did not live long after the sack of Rome, but straightway departed this life.

Therefore while Attila's spirit was wavering in doubt between going and not going, and he still lingered to ponder the matter, an embassy came to him from Rome to seek peace. Pope Leo himself came to meet him in the Ambuleian district of the Veneti, at the well-travelled ford of the river Mincius. Then Attila quickly put aside his usual fury, turned back on the way he had advanced from beyond the Danube and departed with the promise of peace ...

So Attila returned to his own country, seeming to regret the peace and to be vexed at the cessation of war.

B.   PRISCUS DINES WITH ATTILA   448

The seat of honour on the right hand of Attila's couch was occupied by Onégesh.[1] We did not receive even the second place, that on his left, but saw Berich, a Hun of noble birth, placed above us there. Opposite to Onégesh, on a double chair, sat two of the sons of Attila. His eldest son sat on the king's couch, not near to him, however, but on the very edge of it, and all through the banquet he kept his eyes fixed on the ground in silent awe of his father. When we were all seated the cup-bearer came in and handed to Attila his ivy-wood drinking cup, filled with wine. Remaining seated, the king drank wine with the one nearest to him in rank (and then in turn with each guest). . . . For all the rest of the barbarians and for us a costly banquet had been prepared, which was served on silver dishes; but Attila on his wooden plate had nothing else save meat. In all other respects Attila showed the same simple tastes. The other guests had drinking cups of gold and silver handed to them, but his was of wood. His clothes were quite

[1] Attila's chief minister.

plain, distinguished only by their cleanness from those of an ordinary man. Neither the sword which was hung up beside him, nor the buckles of his shoes, nor the bridle of his horse, were decorated, in Scythian fashion, with gold, jewels or any expensive material.

C.   LEO AND THE VANDALS   455

After the death of Maximus, there followed immediately the captivity of the Romans, a thing worthy of many tears. The city was left undefended, and Gaiseric got possession of it. The holy bishop Leo went forth to meet him outside the gates, and his prayers, by God's help, so softened him that though all was in his power, as the city had been handed over to him, he refrained from fire and slaughter and punishment. So for fourteen days they were free and at liberty to search. They spoiled Rome of all its wealth; and many thousand captives, according as age or beauty took their fancy, they carried off to Carthage, including the empress and her daughters.

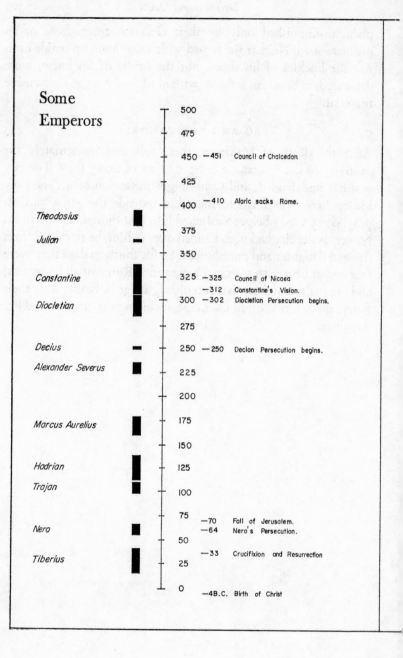

Some Emperors

	500	
	475	
	450	—451 Council of Chalcedon
	425	
	400	—410 Alaric sacks Rome.
Theodosius	375	
Julian	350	
Constantine	325	—325 Council of Nicaea
		—312 Constantine's Vision.
Diocletian	300	—302 Diocletian Persecution begins.
	275	
Decius	250	—250 Decian Persecution begins.
Alexander Severus	225	
	200	
Marcus Aurelius	175	
	150	
Hadrian	125	
Trajan	100	
	75	—70 Fall of Jerusalem.
Nero		—64 Nero's Persecution.
	50	—33 Crucifixion and Resurrection
Tiberius	25	
	0	—4 B.C. Birth of Christ

EGYPT	SYRIA & PALESTINE	TURKEY & the BALKANS	ITALY	ALGERIA & TUNISIA	FRANCE

A timeline chart spanning years 0 to 500 (marked at 50-year intervals: 0, 50, 100, 150, 200, 250, 300, 350, 400, 450, 500) showing the lifespans of early Christian figures by region:

EGYPT: Clement of Alexandria, Origen, Antony, Arius, Athanasius, Cyril

SYRIA & PALESTINE: Ignatius, Gregory Thaumaturgus, Eusebius, Chrysostom, Jerome, Nestorius

TURKEY & the BALKANS: John the Apostle, Polycarp, Lactantius, Ulfilas, Basil, Gregory of Nyssa, Gregory of Nazianzus

ITALY: Clement of Rome, Justin Martyr, Hippolytus, Ambrose, Leo the Great

ALGERIA & TUNISIA: Tertullian, Perpetua, Cyprian, Augustine

FRANCE: Irenaeus, Martin, Apollinaris Sidonius

311

Map 1
PREFECTURES:

A The East
B Illyricum
C Italia
D The Gauls

Eboracum (York)

D

AUGUSTA
TREVIRORUM
(Trier)

r. Rhine

D

MEDIOLANUM (Milan)

Vienne

C

Rome

D

Hispalis (Seville)

Carthage

D

C

SEA TRAVEL. Unsafe, 11th Nov. — 10th March.
    'High Season, 26th May – 14th Sept.
LAND TRAVEL. From the Antonine wall in Scotland
  to Jerusalem via Rome & Byzantium (Constantinople)
  is 3740 miles. An Imperial Courier could travel
  over 100 miles a day if pressed, going from Antioch
  to Constantinople, 665 miles, in 5½ days.

ROMAN EMPIRE C. 330

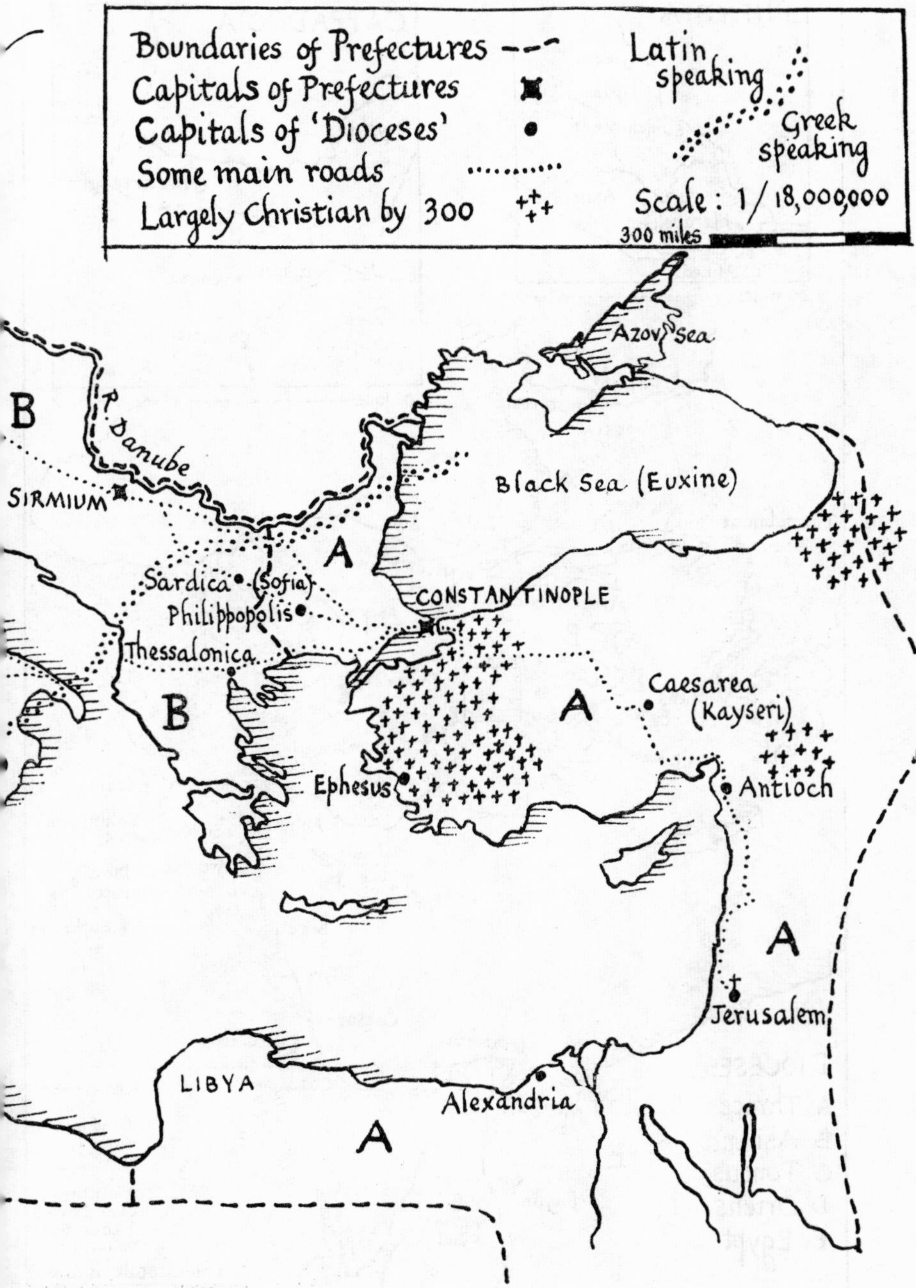
Boundaries of Prefectures
Capitals of Prefectures
Capitals of 'Dioceses'
Some main roads
Largely Christian by 300
Latin speaking
Greek speaking
Scale: 1/18,000,000
300 miles
Azov Sea
B
R. Danube
SIRMIUM
Black Sea (Euxine)
A
Sardica (Sofia)
Philippopolis
Thessalonica
CONSTANTINOPLE
Caesarea (Kayseri)
Ephesus
Antioch
Jerusalem
LIBYA
Alexandria

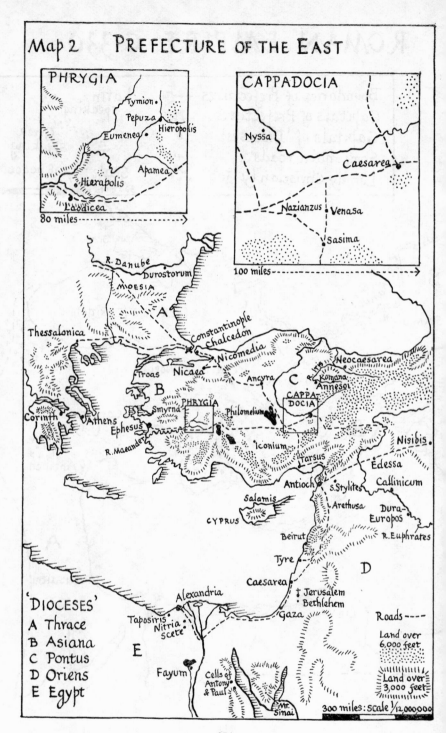

Map 2 PREFECTURE OF THE EAST

PHRYGIA

Tymion
Pepuza
Eumenea
Hieropolis
Hierapolis
Apamea
Laodicea

80 miles

CAPPADOCIA

Nyssa
Caesarea
Nazianzus
Venasa
Sasima

100 miles

R. Danube
Durostorum
MOESIA
A
Thessalonica
Constantinople
Chalcedon
Nicomedia
Nicaea
Troas
B
Smyrna
PHRYGIA
Corinth
Athens
Ephesus
R. Maeander
Philomelium
Iconium
Ancyra
C
CAPPADOCIA
Neocaesarea
Komana
Annesoi
Tarsus
Nisibis
Edessa
Antioch
S. Stylites
Callinicum
Salamis
Arethusa
Dura-Europos
CYPRUS
R. Euphrates
Beirut
D
Tyre
Caesarea
† Jerusalem
· Bethlehem
Gaza

'DIOCESES'
A Thrace
B Asiana
C Pontus
D Oriens
E Egypt

Alexandria
Taposiris
Nitria
Scete
E

Fayum
Cells of
Antony
& Paul
Mt.
Sinai

Roads ----
Land over
6,000 feet
Land over
3,000 feet
300 miles: scale 1/12,000,000

314

Map 3 — PREFECTURE OF ITALIA

'DIOCESES'
A Italia Annonaria
B Italia Suburbicaria
C Africa

Land over 6,000 feet
Land over 3,000 feet
Roads ---
Scale: 1/8,000,000

R. Danube

A

Aquileia
Milan
R. Mincio
R. Frigidus

A
Ravenna
Rimini

Split

Rome
Ostia
Antium
B
Nola
Eclanum
Brindisi

SARDINIA

B

Thibiuca Carthage
Cirta Hippo Tuniza
Calama Abithinae
Tagaste Vita
NUMIDIA
C

200 miles:

315

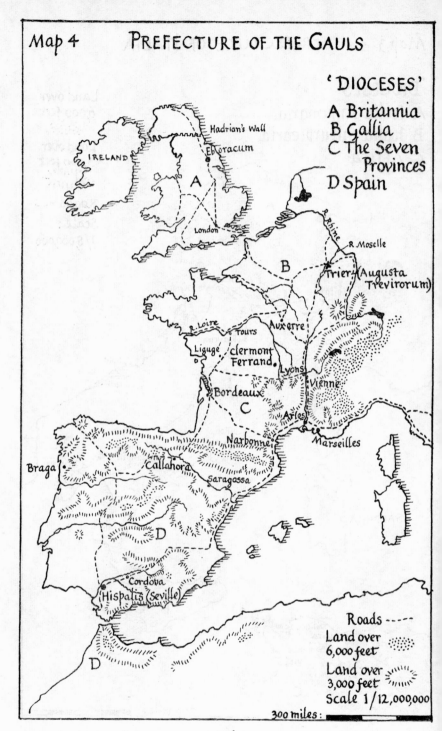

Map 4   PREFECTURE OF THE GAULS

'DIOCESES'
A Britannia
B Gallia
C The Seven
   Provinces
D Spain

IRELAND

Hadrian's Wall
Eboracum

A

London

R. Moselle
Rhine

B

Trier (Augusta
Trevirorum)

R. Loire
Tours   Auxerre
Ligugé   clermont
          Ferrand.
                    Lyons
Bordeaux   Vienne

C   Arles

Narbonne   Marseilles

Braga
        Callahora
        Saragossa

D

Cordova
Hispalis (Seville)

D

Roads -----
Land over
6,000 feet
Land over
3,000 feet
Scale 1/12,000,000
300 miles :

Panel from the Arch of Titus

PLATE I

a. Judaea Capta. (Coin Struck by Vespasian)

b. The Emperor Vespasian

PLATE 2

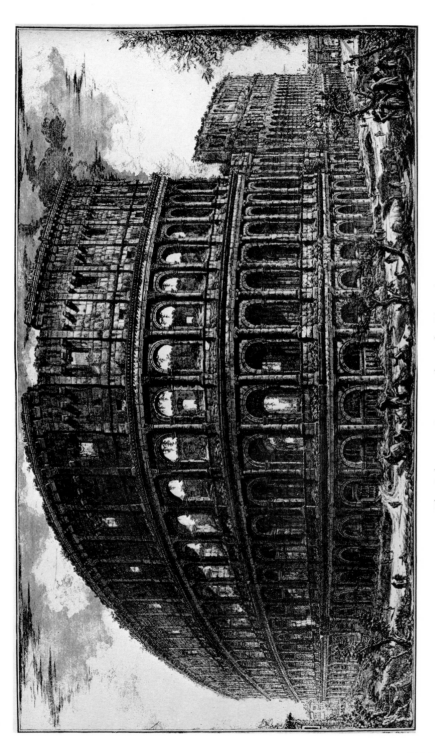

The Colosseum, Rome, as drawn by Piranesi *c.* 1750

PLATE 3

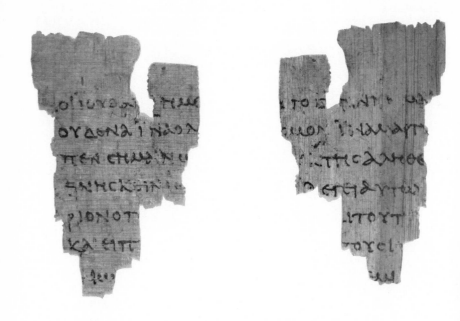

Papyrus fragment of St John's Gospel, before 150

PLATE 4

Mithras slaying the Bull

PLATE 5

Font of House–Church at Dura–Europos *c.* 240

PLATE 6

Statue of Hippolytus *c.* 230

PLATE 7

Shepherd milking sheep, 3rd Century

PLATE 8

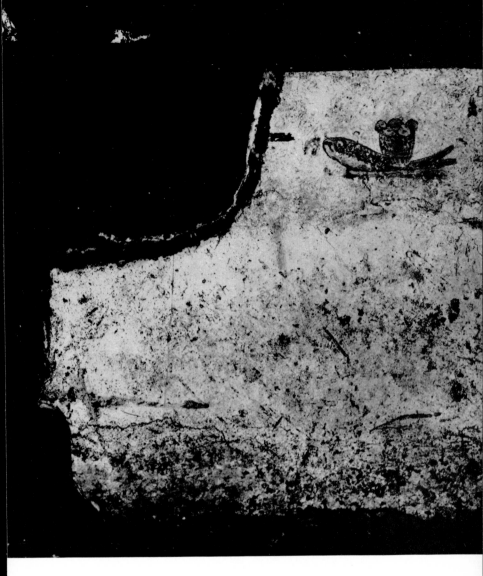

Eucharistic Symbol. Catacomb of Callistus *c.* 210

PLATE 9

Child Ciriaca's Epitaph. Catacomb of Domitilla, early 3rd Century

PLATE 10

Memorial of Rufina and Irene. Catacomb of Callistus, early 3rd Century

PLATE II

Memorial of Apuleia Crysopolis, Catacomb of Callistus

PLATE 12

Memorial of Gerontius. Catacomb of Domitilla, end of 3rd Century

PLATE 13

Coin of Diocletian

The Empress Helena

PLATE 15
The four Emperors c. 314

PLATE 14

Constantine the Great *c.* 315

PLATE 16

Floor Mosaic at Aquileia, 315-320

PLATE 17

Apse mosaic of Saint Pudenziana Church, Rome c. 400

PLATE 18

Sarcophagus Panel: Peter and the Cock, 4th Century

PLATE 19

Church of the Nativity, Bethlehem

PLATE 20

St Paul outside the walls, Rome, engraved by Piranesi *c.* 1750

PLATE 21

Memorial Church of Cyprian, outside Carthage, 4th Century

PLATE 22

Hermits' caves, South Lebanon

PLATE 23

Base of Simeon Stylites's Pillar

PLATE 24

The Monastery of St Catherine, Mount Sinai

PLATE 25

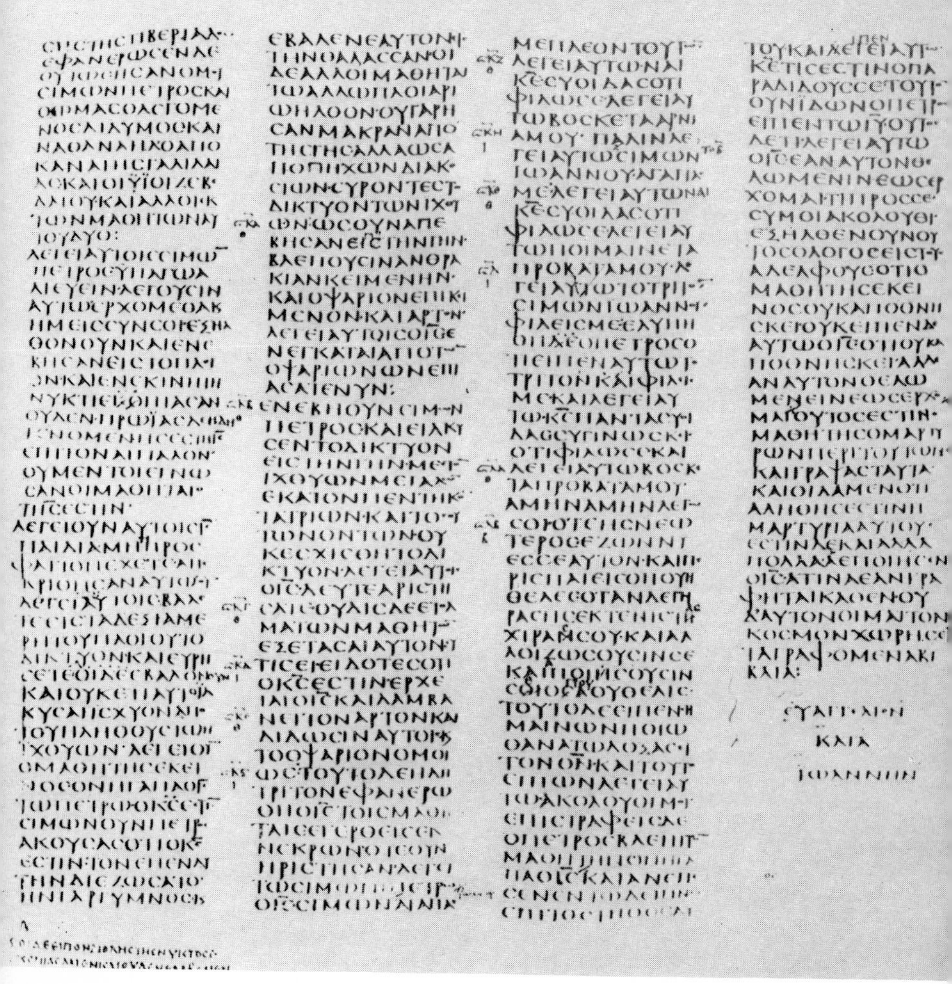

Codex Sinaiticus. End of St. John's Gospel, 4th Century

PLATE 26

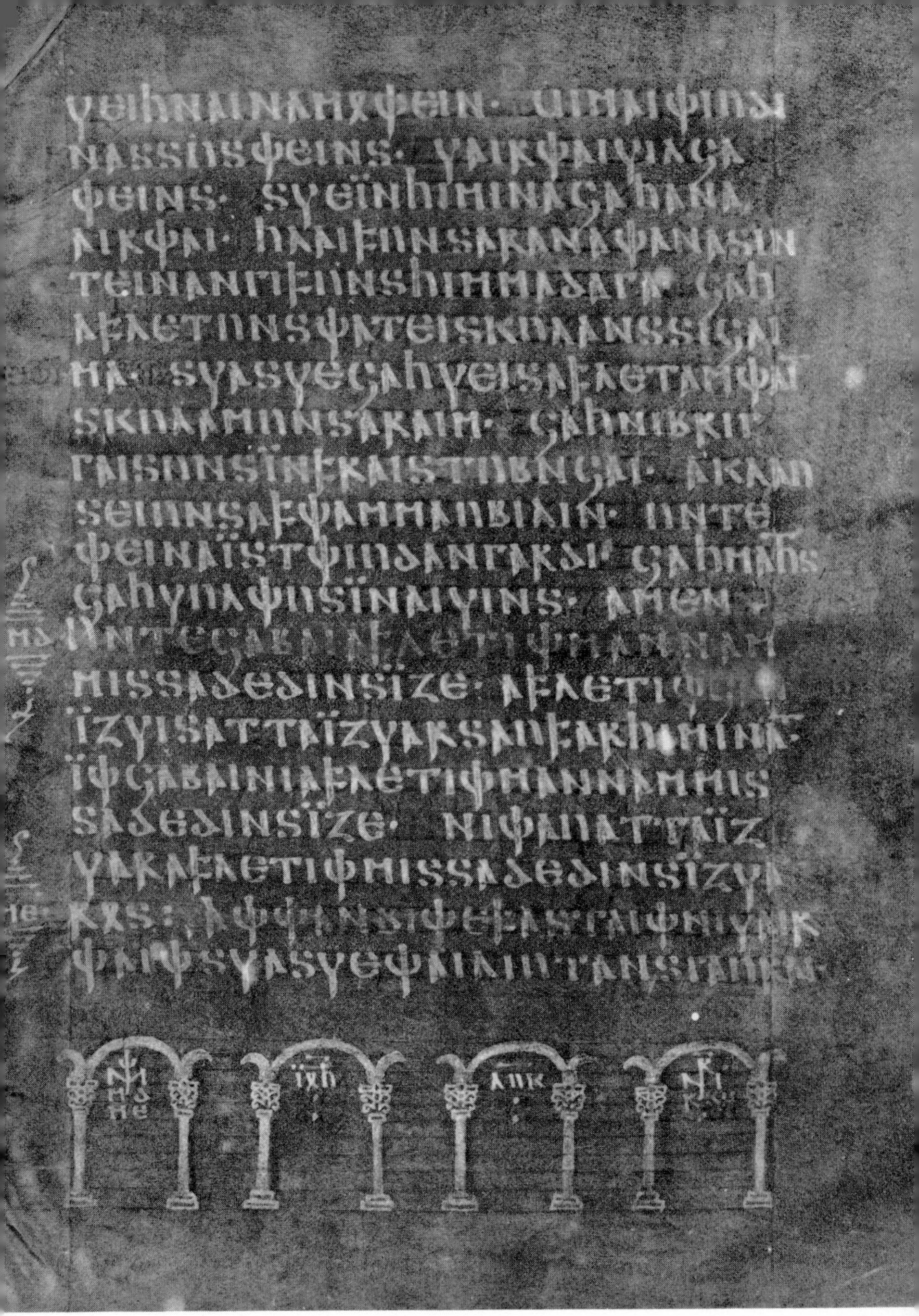

Codex Argenteus, 6th Century

PLATE 27

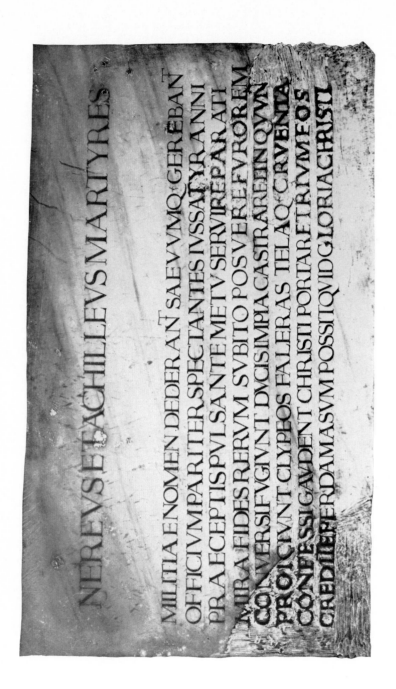

Epitaph of Nereus and Achilleus made by Bishop Damasus c. 366

PLATE 28

The Emperor Theodosius. 388

PLATE 29

Ambrose

PLATE 30

INNOCENTI SPO QVEM
ELEGIT DOMS PAVSAT Q
IN P   AC E
FIDE   LIS
X KA   I SEPT
SEPT   EMBR

Mausoleum of Galla Placidia, Ravenna *c.* 440

PLATE 32

NOTES ON THE ILLUSTRATIONS

Plate 1   Panel from the Arch of Titus, Rome, A.D. 71
Laurel-wreathed Romans are carrying loot from the Temple at Jerusalem.
Notice the gold seven-branched candlestick called the Menora, the golden
table of showbread and the silver trumpets. Pages 9, 307.

Plate 2A   Judaea Capta
A coin struck by Vespasian to commemorate the capture of Judaea and
Jerusalem, 67–70.

Plate 2B   The Emperor Vespasian, 71

Plate 3   The Colosseum, Rome, as drawn by Piranesi, *c.* 1750
Used for many years as a quarry for building stone, there is much less to see
today.

Plate 4   Papyrus Fragment of John's Gospel; before 150
This is the earliest New Testament fragment yet discovered. It is in the
John Rylands Library, Manchester. The words are from chapter 18 and parts
of verses 31–3 are on one side and parts of verses 37–8 on the other.

Plate 5   Mithras slaying the Bull
This relief is from a frontier post, Osterburken on the German border.
Monuments of Mithraism are most often found where Roman soldiers were
stationed.

Plate 6   Font of a House-church at Dura-Europos, *c.* 240
This is the oldest church building to survive. It was against the wall of this
Roman fortress on the river Euphrates (see Map 2), and got buried in a rebuilding of the ramparts in 256. Excavated in 1934. A faint fresco is still
visible of the story of Christ healing the paralytic (Matt. 9. 2–8), and the
man carrying away his bed.

Plate 7   Statue of Hippolytus, *c.* 230
This is generally accepted as a contemporary portrait, see p. 99. The table for
calculating Easter can just be seen engraved on the left side of the seat. On the
right side of the seat is a list of his writings. Lateran Museum, Rome.

W

Plate 8   Shepherd milking sheep, 3rd century
Fragment of a Sarcophagus in the National Museum, Rome. One of many scenes of the Good Shepherd's garden of Paradise carved on Christian tombs. This scene closely illustrates Perpetua's vision, see page 107.

Plate 9   Eucharistic symbol. Catacomb of Callistus, *c.* 210
The Eucharist was a mystery to be hidden from the heathen. The favourite sign of it was the feeding of the 5,000. Hence the bread, fish and basket (see John 6).

Plate 10   Child Ciriaca's Epitaph. Catacomb of Domitilla, early 3rd century
The symbolism of the cut branch, here and in Plates 12 and 13, may not be specifically Christian, but the joy of the picture and the words 'in peace' are very different from the pagan memorials in the catacombs.

Plate 11   Memorial of Rufina and Irene. Catacomb of Callistus, early 3rd century
Note that the letters are Greek; the simple cross is very rare in such early times and this must be one of its earliest appearances.

Plate 12   Memorial of Apuleia Crysopolis, Catacomb of Callistus.
'Who lived 7 years, 2 months. The parents most lovingly have made this for their daughter'. Note that the good Shepherd is beardless and carries the lamb on his shoulder as in scores of other memorials.

Plate 13   Memorial of Gerontius. Catacomb of Domitilla. End of 3rd century
'Gerontius, live in God'. Vibas or Vivas often appears alone. The Christian would remember the words of John (1, 4): 'In him was life'.

Plate 14A   Coin of Diocletian

Plate 14B   The Empress Helena
For Diocletian see pages 130–5.
For FL(avia) Helena, mother of Constantine, see pages 148–52.

Plate 15   The Four Emperors, *c.* 314
Diocletian, Galerius, Maximian, Constantius carved in porphyry, now on the front of St Mark's, Venice. This grim group of tetrarchs seems more barbaric than Roman, see page 130.

Plate 16   Constantine the Great, *c.* 315
This is a fragment of a colossal statue that stood in the Basilica of Constantine in the Forum at Rome.

Plate 17   Floor Mosaic at Aquileia, 315–320

This is the floor of the first church, revealed beneath the present 11th-century cathedral, the third church on the site. It was laid down by Theodorus, bishop of Aquileia, as shown by the dedicatory inscription in the 'clipeus' (round shield):

'O Theodorus, happy one, with the help of God Almighty
and of the flock entrusted to you from heaven
you have made everything beautifully, and gloriously
dedicated it.'

It is a lovely anthology of all the baptismal motifs, the christians born of water, the fishers of men (Matt. 4, 19), even the often-shown story of Jonah, saved through water, and reclining under a paradisal gourd. Notice the chi-rho above the inscription, and the translation of pagan cupids into amorini— little loves.

Plate 18   Apse Mosaic of S. Pudenziana Church, Rome, *c.* 400

Christ the Teacher, enthroned, between Peter and Paul, surrounded by symbols from Revelation; the four living creatures (Rev. 4, 7) and the New Jerusalem (Rev. 21, 2). And naturally the artist has pictured the new Jerusalem built by Constantine and Helena (see pages 148–57). By Christ's right hand is the dome of the Anastasis over the tomb, with the basilica behind it. Then there is the rocky top of Golgotha and the 'staurotheca' containing a relic of the cross. Under the winged ox is the Imbomon church at the place of the Ascension on the Mount of Olives. Note the 'oculus', the open eye in the centre of the roof, through which the worshippers could 'gaze up into heaven' (Acts 1, 10).

Plate 19   Sarcophagus Panel: Peter and the Cock, 4th century

The building on the left is the oldest clear picture of a baptistery. Notice the chi-rho on the top, the bronze doors with a lion's head and open trellis above, the curtains over the doors, which always remained open so that Christians could enter and renew their baptismal vows.

Behind the cock is probably the church of the Anastasis at Jerusalem and its basilica, and on the right, outside the (south) city wall and at a lower level, is the church of St Peter of the Cock-crowing.

Plate 20   Church of the Nativity, Bethlehem

The inner south aisle is shown with, almost certainly, the original pillars of Helena's church.

Plate 21   St Paul Outside the Wall, Rome, *c.* 400

From an engraving by Piranesi, *c.* 1750. The church was burnt down in 1823. Prudentius described its 'imperial splendour' in a poem. The ceiling, he said, was covered with gold leaf so that the light should resemble the morning sun, while pillars and arches were of coloured marbles, like meadows filled with flowers in the spring.

Plate 22 Memorial Church of Cyprian, outside Carthage, 4th century
This had seven aisles instead of the usual five. We can see where the altar table stood in the nave. From a 'cathedra', chair, in the apse, Augustine preached.

Plate 23 Hermits' caves. In the south Lebanon mountains east of Tyre

Plate 24 Base of Simeon Stylites' Pillar
At Qalat Sem'an in Coele-Syria. A great monastery was built around it in about 480 to care for the many pilgrims.

Plate 25 The Monastery of St Catherine, Mount Sinai
The present monastery claims to have been founded in 527, and in its remote desert mountains has been marvellously preserved, but there was an earlier monastery here which Etheria visited. See page 152.

Plate 26 Codex Sinaiticus, 4th century
This is the oldest MS of the Greek Bible and was discovered in 1859 by the scholar Tischendorf at St Catherine's monastery at Mount Sinai. He acquired it for the Tsar of Russia and the Soviet Government sold it to the British Museum for £100,000. It has lost many leaves in its adventures. It contained the *Shepherd of Hermas* at the end of the N.T. The plate is of the end of St John's Gospel.

Plate 27 Codex Argenteus, 6th century
Ulfilas' Gothic Bible. The writing is in gold and silver on purple parchment. This page shows the Lord's Prayer from VEIHNAI NAMO THEIN, hallowed be thy name. See p. 260.

Plate 28 Epitaph of Nereus and Achilleus made by Bishop Damasus, *c.* 366
Damasus (see p. 241) delighted in records of Christianity and tidied up the catacombs, composing epitaphs for some of the dead. This one was carved by his calligrapher Filocalus in letters of his own design. It is for two soldiers who, by a miracle, suddenly deserted their cruel trade, fled the barracks, threw away their weapons and gladly confessed their faith in Christ and bore his sign of victory. 'Believe from Damasus what the glory of Christ can achieve'. Catacomb of Domitilla.

Plate 29 The Emperor Theodosius, 388
The last emperor to rule the whole empire. This silver presentation plate shows him suitably enthroned between his two sons with a halo of glory around his head, a new court convention, later adopted for Christ and the saints, especially in Byzantine art.

Plate 30   Ambrose

A mosaic portrait, made a few years after his death in 397. S. Vittore, Milan.

Plate 31   Tombstone of Innocent, *c.* 400

'Innocent our dear boy whom the Lord has chosen rests in peace in the faith. On the 10th day before the calends of September'. The picture is of baptism, but even an adult was shown as an infant, a new-born soul, under the 'living' water, here shown as coming from the mouth of a dove, symbol of the Holy Spirit. Stone in the museum at Aquileia.

Plate 32   Mausoleum of Galla Placidia, Ravenna, *c.* 440

This seems to be the earliest cruciform building, and the sarcophagi are still in their original position in the arms of the cross. Who was buried here is unknown—but it was not Placidia. Perhaps the building was a 'memoria' of the deacon Lawrence shown in this lunette standing beside the grid where he was supposed to have been roasted. He holds a Gospel in his hand, as Deacons read the gospel in the Eucharist, and the cupboard on the other side of the fire shows the four Gospels clearly labelled Mark, Luke, Matthew, John. The whole mausoleum has walls covered with marble and is vaulted with beautiful mosaics.

INDEX OF BIBLICAL REFERENCES

INDEX TO PLACES

The numbers in italics refer to the four maps on pages 312–16. Only the chief references are given for Alexandria, Antioch, Carthage, Constantinople, Milan and Rome.

INDEX OF PERSONS

Note: Where many references are given, the most important are in italics.

INDEX OF SUBJECTS